Popular Science

Do-it-yourself Yearbook

Popular Science

Do-it-yourself Yearbook

1983

 New York

 VAN NOSTRAND REINHOLD COMPANY
New York   Cincinnati   Toronto   London   Melbourne

Published by

Popular Science Books
Times Mirror Magazines, Inc.
380 Madison Avenue
New York, NY 10017

Distributed to the trade by

Van Nostrand Reinhold Company
135 West 50th Street
New York, NY 10020

ISSN: 0733-1894

ISBN: 0-442-27454-8

Manufactured in the United States of America

introduction

Welcome to the first *Popular Science Do-it-yourself Year-book*. It begins an annual series on trends and techniques in house construction, remodeling, and repairs, while also offering over 50 woodworking projects. The projects range in challenge from a simple footstool to cabinets and outdoor structures. Most of the projects are accompanied by dimensioned drawings, materials lists, and step-by-step instructions. Concluding sections of the yearbook cover finishing techniques, tool innovations, and tips on buying lumber.

In construction and remodeling, energy efficiency is now a fundamental concern. Here design and materials play basic roles, certainly. But, as you'll see, craftsmanship is vital in achieving highest energy savings. The yearbook also reports on passive solar options, earth-shelter dynamics, and hi-tech insulating materials. There's guidance on deciding between retrofitting for solar heat gain and superinsulating for greater heat retention. Here, surprisingly, if you spend as little as 3 to 8 percent of your new home's price on superinsulation, you can save over 75 percent on eventual energy costs that would have resulted from merely average insulation.

In the event you'd like to neaten up your workshop and improve your efficiency there, you'll find plans for workbenches and an elaborate shop-tool ensemble with fold-out double-layered wall cabinets. Later comes a chapter on shop wiring as well.

The chapters were selected from recent issues of *Popular Science* magazine and *Homeowners How To* magazine. But the chapters aren't simply reprints. Authors, manufacturers, artists, and editors updated and adapted the material just before we went to press. In selecting the articles, we weren't surprised to note that the authors tend to rank among the best-known in their fields—as evidenced in the biographical capsules on the next two pages.

Why people do it themselves

Consumer surveys indicate that do-it-yourselfers are motivated differently at various times. Of course, financial savings is often a big factor. With today's high interest rates, sweat equity can cut that initial loan principal for remodeling and construction by 30 to 50 percent. Yet aside from interest rates, you can save plenty by doing work around the home rather than hiring for it, building instead of buying, and repairing rather than discarding.

Other motivators? Sometimes it's just unavailability of a manufactured furnishing that leads to do-it-yourself designing and building. Then too, many people undertake projects because they've been disappointed with pro workmanship, as today's legal claims give testimony. Still, many people simply enjoy learning how to approach new projects and doing the work themselves. In the end—whether it's a large project or small, whether it's woodworking, wiring, plumbing, or repairs—there's that sense of pride in accomplishment: "Hey, that chair you're sitting in? You say you like it? I built it myself."

A vital tip

Although this yearbook will help keep you up to date, some things of course never change and will apply to do-it-yourself tasks forever. In this regard we offer this reminder from the oldest and wisest of craftsmen: "Measure twice before you cut once."

An invitation

We hope you'll put this initial yearbook to use—learn from it, save with it, and enjoy the tasks it guides you through. Then, please drop us a line to let us know how you liked this issue and what subjects you'd like to see in upcoming annual issues.

The editors

the authors

Below is an alphabetical sampling of the authors for this issue. They include prominent freelancers as well as members of the *Popular Science* New York and field staff.

Paul Bolon took a humanities and science degree from M.I.T. before working several years as a cabinetmaker and carpenter. Later, in New York as an associate editor for *Popular Science,* he wrote and edited articles on science, consumer products, and do-it-yourself projects. He's now writing full-time, also renovating his condo and readying its basement workshop—efforts that will lead to more magazine articles.

George Daniels is a former how-to editor of *Mechanix Illustrated* and *Science Illustrated.* He has also served as editor-in-chief of four modeling and handyman publications and as a consulting editor for many others. His 19 books include *Home and Workshop Guide to Glues and Adhesives; How to Be Your Own Home Electrician; How to Use Hand and Power Tools;* and *Home Guide to Plumbing, Heating and Air Conditioning.*

Richard Day, contributing editor for home and shop at *Popular Science,* was the owner of an auto-repair shop before he turned to writing. Considered an expert in many subjects beyond auto repair, such as masonry, plumbing, shop work, and tools, Day is a prolific writer of magazine do-it-yourself articles and the author of over a dozen related books, including *How to Build Patios and Decks* and *How to Service and Repair Your Own Car.*

R. J. De Cristoforo has long been one of the leading woodworking writers. He is widely recognized as a master of tools, a shopwork genius, a highly accomplished photographer, and a skilled draftsman. Besides serving as consulting editor for tools and techniques for *Popular Science,* he is the author of countless articles and over two dozen books, including *How to Build Your Own Furniture; Build Your Own Wood Toys, Gifts and Furniture;* and *De Cristoforo's Housebuilding Illustrated.*

C. P. (Ken) Gilmore, editor-in-chief of *Popular Science,* became a freelance writer in 1958. He joined *PS* in 1971 and assumed his present post in 1980. Ken specializes in science and technology writing. He also serves as the on-camera science editor for WNEW-TV in New York and conducts his syndicated science radio show. He is the author of *Exercising for Fitness* and *The Scanning Electron Microscope.*

A. J. Hand began preparing for a career as a writer-photographer at the age of six by assisting his writer-father, Jackson Hand, with photo set-ups. A. J. later served on the *Popular Science* staff, winding up in 1975 as the magazine's home workshop editor before he began freelancing full-time. His photos have appeared on many magazine covers, and his articles appear in magazines and in his syndicated newspaper column, "Hand Around the House." He is the author of *Home Energy How-to.*

Jackson Hand, who died as this book went to press, had long been one of the leading writers on tools, workshop techniques, and home improvement. He began his career as editor of a furniture trade magazine, where he specialized in wood finishing and antique restoration. Jack had also edited do-it-yourself yearbooks and an encyclopedia and had sold countless magazine articles. Among his books are *How to Do Your Own Wood Finishing* and *How to Repair, Renovate, and Decorate Walls, Floors, and Ceilings.*

William J. Hawkins, senior editor for electronics, came to *Popular Science* in 1970 after winning a national contest for the design for better car antitheft devices. Since then Bill has reported mainly on electronics technology. Yet, as this issue gives evidence, Bill is also a knowledgeable and adept writer on general home improvements. Bill recently computerized his entire home.

Herb Hughes is a technical writer for Intergraph Corporation and has worked in home-design and construction fields since the mid-1960s. Herb's many articles have appeared in the major do-it-yourself magazines, including *Homeowners How To.* He has published two books: *More Living Space* and *Home Remodeling Design and Plans.*

John H. Ingersoll has been an editor and writer for over 30 years, specializing in housebuilding, remodeling, energy, architecture, and science. Formerly senior editor of *House Beautiful,* John has written nearly 1,000 articles for many magazines including *Homeowners How To* and *Popular Science.* He is the author of four books, including *How to Buy a House.*

Thomas H. Jones is a full-time writer who specializes in furniture making, home improvement, and woodworking techniques. Before taking up writing full time in 1970, Tom was an aerospace engineer. He has sold hundreds of articles on do-it-yourself subjects and is the author of three books, including *How to Build Greenhouses, Garden Shelters and Sheds.*

Alfred W. Lees, the *Popular Science* group editor for reader activities, is in charge of all do-it-yourself instruction. He designed and built the Lockbox leisure home, which was the focus of 19 feature articles during the 1970s. He also created the *PS* "Leisure-Home" and "Storage from Scratch" series and the national design competition for plywood projects, which he judges annually. His several books include *Popular Science Leisure Homes* (with Ernest V. Heyn).

E. F. (Al) Lindsley is the *Popular Science* senior editor for engineering. He's also been a steeplejack, a semi driver, a carpenter, a meteorologist, a test pilot, an industrial engineer, and an editor with *Scientific American*. For *PS* and *Homeowners How To,* he covers motors, engines, vehicles, house repairs, and woodworking. Al is the author of the long-time standard *Engine Installation Manual* for the Internal Combustion Institute as well as *Electric and Gas Welding*.

Mike McClintock, as a general contractor for almost 10 years, designed and built houses, additions, and custom furniture. Later he was head of the home-and-shop department at *Popular Mechanics*. He now writes on home how-to subjects for a wide range of magazines and has published four books, including *Homebuilding* and *Getting Your Money's Worth from Home Contractors*. In addition, Mike hosts "The Home Show" on New York's WMCA radio and is the home care and repair editor for Warner/Amex cable TV.

Everett H. Ortner, editor of *Popular Science,* joined the staff in 1953. The magazine's photography columnist, Ev has written on all facets of that subject. He also has a strong interest in architecture that has led to leadership roles in various historical and preservationist organizations. Over the years, he has written many articles on innovative home architecture—two of those articles appearing in this issue.

Evan Powell, southeast editor for *Popular Science* and *Homeowners How To,* specializes in home repairs, equipment, remodeling, and energy systems. Earlier Evan was technical service director for Sears, Roebuck and Co. Currently he is also a product consultant to General Electric and produces home equipment features for Multimedia TV. He is the coauthor of *The Complete Guide to Home Appliance Repair* (with Robert P. Stevenson).

Bernard L. Price, a former mechanical engineer and head technical writer for Edmund Scientific Corporation, has worked 12 years in automotive repair and 10 years in cabinetmaking and general construction. A full-time freelance writer now, Bernie is a principal contributor to major do-it-yourself magazines and book collections. His specialties include tools, machines, plumbing, wiring, cabinetmaking, remodeling, and outdoor structures.

Susan Renner-Smith, a senior editor at *Popular Science,* began work as a science and English teacher before becoming an editor for Scholastic Magazines and for the EPIE Institute, a consumer's union for educators. For *PS,* Susan covers many beats from the sciences and electronic technology to house design and renovation. She and her husband recently bought a "handyman's special" house that promises to figure in do-it-yourself articles.

John Robinson believes he owns all the power tools ever invented. He's worked many years as a writer, editor, and photographer in the architectural and home fields. He says he usually generates do-it-yourself magazine articles as by-products of a home problem he's been forced to solve, simply photographing his steps in case somebody else might need guidance. He is the author of books on travel and *Highways and Our Environment*.

Benjamin T. (Buck) Rogers is an engineer in private practice with special expertise in solar design. He was a founding member of the Los Alamos National Laboratory (LANL) Solar Group and is now serving LANL as a consultant in the development of solar analysis methods. He served with the University of California's Solar Lab at Los Alamos for nearly three decades and has taught energy efficient architecture for Arizona State University and Pratt Institute College.

Daniel J. Ruby, an associate editor at *Popular Science,* writes and edits articles on technology, energy, the physical sciences, house design, and home do-it-yourself projects. Over the past two years, he has honed his construction and home-improvement skills by converting raw warehouse space into a living loft.

V. Elaine Smay, a senior editor at *Popular Science,* writes and edits stories on diverse subjects including house design, home heating systems, camping equipment, and electronic watches. She's become the magazine's expert on earth-sheltered housing, a feature in this issue. She began jogging in 1968, when jogging wasn't cool, and has since competed in marathons. At home she enjoys tending her hydroponic garden.

Richard Stepler, formerly the home and shop editor for *Popular Science,* is now group editor for consumer information. He has written on a variety of home-improvement subjects, ranging from house design and construction to lighting, wall systems, and built-ins. He is also an expert on alternate energy—particularly solar and wind power—and in that capacity has helped establish *Popular Science* as a leading information source.

Peter and **Susanne Stevenson** are the husband-and-wife team behind Stevenson Projects, Inc., a California company that supplies do-it-yourself plans for scores of projects ranging from furniture to sailboats. Many of their projects, which combine beauty and utility, have been featured in national magazines. According to the Stevensons, Pete's the designer, builder, and writer. Susie's the business manager and publications director.

CONTENTS

I. Energy-saving House Designs
and Construction Techniques   2

Super-insulated Houses   2
Thermally Layered Retreat   4
High-tech Houses   6
Passive Solar Kit Homes   14
Earth-sheltered Housing   17
Passive Solar Design   20
Slant for Solar Panels   24

II. House Remodeling   26

Know What You're Getting Into   26
Two Ways to Insulate Basement Walls   29
Cut the Cost of Adding On   32
Remove a Supporting Wall   37
Add a Screened Porch   40
Converting a Garage to Living Space   42
Add a Spa Wing   48
How to Handle Condensation Problems   50

III. Woodworking Projects: Indoors and Out   52

INDOORS PROJECTS
Basic Workbench   52
Shop Tool Storage Units   54
Table-saw Alignment   58
Tricks for a Radial-arm Saw   61
Over-hood Garage Storage   64
Home Computer Center   66
Rolltop-desk Kit   68
Modular Storage Units   72
Fold-up Stool   77
Appliance and Wine Rack   78
Kitchen Island   80
Closet-door Pantry   81
Stereo Tower   82
Free-standing Closet   84
Darkroom Work Cabinet   86
Magazine Cradle   87
Wine Rack   87
One-wall Vanitory   88
Bathroom Built-ins   92

Early American Medicine Chest **94**
Airtight Attic Door **95**
Sewing Center **96**
Yarn Box **99**
OUTDOORS PROJECTS
Hot-tub Deck **100**
Butcher-block Construction **102**
Solar Concentrator with a Twist **103**
4-in-1 Backyard Center **104**
Weatherproof Chairs **106**
Projects for Fiberglass-reinforced Plastic **108**
Rustic Planter **113**
Cold-frame Hot Bed **114**
Easy-to-build Outdoor Furniture **116**
Drop-leaf Swim Deck **119**
Weekender Sloop **120**
Berming Your Yard **122**

IV. Woodworking Techniques

125

Wall Accents with Wood Moldings **125**
Furniture Repairs **128**
Care and Refinishing of Wood Floors **132**
Silence Squeaky Floors and Stairs **137**
Fast Furniture Finishes **141**

V. Wiring and Plumbing

144

How to Wire a Home Workshop **144**
How to Solvent-weld Plastic Pipe **147**

VI. Latest in Tools, Hardware, and Materials

150

Air Tools **150**
Computerized Drill Press **155**
Power Screwdriving **156**
A Hotter Torch **159**
Sander/Stripper and Specialty Cutter **162**
Better-grip, Different-twist Wrenches **164**
Choosing Door Hinges **168**
How to Buy Lumber **172**

Index **179**

super-insulated houses

The conventional-looking house pictured here has very unconventional fuel bills. During an entire icy Saskatchewan winter, Peter and Judy Fretz's house used only as much fuel as a standard house would have needed in two weeks.

The secret is under the skin: 12 inches of insulation stuffed into double exterior walls; greatly increased insulation in the floors, ceilings, and foundation; a tightly sealed vapor barrier; and vestibule entries.

The Fretz house is one of a relative handful of homes in the United States and Canada that are pointing the way to a new trend in building. Super-insulated houses—also called low-energy or conservation houses—approach home heating by cutting energy demand instead of increasing supply. People who have built and lived in them believe that they perform better and cost less to build than houses with complicated active or passive solar systems.

In fact, super-insulation is a kind of passive solar design. Multiple-glazed windows are concentrated on the south side, and direct solar gain is an important source of heat. But, because heat travels both ways through windows, much less glass is used than in most passive homes. Also, no special attention is given to adding heat-storage mass.

Instead, dramatically increased insulation and decreased air leakage

seal in the modest solar gain and the internal heat given off by human bodies and electrical appliances. The result is an energy saving of at least 75 percent over a house with average insulation (see heat-loss drawing). A similar saving results in summer: By keeping hot air out, air-conditioning cost approaches zero.

Some super-insulated houses can even get by without a backup heating plant. "That's the quantum jump," says Harvard researcher William Shurcliff. "That $4,000 saving makes up the cost of the other features."

So far, few builders have been

confident enough to eliminate the furnace, and most super-insulated houses have cost 3 to 8 percent more to build than homes with average insulation.

The slight capital-cost penalty does not dampen enthusiasm, though. "Within a few years, super-insulation will be the commonplace of building," says Wayne Shick, a retired University of Illinois architect whose Lo-Cal House design is credited with starting the super-insulation boom.

After Shick published his design, other academic and scientific groups took up the crusade. The Saskatche-

In the Fretz house walls, two sets of 2×4s separated by plywood plates and sheathing were constructed in sections, then raised into place. A continuous vapor barrier covers inside of plywood. Windows are concentrated on south; overhangs prevent overheating in summer. The Fretzes modified the Cape Cod design with help from Saskatchewan Research Council.

wan Research Council built and monitored a demonstration house that incorporated many of Shick's ideas. The same group is now sponsoring a "parade" of energy-efficient homes in Saskatoon.

But the breakthrough came when a number of independent owner-builders applied the concept in actual homes.

"I call those people the granola boys," says Harry Hart, a commercial builder in Lorton, Virginia. "Now it has gone beyond that stage." Hart has developed two subdivisions of houses based on the Lo-Cal design, and Enercon Builders, in Regina, Saskatchewan, has sold many super-insulated homes and licensed its design to other builders.

"Business is flying," says Enercon's Leland Lange. "In our area, all sectors of the industry—from the subtrades to the financial institutions—are getting involved."

Harry Hart is not so sanguine. He says that only about 20 percent of his buyers were sold by the energy efficiency of his houses. "The consumer is a funny cat. Many buyers say they are interested in energy, but they base their decisions on items like fancy bathroom fixtures."

"Energy awareness in building may have to work its way from the North down," comments Shick. "But as energy prices continue to soar, there will be a moment of awakening."

While super-insulation backers are universally excited about the concept, specific designs vary. Some favor double walls with 8½ inches of insulation, some 12 inches. Others get by with single 2×6 or 2×8 walls with exterior sheet insulation supplementing standard fiberglass batts. Some require an airtight seal, heat exchangers, and vestibule entries. Others say these aren't needed. There are many pieces to the super-insulation puzzle. How they go together makes a big difference.

Right now, many super-insulated houses are rather plain looking. But this is a result of builders and buyers trying to reduce cost, not of design limitations. Within certain constraints, such as the number of windows and overall size of the house, super-insulated houses could be architectural eyecatchers.

Will they replace other types of solar design? Shurcliff says there will still be a role in very sunny areas for passive houses with huge amounts of glass and thermal storage. "But almost every kind of house has some sort of catch," he says. "With super-insulated houses, nobody has found an Achilles' heel"—*Daniel Ruby.*

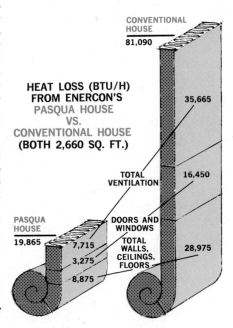

HEAT LOSS (BTU/H) FROM ENERCON'S PASQUA HOUSE VS. CONVENTIONAL HOUSE (BOTH 2,660 SQ. FT.)

CONVENTIONAL HOUSE 81,090

PASQUA HOUSE 19,865

TOTAL VENTILATION 35,665 / 16,450

DOORS AND WINDOWS 7,715 / 3,275

TOTAL WALLS, CEILINGS, FLOORS 8,875 / 28,975

Pieces of the puzzle

Typical insulation values and other features of a super-insulated house are shown in the drawing, but designs vary widely. "The key to a cost-effective design is striking a balance among the many elements," says David Robinson, a Honeywell development engineer who devised mathematical techniques to help designers. "If you are going to use only double glazing in the windows, for example, then it's a waste of money to put more than R-21 of insulation in the walls." The required R-values will determine what kind of wall construction is needed. Robinson's guidelines also indicate that you should spend the same amount of money on energy-saving installations as you'll spend on fuel over the life of the house. But his methods don't yield easy decisions on some other features. Airlock doors? The experts are split. They also dispute the importance of a perfectly sealed vapor barrier. Wayne Shick says a barrier is important mainly to protect insulation from humidity; perfect seal is less cost-effective than using superior windows. Leland Lange says sealing is crucial. "Upward of 40 percent of the energy load in an average house comes from heating infiltrated air." If sealing drops air-change rate to under 20 percent an hour, a fresh-air heat exchanger may be needed to combat indoor pollution.

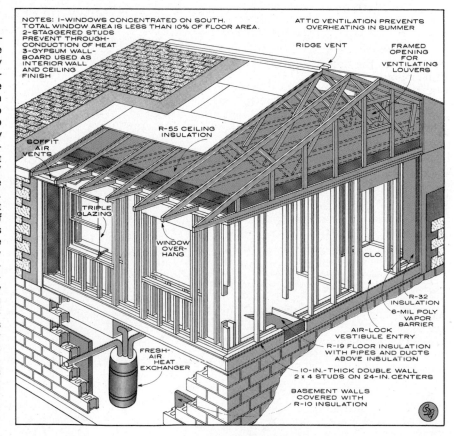

NOTES: 1-WINDOWS CONCENTRATED ON SOUTH. TOTAL WINDOW AREA IS LESS THAN 10% OF FLOOR AREA. 2-STAGGERED STUDS PREVENT THROUGH-CONDUCTION OF HEAT 3-GYPSUM WALL-BOARD USED AS INTERIOR WALL AND CEILING FINISH

ATTIC VENTILATION PREVENTS OVERHEATING IN SUMMER

RIDGE VENT

FRAMED OPENING FOR VENTILATING LOUVERS

R-55 CEILING INSULATION

SOFFIT AIR VENTS

TRIPLE GLAZING

WINDOW OVERHANG

CLO.

R-32 INSULATION

6-MIL POLY VAPOR BARRIER

AIR-LOCK VESTIBULE ENTRY

R-19 FLOOR INSULATION WITH PIPES AND DUCTS ABOVE INSULATION

10-IN.-THICK DOUBLE WALL 2 x 4 STUDS ON 24-IN. CENTERS

FRESH-AIR HEAT EXCHANGER

BASEMENT WALLS COVERED WITH R-10 INSULATION

thermally layered retreat

Whatever the temperature and wind conditions outdoors, thermosiphoning ensures comfort throughout this unique multilevel house. The rising of heated air generates currents that work to dissipate heat in summer or capture it for reuse in winter.

Award-winning architect Alfredo De Vido, who designed this passive solar house, describes it this way: "There are two basic heating modes and two for cooling.

"A. Cool weather: Shades to the greenhouse are opened; living spaces benefit from direct solar gain and nighttime radiation from thermal mass. Shades are pulled down over the greenhouse roof at night to conserve heat.

"B. Cold weather: In addition to the above, the 'double roof' between atrium and skylights collects a good deal of heat near the peak; a fan pulls this heat back down.

"C. Warm weather: The greenhouse shade is drawn against the sun, and the vent at the top of the air chimney is opened. As air here heats and rises through the vent, it pulls cool air into the house through underground vents.

"D. Hot weather: Atrium shades block the sun's penetration, and a fan in the plenum exhausts air through the house. The 'layering' of the house, plus all these controls, lets you fine-tune the thermosiphon system to match the season."

The key word in this design is *control*. The various options guard against overheating in summer and underheating in winter. The backup wood stoves that flank the open kitchen concentrate their heat in the activity areas. These are isolated from the three bedrooms, which are set halfway into the earth platform, below—*Al Lees*.

Stairs coil up through layered levels, rising from sunken solar greenhouse and bedroom hall to room under ridge. Another stair climbs from mid-level entry. Atrium offers sun-tempered area for winter work/play, wood storage; in summer it's a breezeway.

How to order your plans

For architect's working drawings of this house, send your check to Alfredo De Vido, 699 Madison Avenue, New York, NY 10021. A single set is $90; four sets are $105. Complete materials list is $15 additional. Three other De Vido houses are featured in *Popular Science Leisure Homes*—a book of fifty-six of the best designs in this series. Send $18.95 plus $1.95 for postage and handling to PO Box 2018, Latham, NY 12111.

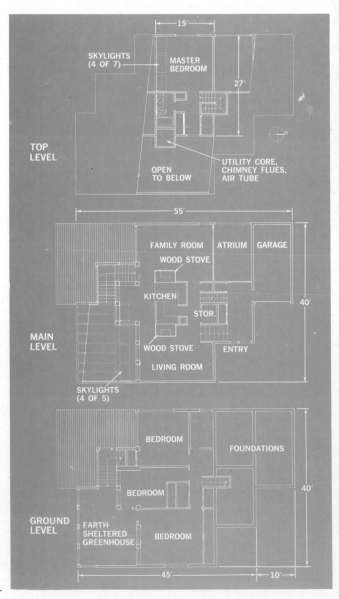

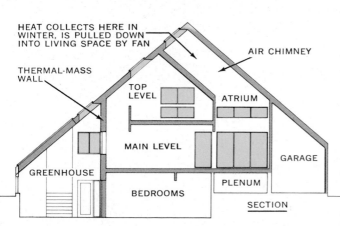

HEAT COLLECTS HERE IN
WINTER, IS PULLED DOWN
INTO LIVING SPACE BY FAN

AIR CHIMNEY

THERMAL-MASS
WALL

TOP
LEVEL

ATRIUM

MAIN LEVEL

GARAGE

GREENHOUSE

PLENUM

BEDROOMS

SECTION

Front section of house nests into an earth pedestal: Greenhouse
and three bedrooms are all earth-sheltered. Sun through in-
clined south glazing heats thermal masses of partition wall and
tile floors of main level. Heat travels up air chimney at back.
During summer, it's vented outside through openable skylights
at peak, acting on thermosiphon principle for cooling.

5

high-tech houses

The liftplate house

The system is magnificently simple: Cast all the concrete floors in the same form at ground level, one on top of the other, then lift them into place one at a time. This technique has been used for some time in big multistory buildings. But with complex and expensive machinery, the system that is economical for large buildings is impractical for houses.

Or was. Now architect Peter M. Vanderklaauw of Coral Gables, Florida, has scaled down the machinery and the cost, and has devised new control devices that make the lift-slab system—he calls his version Liftplate—practical and economical for individual houses.

Let's start with the concrete form at ground level. Vanderklaauw pours a slab 6 to 8 inches thick, lets it cure a day or so, then spreads a bond-breaking compound (a waxy substance that keeps the layers separate) over it and pours again. And again. He ends up with a stack of slabs— or plates, as Vanderklaauw calls them because post-tensioned steel reinforcement keeps them thin as well as rigid. He has plates for the foundation floor, the ceiling/floor above it, the ceiling/floor above that, and the topmost ceiling. With the stack at ground level, workmen frame a roof over the top plate. Then Vanderklaauw starts lifting.

The lifting controls, invented and patented by Vanderklaauw, are the heart of his Liftplate system. "Lifting is nothing," he says. "With hydraulics, you can lift the Empire State Building." The problems lie in controlling the hydraulic jacks and in protecting against fall-backs.

He designs his houses with a specific number of "lifting points"—the steel poles that will support the hydraulic jacks as they pull the plates up, and that will end up supporting the house. For the house shown there were four. The trick is to have all jacks lift at exactly the same rate.

To ensure that, Vanderklaauw runs thin wire from his lifting mechanisms through pulleys on the floor toward a central point and puts weights at the end of the wires. The wires pull against small metal tabs as they run through a sensing device Vanderklaauw invented.

"If I have a synchronous lift, all the wires should travel across the floor at the same speed," Vanderklaauw says. If one wire moves faster than the others, its tab moves out farther, cutting out its pump until the others catch up. If one wire moves slower, the other pumps cut out until all are even. To prevent fall-back, a nut is automatically turned under the plate as it is lifted. The cost of Liftplate? About $4,000 per lifting point. The saving using his system? Vanderklaauw estimates 20 to 25 percent—*Everett H. Ortner.*

Sprayed-concrete sandwich

It's a deceptively plain sandwich: a thick slab of insulation board between thin slabs of structurally reinforced, sprayed concrete. But walls made this way cut energy costs from 50 to 80 percent, reports Solarcrete Corporation (3635 Turfway Road, Erlanger, KY 41018). And a sandwich-wall building is cheaper to erect than a conventional one.

Architect/inventor Vanderklaauw points to nut that prevents fall-back. Below it are sensor and counter. The house, shown just after lift and completed, is in the Florida Keys.

To create the energy-trapping wall, Solarcrete locks 2- to 6-inch-thick polystyrene boards inside a framework of reinforcing steel bars (see drawing). The rebar frame lets the insulation butt together without gaps. For added structural strength, reinforcing wire mesh is stretched over the unit. Then the wall is sprayed inside and out with a layer of high-density shotcrete.

R-values of this infiltration-free wall range from R-19 to R-37, depending on insulation thickness. The wall uses only one-third the concrete of a poured wall and is cost-competitive with insulated concrete-block walls. Mark Graham, one of the system's developers, cites a further advantage: "The concrete supply is local, the insulation is lightweight. Materials that have to be hauled in because they're manufactured someplace far from the job have caused building prices to go out of sight."

Best of all, Solarcrete proves that energy-efficient concrete-slab houses need not look dreary (see photo). The simple construction encourages creative design. "You just carve the styrene panels into arches or rounded walls at the site," says Solarcrete President Bruce Poston.

Construction-cost savings can be substantial. One Solarcrete building in Indiana cost 33 percent less to build than a comparable concrete-block structure. The owners report a hefty 84 percent saving in yearly energy costs, though this is partly due to the building's passive solar design.

In fact, the Solarcrete wall was part of an all-solar system until the company realized the construction method had its own merit. But Solarcrete still offers an optional—and unique—active solar-heating design. The solar collector is built right into the south wall. Poston describes the process: "You just cut channels in the styrene for collector pipes and set them in place before you finish the wall. Then you paint the concrete a dark color and add a glass or plastic windbreak to keep wind from stealing the heat." The solar-heated water is piped to a storage tank that serves as energy bank for a water-source heat pump.

The Solarcrete system can also revitalize older, energy-gobbling buildings. Using specially designed clips, workers attach the insulation board directly to the building's exterior walls, then spray on the shotcrete. Such a rehabilitation can dramatically improve a building's looks—but the energy savings are even more dramatic. One owner, whose renovation job included building a 912-square-foot addition, still reported an average $325 monthly saving on electric bills after the Solarcrete overhaul—*Susan Renner-Smith.*

Factory-made foam-core walls

What do you do if you're a "stick builder" and want to build houses in the Middle East—where there are no sticks?

Covington Technologies, a Southern California house-

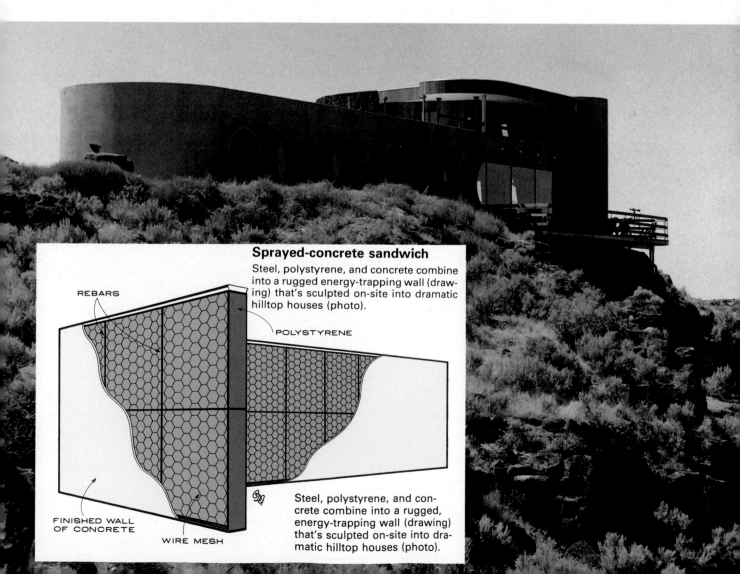

Sprayed-concrete sandwich
Steel, polystyrene, and concrete combine into a rugged energy-trapping wall (drawing) that's sculpted on-site into dramatic hilltop houses (photo).

REBARS

POLYSTYRENE

FINISHED WALL OF CONCRETE

WIRE MESH

Steel, polystyrene, and concrete combine into a rugged, energy-trapping wall (drawing) that's sculpted on-site into dramatic hilltop houses (photo).

Factory-made foam-core walls

Structural-foam panels, sprayed with plaster, form walls of this house. Mechanicals are all in prefab core module.

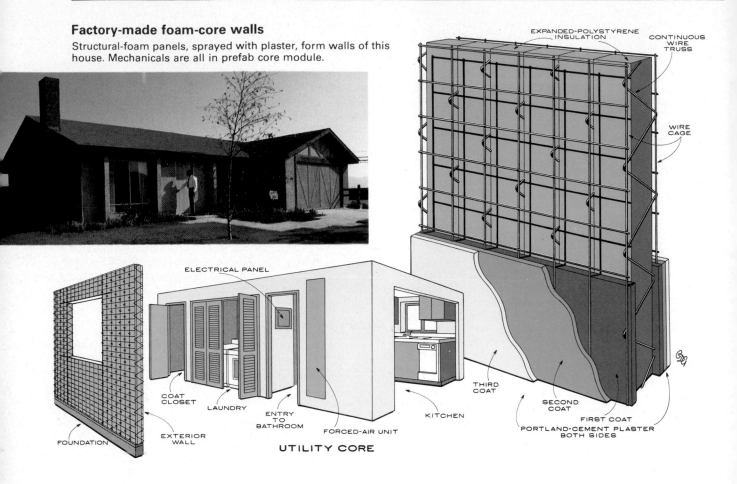

building firm, solved the problem by devising a construction system based on foam-and-concrete wall panels called Therml Impac panels. They're similar to Solarcrete walls, but these are structural panels built in a factory. Walls require no steel-rebar framework or any site-installed wire mesh. It's all done at the plant.

"By the time Covington got into production with the panels, the housing market in the Mideast had begun to cool down," Bob Mulvin, vice-president for marketing, told me, "but the California market had really started to go." So Covington decided to build Therml Impac houses locally.

In a small factory near Riverside, California, stacks of 2¼-inch expanded polystyrene-foam sheets are converted to stacks of Therml Impac panels. First, hot knives slice the foam sheets into strips. Then a machine stacks the strips, alternating them with 14-gauge-wire trusses. Another machine welds on vertical and horizontal wires to form a grid on both sides of the foam (see drawing). The 4×8-foot, 26-pound panels can be easily handled and cheaply shipped. (The company sells the panels to other builders, too.)

At the building site, the Covington houses start with a core module, also factory-built, which contains the heating, plumbing, and electrical equipment; two bathrooms; and a fully equipped kitchen. "Even the light bulbs are in place," Mulvin said, pointing to the luminous ceiling in the spacious kitchen of a three-bedroom model.

To form the walls, the Impac panels are slipped into U-channels around the footings. They're temporarily braced while the crew staples them together using a special ma-

chine. Then the walls are sprayed, inside and out, with about an inch of portland-cement plaster.

"These houses go up in about half the time it takes to build a wood-frame house," Mulvin said. That means lower labor costs and less interest paid on the construction loan. Another saving: Most of the labor can be unskilled.

Covington houses are among the least expensive in Southern California. Three-bedroom models with fireplace, draperies, and carpeting are priced at around $60,000 in some developments, land included. In Southern California—believe it or not—that's a bargain.

The houses are sound-resistant and vermin-proof, and need little maintenance. They also have excellent seismic properties, according to Mulvin. And a fire that raged through the San Bernardino National Forest last November leveled a wood-frame subdivision but left the adjacent Covington tract nearly unscathed.

The Impac-panel houses may also be more energy efficient than conventional houses. "It may be the relatively high thermal mass and low infiltration rate, but for some reason our houses seem to be using less energy than the R-value of the walls [R-11] would suggest," said Mulvin. But the company is not making specific claims until an analysis of heating and cooling bills—from Covington and conventional houses—is complete. Meanwhile, Gerald B. Steel, an engineering consultant, has studied the houses and concluded that with some attention to passive solar design they could realize energy savings of at least 40 percent. Covington Technologies (2451 E. Orangethorpe Avenue, Fullerton, CA 92631) is now working on such designs—*V. Elaine Smay.*

Passive solar—and mostly steel

Galvanized-steel C-joists, steel I-beams, steel columns, concrete-block walls—this is the stuff of warehouses. But it's also the stuff of an elegant house designed by architects Joseph Linton and Wayne Bingham (62 S. 300 East, Salt Lake City, UT 84111)—home to Linton and his family.

The main entry to the house is through a soaring, two-story greenhouse, topped by a sloping skylight. In winter, heat from the top can be circulated to warm the house. In summer, a vent dumps the heat outside. The north wall of the greenhouse is made of 12-inch concrete blocks reinforced with steel rebars. The wall acts as thermal mass, absorbing and releasing heat to even out diurnal temperature variations. But this exposed block wall, which extends through the house, is no ugly duckling. It's smooth, with a slight luster. "We discovered that if you hone the face of a block, you have a handsome stonelike surface," Linton explained. To avoid mortar lines they assembled the blocks with construction adhesive. Another block wall adds more thermal mass at the back of the two-story house. It forms the windowless north side, which nestles into a hillside to reap the benefits of earth-sheltering. The open living-dining area at the front has large south-facing windows that admit the low winter sun, but they're recessed to keep out the high summer sun. A curving wall is punctuated by bands of glass blocks, which were installed with clear silicone caulking to avoid grout lines.

The interior walls are faced with linen-covered acoustic panels. Partition walls stop short of the ceiling for better air circulation. "That's why the acoustic panels were necessary," Linton said. "We have five children, and Joe likes it as quiet as a bachelor's place," his wife added.

The house is heavily insulated. The galvanized-steel C-beams that form its skin are stuffed with 3½ inches of polyurethane. Next comes 3 inches of cellulose, which adds acoustical insulation and covers the polyurethane with a one-hour fire barrier. It also separates the steel studs from the steel skin. The total R-value of the walls is about R-29; the roof's is about R-35. The foundation is also insulated, but the concrete floor is not, which ties the house into the thermal mass of the soil. "It's a 5,000-square-foot house, and we could heat it with three fireplaces if we wanted to," Linton said. Normally, however, they use a water-source heat pump—*V. Elaine Smay.*

Solar hybrid—in copper

How do you condense into a few lines a report on a house with everything? I'm still reeling from my visit to the Sun/Tronic showcase house of the Copper Development Association, built on a Connecticut lake bank, just outside Greenwich. One of the most sophisticated solar homes yet built, it boasts a hybrid energy system that takes advantage of both direct and indirect solar gain by means of both active and passive collectors. The south face features a two-story greenhouse flanked by banks of all-copper flat-plate collectors, each 320 square feet in area. Off to the left is a 150-square-foot photovoltaic array that powers all pumps and fans for the entire computerized system—and provides emergency power through battery storage. Note

Passive solar—and mostly steel

SOLAR HYBRID— IN COPPER

all banks were placed at grade, rather than on the roof, so they could be adjusted to the site's optimum 55-degree pitch and remain accessible for tuning.

The entry wall, on the north (not shown), is sunk into the hill to minimize exposure to cold winds. Here the 12-ounce standing-seam copper roofing folds down to clad the short wall. Elsewhere the redwood walls are backed with rigid foam and fiberglass, for an R-30 rating; similar insulation is beefed up to an R-40 in the cathedral ceilings.

Step through the low air-lock entry and you confront an open-plan, multilevel living space with all the pizazz of a Hyatt hotel lobby. Tying it all together is a towering "energy column" with a powered grille at the top to suck in heat that accumulates at the peak. During summer this heat is exhausted; on cold days it's drawn inside the column and circulated through cavities in the concrete floors.

The left third of the house (behind the geranium pots in the photo) is a master bed/bath suite designed for winter comfort independent of the rest of the space (which could be kept at the less cozy, no-cost temperatures provided by the automated solar systems alone). Built into the south wall of the master bedroom is an innovative collector (inset photo) with Freon tubes run through stacked copper cylinders and out through an insulated barrier to a glazed collector plate. The Freon vaporizes on exposure to solar heat, then gives up this heat to the water cylinders and returns to the collector. The dark-stained cylinders, which look like sculptural decor, continue to radiate heat long after the sun goes down. When no heat's needed, a shutter automatically masks the collector—*Al Lees.*

Balloon-form dome

If you were to design a house with energy efficiency as a prime consideration, you might choose to make it a dome, since that shape encloses more volume with less surface area than any other. You might also make it a monolithic structure, with no cracks or joints that would leak heat and no structural steel or wood that would act as breaks in the insulation. You'd probably want to build it of some high-thermal-mass material that would store heat and moderate temperatures. And to take advantage of the thermal mass, you'd wrap the dome in a cocoon of insulation.

The result would closely resemble a Tecton Corporation dome. This Colorado Springs company holds the patent for a dome-building system invented by California architect Lloyd Turner. Not only are these domes energy efficient, they are strikingly handsome, inside and out. They can be built in many shapes and sizes. And the way they are built is as elegant as the final product.

A Tecton dome starts as a giant, custom-made vinyl balloon—the form for what will be a sprayed-on polyurethane-and-concrete structure. The balloon is attached to a poured-concrete footing and pressurized with large fans. If the house is to be something other than a hemisphere (such as the "flying saucer" in the photo) a compression ring is put in to shape the balloon. "Sometimes we put lights inside those at night and listen for reports of UFO sightings," said Tecton Vice-President John Smith with a chuckle.

Working inside the balloon, the construction crew

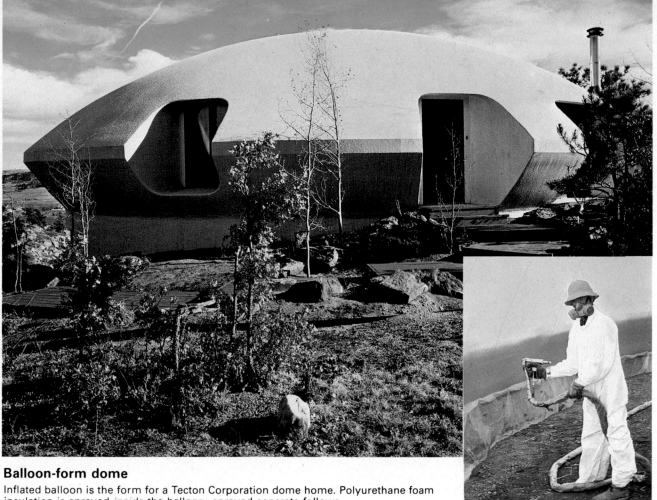

Balloon-form dome

Inflated balloon is the form for a Tecton Corporation dome home. Polyurethane foam insulation is sprayed *inside* the balloon; sprayed concrete follows.

sprays on polyurethane-foam insulation, building it up to a 3- or 4-inch thickness. Next, they spray on shotcrete to form a 1½-inch shell. A clever, automated scaffolding system aids these operations. The scaffolding has powerful lights attached. "Once you spray on the shotcrete, it's darker than the inside of a cow in there," said Smith.

The shotcrete Tecton uses is reinforced with steel fibers. The company built its first dome without the fibers, using wire-mesh reinforcing instead. "We must have done thirty man-days of mesh-hanging on that dome," said Smith. "With the fibers, you just dump them into the concrete and mix—it takes five minutes." When the shotcreting is complete, the balloon is removed. Generally, the shell can be put up in a week to ten days. But the next step—finishing the openings—requires a lot of hand work.

The polyurethane exterior gets a three-layer coating of elastomeric roofing material, which protects the ultraviolet-sensitive foam from the sun, has a Class-A fire rating, and contains ground walnut shells to add texture and impact resistance. The coating is also quite elastic, as it must be since the foam expands and contracts.

Construction costs of a Tecton dome are about equal to those of a conventional house with similar amenities and square footage. The company expects those costs to dip. "Only about thirty of our domes have been built so far, so we're barely beyond the prototype stage," Smith explained. A number of labor-saving techniques that are now on the drawing board should make construction cheaper.

Lifetime costs, because of the energy efficiency, should be much lower than for conventional houses. Based on cal-culations and on reports from dome owners, Tecton figures the domes will use only 25 to 35 percent as much energy as a well-insulated conventional house of similar size.

For more information, write Tecton Corporation, 111 W. Fillmore, Colorado Springs, CO 80907—*V. Elaine Smay.*

Foam dome

Glaringly white against a brilliant blue winter sky stood Xanadu. Its upthrust spire and convoluted domes suggested the bleached bones of a gargantuan animal.

This plastic-foam house just outside of Wisconsin Dells, Wisconsin, was named after the site of the "stately pleasure dome" decreed by Kubla Khan in Coleridge's poem. A tourist attraction, it encompasses 4,000 square feet in twelve rambling rooms and domes, and contains a host of novelties ranging from a Kohler climate-controlled Habitat to an Apple computer.

Foam dome

Polyurethane foam is insulating and structural material for experimental Xanadu.

But what I was interested in was the construction method and materials and their adaptability to houses where people might really live. So far, no one has lived in Xanadu. But Tom Gussel (Box 447, Wisconsin Dells, WI 53965), the prime mover behind it, has friends who have lived in foam houses and liked them. So Gussel and two partners built Xanadu as an experiment.

The basic domes were created by spraying polyurethane foam inside inflated plastic balloons, much the way Tecton (preceding story) starts its domes. But Gussel stopped with the 4- to 12-inch foam shell. No shotcrete was used. An acrylic-latex paint protects the ultraviolet-sensitive foam on the outside, and a fire-resistant Thermatek coating was sprayed inside. Construction took only days.

So far, there have been no real studies of Xanadu's energy requirements. Over several summers, when it has often been packed with tourists, the air-conditioning needs have reportedly proved trivial. It has never been heated during winter. The builders claim that other foam houses have shown remarkably low heating bills, but there have been no thermal studies of them, either. One can guess that the lack of seams and cracks, plus the high insulating value of the foam (R-28 or greater, depending on thickness) would keep heating costs low if the concrete ground slab and perimeter were properly insulated.

But a foam home raises a number of safety questions. Would an intruder be able to cut through the walls?

The tough interior and exterior coatings provide an adequate barrier, Gussel believes. "A burglar could cut through with a chain saw, but he could cut through the walls of a wood house, too," he pointed out.

A more important concern is the flammable nature of polyurethane and the toxic fumes it emits in a fire. The builders of Xanadu feel that the Thermatek minimizes the hazard. I was not convinced, mainly because the Thermatek was cut away in places for electrical hookups.

But Gussel is now working with a subsidiary of Pennzoil Corporation to develop an alternative foam made from a byproduct of copper mining. The company is building a model house near Tucson to test the foam. "There are still problems to be solved," Gussel reported, "but the foam appears to be fire resistant, and it should be inexpensive."

Xanadu was built at low cost, but the price of the petroleum-base polyurethane foam has risen considerably since then. "If we succeed with this new foam," Gussel said, "I think we'll have a process that will be about half the price of conventional construction"—*E. F. Lindsley.*

Cost-cutting concrete waffles

"This could become the plywood of the concrete industry," predicts one expert about Waffle-Crete. Like plywood, these precast-concrete panels make efficient use of raw material, cost less, and have a high strength-to-weight ratio.

"We use the same amount of concrete in a Waffle-Crete panel wall as we'd normally use to build a 3½-inch-thick solid wall," says Richard Malmberg of Van Doren Industries (Box 1008, Hays, KS 67601). "But the Waffle-Crete panel has 8-inch-thick sections and, in most applications, performs more like an 8-inch-thick solid wall than one half as thick," he adds.

To make a panel, concrete is poured into a waffle-shaped, plastic-and-aluminum mold, then covered with an insulating top. The top seals in heat so the concrete cures overnight. The final product is a grid of 8-inch-thick, steel-reinforced joists linked by 2-inch-thick rectangular slabs reinforced with wire mesh. The panels can be used for load-bearing walls and floors and, according to Malmberg, are much stronger than thinner, solid slabs.

Waffle-Crete molds are reusable and light enough to truck to a site if shipping the panels would be too costly. To cut construction time, molds have built-in formers for bolt holes, rebar channels, and wiring and plumbing runs. Workers bolt the panels together as they are set in place, reducing the amount of temporary bracing usually required when installing precast walls.

But Waffle-Crete is more than a cost-saving building system. "Precast-concrete construction reduces air leaks in exterior walls to near zero," says Dave Van Doren, Van Doren Industries' president. "Because of its mass, concrete also stores and releases heat in a thermally efficient way," he adds.

Van Doren capitalized on these thermal qualities when building his own home (see photo). Its walls have an R-value of R-17.9. The interior cavities contain standard fiberglass batts, but the exterior has an extra layer of foamboard insulation covered with a thick coating of fiberglass-reinforced concrete. With the aid of an efficient, solar-assisted heat pump, Van Doren says he heats and cools his 4,500-square-foot home for less than a dollar a day.

The company now has forty authorized Waffle-Crete producers in the United States and Canada and hopes to expand that number to two hundred fifty in the next five years—*Susan Renner-Smith.*

Cost-cutting concrete waffles

Conventional-looking house (above) has unconventional waffle-shaped, precast-concrete walls (left), which block air leaks.

The vented-skin house

Basically, the concrete-block house built by George J. Antonich and Charles W. Barcelo, principals in the Red Carpet Development Corporation, Ormond Beach, Florida, is a sister under the skin to hundreds of thousands of other concrete-block houses in the South. But what a difference in that skin! It starts with the insulation: They put it *outside* the block. Then they nailed on 1×2 furring strips. Over that they put a veneer—cedar siding and brick. Along the bottom of the house they ran a continuous grille. They put a vent in the roof ridge.

The result: "We estimate, based on a computer model, that this skin system operates 30 percent more efficiently than a conventional system with furring strips and insulation inside," says Antonich.

It works by lightening the heat load—picking up the heat of the sun before it can penetrate into the house. "Those furring strips give us ¾-inch-deep channels," says Barcelo. "Air flows in at the bottom between the insulation and the skin, is heated, and rises naturally to the eave line. Then it continues into the truss space, where it hits a reflective shield—composition board with aluminum facing—and goes out through the ridge vent."

In the hot Florida summer, Antonich and Barcelo figure that their system, plus the thermal mass of the concrete block, cools the inside surface of the block by 4 to 6 degrees. It is not a total cooling system; it is designed to reduce the heat load on a house that will—for humidity as well as heat—be air-conditioned.

A new idea? "The double-skin roof is an old idea in the South," says Philip W. Fairey of the Florida Solar Energy Center, Cape Canaveral, who suggested it to the two builders. "It was used in the design of ice houses."

What about winter? In Palm Coast, Florida (an ITT community development on the Atlantic coast, just north of Daytona), where the vented-skin house stands, cold weather is less of a problem. Even so, the concrete block with the insulation outside becomes a collector, storing interior heat—from people, cooking, lights, and sun.

The idea could also be applied to an existing house: "Just tack on an additional skin," says Barcelo. "You really don't need it on *all* sides—just the walls that get maximum sun exposure"—*Everett H. Ortner.*

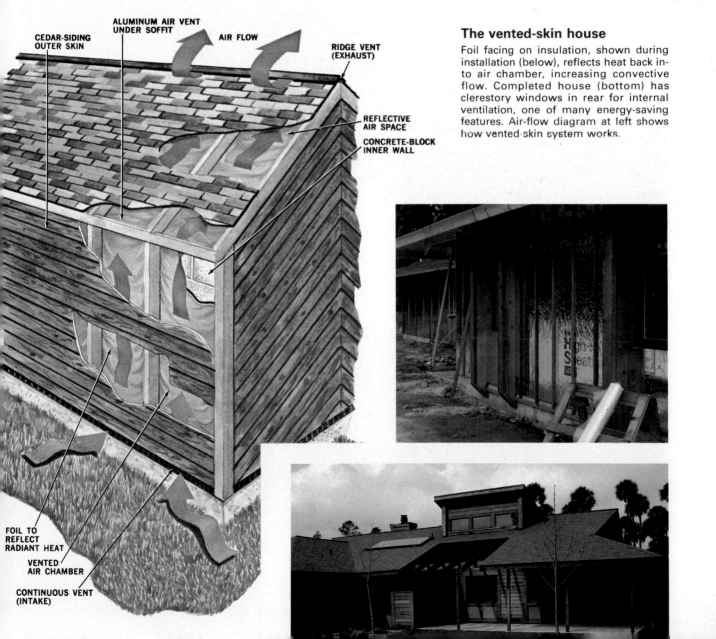

CEDAR-SIDING OUTER SKIN
ALUMINUM AIR VENT UNDER SOFFIT
AIR FLOW
RIDGE VENT (EXHAUST)
REFLECTIVE AIR SPACE
CONCRETE-BLOCK INNER WALL
FOIL TO REFLECT RADIANT HEAT
VENTED AIR CHAMBER
CONTINUOUS VENT (INTAKE)

The vented-skin house

Foil facing on insulation, shown during installation (below), reflects heat back into air chamber, increasing convective flow. Completed house (bottom) has clerestory windows in rear for internal ventilation, one of many energy-saving features. Air-flow diagram at left shows how vented-skin system works.

passive solar kit homes

A passive solar home used to mean a custom-built, architect-designed structure. Getting one built usually presented problems. Even a few years ago, just finding an architect knowledgeable in solar design wasn't easy. And once you had an architect and a design, contractors made costly mistakes because they were unfamiliar with special building techniques.

Today all that may be changing. The companies that sell manufactured homes are now adding passive solar models to their catalogs. These are precut, panelized, or modular buildings that are partially or completely prefabricated in factories and then trucked to building sites where they are quickly assembled by trained crews. Manufactured homes account for more than 30 percent of new construction. Here's a sampling:

• Deck House, a Massachusetts-based maker of precut contemporaries, recently unveiled a hybrid passive design wrapped around a two-story solarium (below) that features Heat Mirror insulating glazing.

• Acorn Structures announced its Independence series of four passive solar models. Among the four, there are price options based on finished homes, rough finishes, and just erected shells. Prices: $50,000–$130,000 and up.

• One home company's design won an award in the First National Passive Solar Design Awards Competition. It's a precut post and beam made by Sawmill River Post & Beam (page 16). Price is about $80,000.

• Dixie Royal Homes of Cookeville, Tennessee, has developed four designs under contract with the Tennessee Valley Authority. "Building a passive solar home is not an earth-shaking technical marvel," says Solar Consultant Dr. Kris Ballal, "but we decided to build one that is cost-

effective." Price of Dixie Royal's modular 950- to 1400-square-foot homes are $22,000 to $29,000 F.O.B.

• A passive solar log cabin? Yes. Real Log Homes offers a series of four solar models from 1,200 to 2,100 square feet (drawings, overleaf). Price range: $16,800 to $35,500.

Home manufacturers have benefited from the pioneering efforts of others as well as from recent sources of information on passive solar design. References such as Edward Mazria's *Passive Solar Energy Book* (Rodale Press) and computer simulation programs including Total Environmental Action's TEANET and PASCALC, and Princeton Energy Group's PEGFIX, were credited by several companies I talked with.

Help has also come from the Department of Energy's Manufactured Buildings Program, with its goal of mass production and sale of energy-conserving, passive solar buildings. Dr. Fred Morse, director of DOE's Office of

Solar Buildings says: "This is an important experiment in how government can work with business to accelerate the rate and guide the direction of change." Participants in the residential part of DOE's program include such companies as Boise Cascade, National Homes, Northern Homes, Guerdon Industries, and Wick Building Systems. (The program also includes commercial buildings: Butler Manufacturing Company, the world's largest maker of prefab metal buildings, has already developed designs for two climates and completed one prototype.) Most have completed designs and are now building or testing prototypes. Others, such as Acorn Structures, are simultaneously going into test marketing.

There's more than one way to get to Boston, as they say. That's also true for passive solar kit homes. I visited two in Massachusetts that represent different approaches. One, a direct-gain type, is almost entirely passive—no moving parts (that is, unless you're a purist and count a small fan in the attic). The other is more active: a hybrid system in which a sophisticated network of ducts and blowers, all automatically controlled, channels heated or cooled air to where it's needed.

Recently Shirley and Hugh Kirley and their children moved into Solar Woodbox, a 2,000-square-foot precut home made by their company, Sawmill River Post & Beam. The compact, three-level design has 413 square feet of south-facing glass for direct solar heating. Heat is stored in forty 12-inch-diameter-by-8-foot-high fiberglass tubes from Kalwall Corporation, each filled with water that will be dyed a green-blue for appearance and better heat absorption. Mylar insulating shades from the Insulating Shade Company are drawn at night over the windows to prevent heat loss. Hugh Kirley says he designed the house "using criteria from Mazria's book to hold the inside temperature at 70°F on a sunny January day." Sawmill River has built hundreds of post-and-beam homes and distributes east of Chicago and into Canada.

After my visit with the Kirleys in Amherst, I drove to Acton, near Boston. There I was met by Molly Tee of Deck

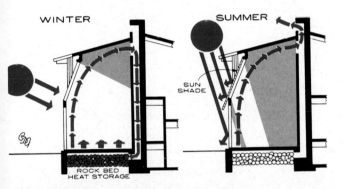

Two-story solarium (interior, facing page) in the Conservatory House collects heat; when temperature reaches 73°F in winter, microprocessor control sends warm air to rock bed (drawing). In summer, excess heat is vented in this Deck House model.

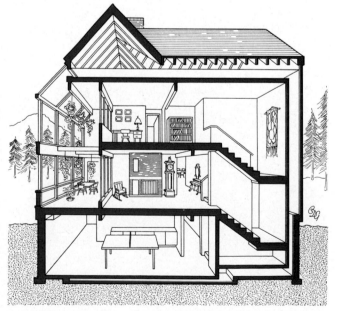

Independence IV, a 1,900-square-foot home from Acorn Structures, is a modified double envelope. In winter a fan ducts warm air from a south-facing solarium to the basement slab. Acorn offers three other models in the Independence series.

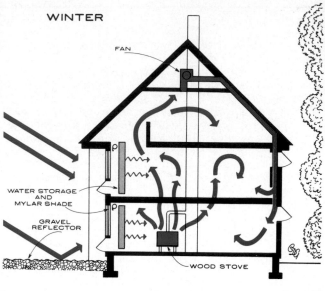

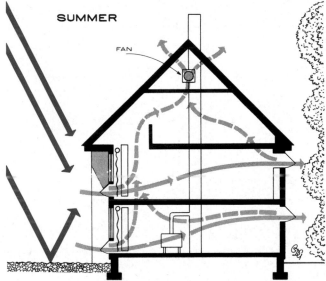

House. Molly showed me a brand-new model that Deck House was just putting the finishing touches on: the Conservatory House, a luxury home built around a two-story-high "conservatory" or solarium. As befits a home that will sell in the $150,000 range, all of its heating and cooling functions are automatically controlled by microprocessor-based control. In winter, excess heat in the solarium is ducted to a rock bed under the family-room floor. In summer, electrically operated sunshades screen the upper sloped glazing, and excess heat is vented outdoors.

The Conservatory House is designed so one or more parts can be closed off when they're not needed. Bedroom wings, for example, can be sealed when children or guests are not at home. Primary living areas—kitchen, family room, and living room—are set on the south side of the house for direct solar gain. Stairs, halls, utility room, and garage are placed on the north side to serve as buffers from cold winter winds. The lower level of the house is sunk into a berm reaching almost to the second story on the north wall.

Deck House sells from three to four hundred homes annually; they are precut at the factory and shipped nationwide. "They're essentially custom homes with factory economics," Molly Tee told me. "We're usually 30 to 35 percent under architect-designed custom houses"— *Richard Stepler*.

Sawmill River Post & Beam's Solar Woodbox (top left photo and drawings above) has a precut, white-pine, post-and-beam frame. Interior temperature swings are moderated by forty translucent fiberglass tubes, each filled with 47 gallons of water.

FOR MORE INFORMATION

Acorn Structures, Box 250, Concord, MA 01742; **Deck House**, 930 Main St., Acton, MA 01720; **Dixie Royal Homes**, PO Box 805, Cookeville, TN 38501; **Real Log Homes**, PO Box 202, Hartland, VT 05048; **Saw Mill River Post & Beam**, PO Box 227, Leverett, MA 01011.

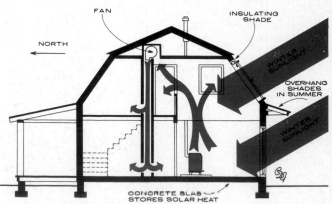

Even log homes, with their solid, high-thermal-mass exterior walls, are being adapted to passive solar. Sequoia B, in Real Log Homes' Solar series, has sophisticated design features (cross section above) that belie its rustic appearance (left).

earth-sheltered housing

Tap an egg lightly and you'll fracture its fragile shell. But bury it in a hole in the ground and the heavy soil pressing on all sides won't harm it. Nature fashioned the eggshell of brittle material, so it has virtually no tensile strength. But she gave it a superb geometry for resisting compressive forces.

While there's not much reason to bury an egg in a hole in the ground, there are plenty of good reasons to bury a house. Chief among them is energy saving. Since the soil remains at a much more moderate temperature than the air above, it takes less energy to keep an earth-sheltered house comfortable. Also, the earth has fairly high thermal mass, which slows down heat flow. That means the soil is coldest not in the winter but in the spring, and warmest in the fall instead of the summer.

Like an eggshell, many building materials are much stronger in compression than in tension. Thus, curving walls and roofs are better than flat ones at resisting the immense weight of the soil over an earth-sheltered house and the lateral pressure against its walls. With geometry on their side, earth-sheltered houses don't have to be so massive. That can save both materials and labor. Curving shapes also enclose a maximum volume with a minimum of wall area. That means less unwanted heat loss and gain.

With these advantages in mind, the designers of the earth-sheltered houses on these pages have avoided boxes and turned instead to domes, cylinders, and arches.

1. Modular domes

Its walls are straight, its corners square, but soaring overhead are 12-foot-high domed ceilings that give this house

Terra Dome's modular houses are made of poured, reinforced concrete. "It's a continuous pour from the base of the walls to the top of the dome," explains Terra Dome staffer Nancy Day (below). "When one module has set, the forms are stripped and set up for the next one." The model home shown, in Independence, Missouri, is 6½ modules.

Dome modules are linked by 16-foot-wide arches (above). Aluminum wall forms and fiberglass dome form load onto a trailer for travel.

an unusual airiness. More to the point, the domed ceilings are strong: "About twenty times stronger than a flat roof," said Gayle Scafe, president of Terra Dome Corporation, Independence, Missouri. The handsome house I was visiting is the original model for Terra Dome, and home to Gayle, his wife Dona, and three of their six children. Now, Terra Dome and its licensed dealers have over 150 houses and commercial buildings built or under construction.

Terra Dome houses are composed of 24-, 28-, or 40-square-foot modules and built by a system Scafe devised. Any number of modules can be massed together to form a house of the desired size.

The modular system means rapid construction and reduced labor costs. Basic cost of a Terra Dome shell is $16 per square foot (with concrete at $38 per cubic yard). Total cost of the house is usually about double that. A new model in Grand Junction, Colorado, cost $31.50 per square foot, for example.

The Scafes heat their house with the sun (most of the windows face south) and a wood stove. An air handler circulates the heat through PVC pipe under the floor. Each module contains approximately 50 yards of concrete, which provides plenty of thermal mass to store the heat and even out peaks and dips in temperature. Polyurethane-foam insulation (1½ to 2 inches) is sprayed or rigid polystyrene board is glued on the outside of the roof and down the walls to a foot below frost line. The bottom of the walls and the slab are uninsulated, which ties the house into the thermal mass of the soil.

An overhang protects the south windows from the high summer sun. A small (1½ ton) air conditioner is used primarily for humidity control. "Before it was installed, we had three weeks of temperatures up to 110 degrees every day," Dona Scafe remembered. "The highest it got in the house was 84 degrees. But the humidity reached a sticky 85 percent." In future years, after the concrete has lost most of its moisture, the house should be much less humid.

2. Cylinder with see-through roof

"You can't build a house like that," the county official told Gordon Young when he presented the blueprints.

"Oh, yes I can," Young assured him. And recently this inventive electrical and nuclear engineer, with extensive experience in solar engineering, invited me to Salt Lake City to see his "impossible" house, now nearly complete.

We drove east from the city into Emigration Canyon in the Wasatch Mountains. "There's the house," Young said, pointing to a broad, whitish cone about two-thirds up the mountain. "People tell me it looks like a flying saucer."

I could see why.

The house is a 71-foot-diameter cylinder made of 8-inch grouted and steel-reinforced concrete block. It's buried to the top of the walls. There are no windows. Gordon Young's solution to lighting an underground house is unique: More than two-thirds of the roof is transparent acrylic. From inside, the view is awesome. Jagged mountain peaks loom all around.

The house has 4,000 square feet of living space on two levels. The lower floor is surrounded by 2,000 square feet of planting beds. A separate "view tower" off the entry foyer will also have an acrylic roof—and a view of Salt Lake City in the valley below.

The see-through roof is supported by radial wood trusses and concentric circles of ⅜-inch guy wire. The acrylic panels are glued on with silicone adhesive. The center of the cone is made of ⅛-inch opaque fiberglass. Originally, Young and his architect, Allen B. Erekson, designed the roof to be entirely transparent and supported only by radial steel cables. But the building site is buffeted with strong, gusty winds. "I ran all the wind-load calculations, and my head knew it was okay—but my stomach wasn't so sure." So Young and the structural engineer devised the alternate design.

Movable insulation—two computer-controlled panels—will hang on tracks under the acrylic roof. The panels can be nested so that anything from half to all of the roof is covered at once. On a sunny winter day, the insulation will cover the northern half of the roof, leaving the southern half exposed. The sun will provide about 75 percent of

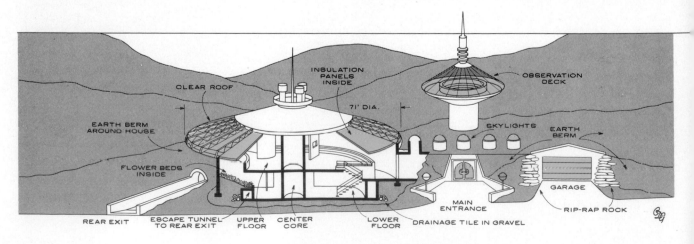

the heat the house requires, Young calculates. "Actually, I think we'll get better than 80 percent," he said, "but it's such an unusual house, I'd be foolish to say." He plans to produce much of his electricity with photovoltaic cells or a windmill.

Young also hopes to build a small village of advanced, energy-efficient houses on his mountainside. Already the holder of two patents, he is working on a roof system that could make a smaller version of a house like his very affordable.

3. Culvert-pipe house

Hermann J. von Fraunhoffer, president of Concept 2000 Inc., an architectural, engineering, and contracting firm in Phoenix, Arizona, builds underground houses of corrugated-steel culvert pipes—the kind used for highway underpasses. Concept 2000's nationwide dealership with Armco Steel Co. allows them to service owner builders. A crane lowers the sections into place and the crew bolts a typical 44×22×16-foot structure together in just 150 hours. Fraunhoffer noted additional advantages: "VA and FHA acceptance, cost-effective waterproofing, limitless earth covering, and full view of front and back yards."

But while concrete gets stronger with age and thus should last for centuries, steel can corrode. "The rate depends on the acidity of the soil," Fraunhoffer noted. "The industrial design life of these culverts is fifty years, untreated." He uses a heavier galvanizing dip and controlled backfill, then wraps them in EPDM membrane. "That at least doubles their life," he said.

Another consideration, especially in a cold climate, is the fact that masonry offers a great deal of thermal mass to store and distribute heat. Steel does not. On the other hand, steel's heat conductivity ties the house into the thermal mass of the soil itself. In the hot Phoenix climate, Fraunhoffer puts no insulation on the houses. "We allow the cooler earth to cool the residence," he explained. "While daytime temperatures can reach 115 degrees, the soil will be around 75 degrees at floor level."

Concept 2000 houses now run about $45 to $65 per square foot, depending on the owner builder's skill and experience.

4. Spray-on dome

Some other folks in Phoenix are going underground— with domes. Consulting Editor Richard Day reports on their system:

"Brothers Gene and Dale Pearcey of Earth Systems, Inc., wanted an earth-sheltered house that would conform to the neighborhood and meet codes and could be largely owner-built.

"Their prototype house is a 1,950-square-foot, two-story, 40-foot-diameter hemisphere. It was built over ten prefabricated steel arches bolted to a center ring at the top. The walls are of sprayed-on shotcrete reinforced with steel rebars. The shotcreting process is the same as that used to build swimming pools. The house, however, required some kind of backing. To avoid the expense of a formed wood backup, the Pearceys covered the frame with wire mesh and a fabric backing.

"After the shotcreting, waterproofing was applied and 2 inches of urethane-foam insulation sprayed over the top third of the dome. Backfill covers it up to the five-sided cupola, which provides light, passive solar heating, and ventilation.

"The floor of the house is 10 feet below grade; the top 10 feet of the dome projects above. This established a street-level elevation so the house blends with those around it.

"With the cupola and the two atria, the dome meets building-code specs for daylighting and ventilation. Ladders in the atria provide egress from the lower-story bedrooms.

"The limited space heating needed in Phoenix is supplied by the sun and a fireplace. To comply with FHA requirements, however, 10-kWh baseboard heaters were installed. The house needs no air conditioning, claims Pearcey. It has been occupied now for six months and the energy bills are 65 to 75 percent below those of above-grade houses, he reports.

"The prototype house cost about $65,000. Most work was subcontracted. The Pearceys have licensed dozens of dealers to build the dome in various sizes, and they also market a single-level do-it-yourself kit. Price for the 40-foot-dome kit is $10,500. According to Pearcey, shotcreting will add another $4,000 to $5,000. Further costs: land, excavation, backfilling, foundation, carpentry, mechanicals, and finishing"—V. Elaine Smay.

FOR FURTHER INFORMATION

Send a self-addressed, stamped envelope to the following addresses: **Culvert-pipe house**—Concept 2000, Inc., 19003 N. 52d St., Phoenix, AZ 85308. **Modular dome**—Terra Dome, Inc., 14 Oak Hill Cluster, Independence, MO 64057. **See-through dome**—Send $5 for brochure and additional $5 for cassette to Box 8551, Salt Lake City, UT 84108. **Spray-on dome**—for details on the construction technique, send $10 to Earth Systems, Inc., Box 35338, Phoenix, AZ 85069.

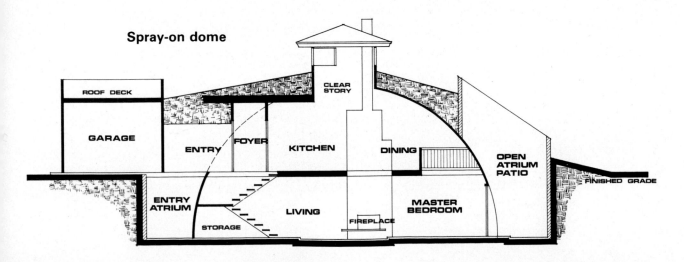

Spray-on dome

ROOF DECK · GARAGE · ENTRY · FOYER · KITCHEN · CLEAR STORY · DINING · OPEN ATRIUM PATIO · FINISHED GRADE · ENTRY ATRIUM · STORAGE · LIVING · FIREPLACE · MASTER BEDROOM

passive solar design

Passive solar design has been around ever since a prehistoric architect first sold a client on the idea that it was all right to put holes in the walls of his house. The ancient Greeks knew that window overhangs would block summer sun but admit winter sun. In America, the Anasazi Indians of the Southwest built adobe huts that stored daytime heat for release at night, and their successors, the Pueblos, lived in cliff dwellings heated by natural convection.

Unfortunately, abundant fuel supplies brought an end to this learning curve, and modern civilization forgot the craft of heating by the sun. Even when dwindling energy supplies startled scientists into taking another look at solar, most attention was focused on active systems (those that use mechanical or electrical energy to move heat.) Passive systems were considered to be inefficient and unsophisticated—not the sort of thing you'd risk writing your thesis on. Only when the Solar Group at Los Alamos Scientific Laboratory (LASL) started detailed computer modeling was it discovered—or rediscovered—that passive heating really works.

But that was only the beginning.

The Kelbaugh House
Passive design: Trombe wall and greenhouse; solar-heating fraction (calculated): 83%

Next they needed to know exactly how it works. How is heat transferred from one area to another? Is one kind of passive design better than others? How do the various components of a system go together to assist or detract from the total effect? Exactly how should a house be designed for best performance and lowest costs?

To find answers, researchers at LASL began a program of monitoring the performance of fifteen passive solar buildings. Their findings are not yet complete, but already some unexpected results have turned up. Certain components of the buildings—storage walls, rock beds, water ponds—performed in ways not always predicted.

Because the LASL researchers were studying existing buildings instead of building them for the purpose of the study, the program is not a neat, controlled experiment. "Suddenly in our neighborhood, a lot of passive solar buildings started going up," recalls Dr. Robert Jones, a member of the LASL solar team, "and we had the opportunity to study them if we got instruments into them when they were being built."

Arrays of thermocouples were embedded inside masonry walls, buried in rock beds, hung in greenhouses. Each building got its own mini weather station to record ambient temperatures and chart daily insolation (amount of sunshine). Also, use of auxiliary fuel was carefully recorded, where possible. But the data were not always comparable.

"The result," says Dr. Jones, "is that for two houses—the Balcombs' and Mobile/Modular II—we know most of the heat-flow paths and how much heat is flowing in them. For the others, the data are limited to one or more components of the total system."

Of the fifteen buildings, eleven are houses, three are commercial buildings, and one is a prototype of a passive solar mobile home. Among them, there is at least one representative of each of the five basic types of passive design—direct gain, thermal-storage wall, attached greenhouse, roof pond, and thermosiphon. However, most use combinations of the five and some even incorporate active components (see drawings). Most of the buildings are located in northern New Mexico (including all of those pictured except the Kelbaugh House, which is in Princeton, New Jersey). Los Alamos doesn't have the climate you might expect (see photo of Balcomb House):

Winters there are generally as cold as in Chicago, though insolation is greater.

Any passive system must have two elements: collectors to gather solar heat and a method of storing heat until needed. The simplest kind of system—called direct gain—uses southfacing windows as collectors and relies on walls and floors for storage. The Williamson House, monitored by LASL, has 290 square feet of south windows, 10-inch-thick adobe walls, and brick floors. Not surprisingly, temperatures measured on the surfaces of the walls and floor correlated closely to variations in insolation. Beneath the surfaces, temperatures stayed at a fairly constant level, but not enough heat was absorbed to keep room temperature from swinging dramatically with solar conditions.

To avoid close correlations between inside temperature and insolation, other types of designs separate the collector from the living areas of the house. In the Balcomb House, the collector is an attached greenhouse, which undergoes temperature swings of 30 degrees or more. But the living area of the house is separated from the greenhouse by 14 inches of adobe wall. Heat is stored in the wall for up

The Hunn House
Passive design: Trombe wall and direct gain; solar-heating fraction (calculated): 57%

The Balcomb House
Passive design: greenhouse; solar-heating fraction (measured): 83%

The Jones House

Passive design: thermosiphon and direct gain; solar-heating fraction (calculated): 84%

Mobile/Modular II

Passive design roof pond; solar-heating fraction (measured): 80%

The Williamson House

Passive design: direct gain; solar-heating fraction (calculated): 72%

to eight hours, and temperatures in the house vary by only about 5 degrees from day to night. Secondary storage is in two rock beds under the floors of the north-side rooms, which are charged by a fan that pulls hot air from the top of the greenhouse. Heat is also transferred to the house through doors in the adobe wall, which are opened during the day and closed at night.

The greenhouse collects 71 percent of incident solar radiation, of which only two-fifths ultimately goes toward heating the house. The rest is either vented or lost through the glazing. In studying what happens to this 40 percent, the LASL researchers found some surprises.

One finding was that the rock beds were not contributing up to their potential because they were losing heat at night by a backward flow to the greenhouse. This was corrected by the addition of back-draft dampers. With reverse thermosiphoning stopped, it was found that the beds were extremely important. They took heat from a place it wasn't needed at a time it wasn't needed and delivered it when and where it *was* needed.

The biggest surprise at the Balcomb House was the behavior of the adobe storage wall. Of the heat conducted into the wall from the greenhouse, a meager 15 percent actually emerged on the other side and contributed to house heating.

The largest contributor to heating the living space in the Balcomb House turned out to be natural convection through the open doors in the adobe walls. Closing the doors at night also played a major role; in the Kelbaugh House, whose attached greenhouse was always open to the house, night heat loss was dramatic.

Some of the unexpected results found in the Balcomb House showed up in other homes, too. For example, the rock bed in the Jones House also experienced reverse thermosiphoning, even though it was equipped with dampers to prevent this. Thermocouples in the rock bed showed that it charged adequately, reaching peak design temperatures five hours past solar noon. But with the blower that circulates this heat turned off, the bed lost 40 percent of its thermal charge overnight. Part of the loss— due to conduction through the walls of the bed and the plywood dampers— was expected. But a greater portion could only be explained by a backward flow of the thermosiphon system. When investigated, it turned out

that small cracks around the edges of the dampers were responsible.

The rock bed in the Hunn House was found to be virtually ineffectual. It was designed as an active-discharge system, but air heated by the Trombe wall reached the bed at a temperature too low to be effective. The two-story Trombe wall, made of 12-inch concrete blocks filled with concrete and covered with glass on the outside, was equipped with thermocouples laid at various depths inside the wall. These showed that the outside of the wall reached a maximum of 160° F and that this heat was conducted through the wall in six hours. Unlike the storage wall in the Balcomb House, about half of the heat passed through the wall to provide a heating effect. Still, backup sources are needed to supply about 40 percent of the heat for the Hunn House.

The performance of the wall would be boosted if night insulation were used over the glass. Also, a selective-surface wall covering that absorbs short-wavelength solar radiation but only weakly emits long-wavelength thermal radiation would cut heat losses. Finally, a wall built of materials with a heat capacity greater than concrete's would help.

One material with a high heat capacity is water, and that is what's used for storage in Mobile/Modular II, an experimental building designed to test the applicability of passive solar heating to mobile homes. Initially, the house exhibited overreaction to insulation changes: Room temperature soared above 90°F in the day and dropped to the low 60s at night.

Most of the excess heat was found to be due to direct gain through south windows. With these windows blocked and all heating supplied by the water bags, the day-to-night temperature swing was reduced to about 10 degrees. The biggest surprise was that the bags absorbed only about 40 percent of incident radiation. Bags of a darker material would raise the already-excellent solar-heating fraction of 80 percent.

The success of Mobile/Modular II may point the way that passive design is going. Although the LANL program will not produce any quick-and-easy answers, the experience will help assure that the next generation of passive homes will perform as well as conventional homes—and cost much less—*Benjamin T. (Buck) Rogers* and *Daniel Ruby*.

Photos: N. M. Solar Energy Assn.

FIVE APPLICATIONS OF PASSIVE SOLAR DESIGN

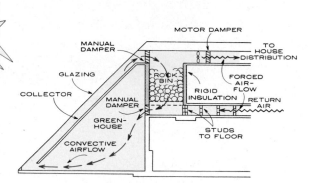

Thermosiphon: the Jones House

Sunlight is absorbed by metal collector, heating air, which rises and flows to rock bin. Air transfers heat to rocks and returns to collector. Fan draws air upward through bin and delivers it to house through ducts. Dampers prevent reverse flow.

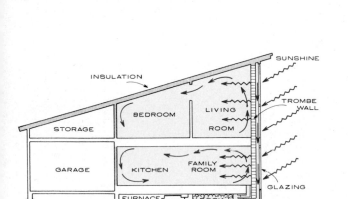

Trombe wall: the Hunn House

Solar energy striking 250-square-foot Trombe wall is partly absorbed and conducted through it, partly reradiated to air space between wall and glazing. Fan pulls heat from air space to charge rock bed. Second-floor wall gaps aid circulation.

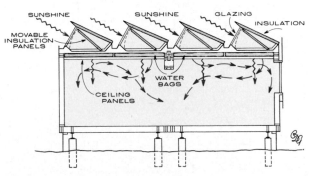

Roof pond: Mobile/Modular II

Sun shining through roof apertures is absorbed by 4,800 gallons of water in plastic bags, storing heat. When house is cold, heat is conducted through aluminum ceiling panels and radiated inside. Insulating panels close at night or when sky is cloudy.

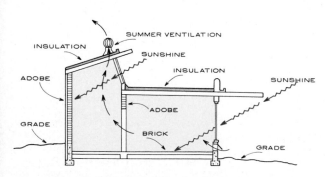

Direct gain: the Williamson House

Sun collected through clerestory windows is absorbed in adobe north wall; sun collected through south windows is absorbed in brick floor. Both store heat and radiate it when house cools. North wall is earth-sheltered and heavily insulated.

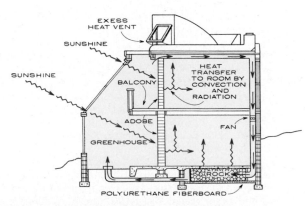

Attached greenhouse: the Balcomb House

Of solar radiation collected through 412 square feet of greenhouse glazing, some is transferred to adobe walls, some is moved by convection through open doors to living areas, some is drawn by fan to charge rock beds. Overheating is prevented by venting.

Drawings by Carl De Groote

slant for solar panels

"I've got a math problem for you," said my friend Warren Cole. He's a solar engineer who takes problem-solving in stride, so I knew it would be something substantial.

"I want to position a solar panel to face south and tilt up at 30 degrees—the latitude here in Austin. But the roof heads 40 degrees west of south, and it has a slope of 4 in 12." I could see what was coming. "Say I start with the panel parallel to the roof," Warren went on. "How far should I first rotate it within the plane of the roof, and then lift it, so it will end up the way I want it? If I knew the formulas, I could prepare the mounting hardware in advance, back in the shop, instead of having to improvise while up on the roof. That would save time, materials, and frustration."

I knew I could work out the formulas, and I was pretty sure they would be complicated. So I also decided to write a computer program that would prepare tables showing typical values. For use in the forty-eight contiguous states, Warren recommended tabulating for tilt angles of 25°, 30°, 35°, 40°, 45°, 50°, 55°, and 60°.

I had some questions for him: "First, do you always want the panel to face due south?" "Usually but not invariably," he answered. Local details such as trees or mountains or atmospheric peculiarities might indicate a modified heading. But we soon realized that would not complicate the tables, because what matters is not the actual headings of the roof and panel but only their difference—the angle between them. The recommendations when the roof heads S 35° W (35° west of south) and the panel is to head S 5° E will be the same as when the roof heads S 40° W and the panel is to head due south. The angle between the headings is the same (40°) in both cases. Warren advised tabulating the results for different angles of 0°, 30°, 45°, 60°, 90°, and 120°.

"Next, how do you ascertain the slope of the roof?" I wanted to know.

"We take a level and tape and measure the rise of the roof in a given run (diagram 1). Most levels are 2 feet long. Say in these 2 feet, the roof rises 8 inches. That's 8 inches in 24. That's called a 4-in-12 pitch." Warren suggested tabulating slopes of 3 in 12, 4 in 12, 5 in 12, 6 in 12, and 8 in 12.

I had another question. In some situations, the formulas might tell us to first rotate the panel 60°, for example, and then lift the rear edge a certain amount. But we could achieve the same aspect by first rotating the panel 30° in the other direction, and then lifting one of the sides (see

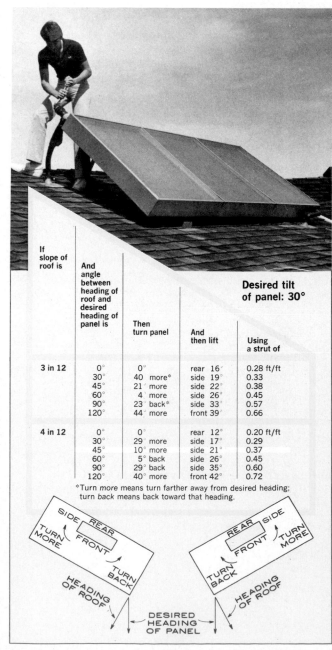

If slope of roof is	And angle between heading of roof and desired heading of panel is	Then turn panel		And then lift		Desired tilt of panel: 30°
						Using a strut of
3 in 12	0°	0°		rear	16°	0.28 ft/ft
	30°	40°	more*	side	19°	0.33
	45°	21°	more	side	22°	0.38
	60°	4°	more	side	26°	0.45
	90°	23°	back*	side	33°	0.57
	120°	44°	more	front	39°	0.66
4 in 12	0°	0°		rear	12°	0.20 ft/ft
	30°	29°	more	side	17°	0.29
	45°	10°	more	side	21°	0.37
	60°	5°	back	side	26°	0.45
	90°	29°	more	side	35°	0.60
	120°	40°	more	front	42°	0.72

*Turn *more* means turn farther away from desired heading; turn *back* means back toward that heading.

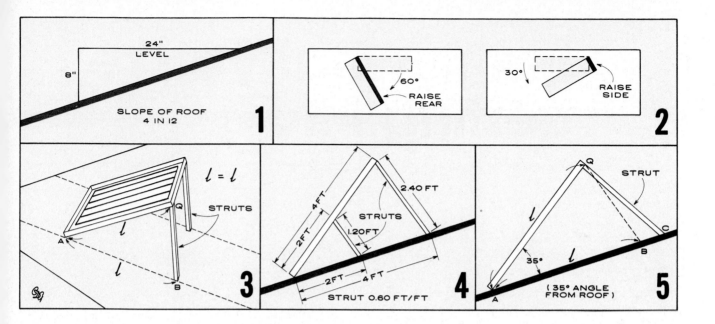

diagram 2). Wouldn't this second way look more pleasing, since the panel would more closely follow the lines of the roof? Yes, Warren said, that's the way they would do it. So I planned to take that into account.

I had one last question: "How do you proceed when you are told to lift the panel so many degrees? Isn't it much easier to be told to use a strut of so many feet to support a particular edge?" Warren agreed.

"And you put the struts at right angles to the roof?"

"No," Warren replied, "the panel receives stronger support when the strut cuts off equal distances along the roof and the panel" (see diagram 3.)

With the panel anchored at point A, fasten the strut at point B, chosen so that the distance AB along the roof is equal to the length of the panel edge, AQ. (In the diagram, both these distances are marked *l*.) What I decided to do, then, was to state the length of the strut in feet-per-foot—that is, the number of feet of strut for each foot of panel (diagram 4).

Warren had a final comment. "We want to fasten the strut to a rafter in the roof. But the rafter may be located not at B but at some other point, say C (diagram 5)." To find the required strut length, QC, just measure it on a scale diagram prepared from the information already available. As a check, I decided to supply the number of degrees in the lift angle, in addition to stating the length of the strut. (In diagram 5, the lift angle is 35°.)

The results

I prepared eight pages of tables, one for each of the panel tilt angles: 25°, 30°, 35°, 40°, 45°, 50°, 55°, and 60°. The accompanying math table shows the beginning of the page for a 30° tilt. Remember: (1) Tilt refers to the desired position of the panel relative to the earth. (2) Turn and Lift are relative to the roof. (3) The information about the strut is a decimal: 0.60 feet per foot is equal to 7.2 inches per foot.

This is the table I used to answer Warren Cole's original question. The relevant entries are shaded: panel tilt angle, 30°; slope of roof, 4 in 12; and angle between headings, 45° (the table does not list 40°, which was the actual angle, so we used the closest one to it). The table then advises: Turn the panel 10° more, then lift the far side 21° by

means of a strut measuring 0.37 feet for each foot along the adjacent panel edge.

The tables are too voluminous to print here, but I will supply them to readers on request. Tell me the tilt angle you want (it should be equal to your latitude for solar water heating and 15 degrees greater for space heating). Also tell me any special needs; for example, if your latitude isn't covered in the tables, I will send what you need. Write to me at Box 5902, Austin, TX 78763, and enclose a dollar to help me cover expenses.

Finally, here are the formulas. If you have a scientific calculator or a computer, you can use them to find the answers yourself. They apply throughout the world.

To start, you need to know the pitch of the roof (R). This is just the arc tangent of the slope—that is, of the fraction rise/run. For example, if the slope is 4 in 12, then $R = $ arctan $4/12 = 18.4°$.

Key factors are the three angles:

P, the desired tilt of the Panel,

R, the pitch of the Roof, and

H, the angle between the measured Heading of the roof and the desired Heading of the panel.

You must find:

T, the angle to turn the panel,

L, the angle to lift the panel, and

S, the length of the strut (per foot of panel edge).

First compute the auxiliary quantities A, B, and C, given by the equations:

$A = \sin P \sin H$,

$B = \cos P \sin R - \sin P \cos R \cos H$,

$C = \cos P \cos R + \sin P \sin R \cos H$.

Before going further, do this check: $A^2 + B^2 + C^2 = 1$.

The desired quantities, T, L, and S, are now given by the equations:

$T = $ arctan A/B,

$L = $ arccos C,

$S = \sqrt{2(1 - C)}$.

T negative means turn back. If T is greater than 45°, you may modify the turn as explained in diagram 2. Also, the formula for T loses its meaning when B = 0; in that case take T = 0°. Finally, the formula for L does not tell you which panel edge to lift; decide that by inspection—*Dr. Leonard Gillman.*

know what you're getting into

Dwight Mallary ran hot water over his razor and peered into a clear spot on the steamy bath mirror, while his wife, Susan, squinted at her hazy reflection and tried to apply eyeliner. They were running late for a dinner important to Dwight's career. Just then, their nine-year-old knocked on the door. "Daddy, I have to go to the bathroom!" Dwight growled his frustration. "Starting tomorrow," he yelled, "we're adding a bath—no matter what it costs us."

Five months later, the second bath—a two-fixture powder room—was in place. The Mallarys now know more about wet walls, stacks, and toilet types than anyone in their area. "If only we knew then what we know now," muses Dwight, "we'd have spent a lot less money."

Knowing the workings of a bath makes sense whether, like the Mallarys, you're adding a new one or you just want to replace aging fixtures. Only electricians get higher union wages than plumbers—and both trades get into major bath remodeling. Obviously, it pays to (1) see how much you can do on your own and (2) understand how a bath goes together so you understand what the pros are doing.

Some bathroom work is simple and inexpensive; some is not; and most falls in between easy and difficult. Here, starting with some of the easier undertakings, is the kind of information the Mallarys learned the hard way—by trial and error.

Decorative changes

You can save more than half the charges a painter or paperhanger would hand you, if you do the painting and the papering yourself.

Moisture-resistance and a scrubable surface are attributes of new high-gloss latex paints and all alkyds. For a super-shiny finish, top the color you apply with a clear coat of high-quality polyurethane.

Use two-component epoxy finishes to alter the color of fixtures or ceramic wall tile. *All* dirt and soap residue must come off first, and apply the epoxy only over a dry base. In any case, what you apply is only a temporary fix. A tub, for example, gets such rugged use that applied finishes don't last more than a few years; on a tile floor, they do not last at all well because of the abrasive use.

To put fresh color on a fiberglass shower stall or tub/shower combo, thoroughly clean the surface and allow it to dry. Then apply a product called Between Coat by McCloskey Varnish. When this is dry, put on a high-gloss alkyd.

Vinyl-coated wall coverings, perfect for the bath, are available in a profusion of designs and colors—enough to please just about any taste. Can you apply them on walls inside a shower stall? While they hold up better outside the shower, the critical factor is installation. What you don't want is the water to work its way under the covering through the vertical seams, or to work its way up from the bottom. One solution: Overlap each joint of the paper on the sidewall away from the direction of shower flow.

new lavatory $90 installed

Bathroom $550 installed

Shower $650 installed

Remodeling existing Bath $3,700

Tile work

Ceramic mosaics for the floor—those tiny squares, hexagons, and octagons of tile—were always ganged on 12 x 12-inch back sheets. They still are, but the new twist is the adhesive that replaces the thick mortar bed used to adhere the tile to the floor. Laying floor tile is a job almost anyone can do with a little practice and patience.

You can buy ceramic wall tile, in 4¼-inch squares, either separate or ganged in sheets. The ganged sheets are the latest wrinkle in continuing efforts to make your job easier. The tiles on the sheet are pregrouted—you need to grout only between butt joints of sheets.

There is still cutting to do with tile nippers or a tile brake. And mastic is applied with a serrated trowel. You'll find tools for rent or sale where tile supplies are sold, along with instructions on how to install tile.

Vinyl tile costs 30 to 50 percent less than ceramic tile and is even easier to install. Much of the 12 x 12-inch production today has the advantage of being self-sticking—you strip off the protection and press down tile. Even sheet vinyl is now designed for easy installing.

One note: The floor under the tile must be level. You may have to lay a subfloor of plywood or hardboard before you lay your tile.

Lighting

Replacing old fixtures with more efficient or better-looking ones is relatively inexpensive and not difficult. Prices for decorative fixtures are in the $20 to $100 range. You might, for example, replace a single incandescent ceiling light with a circular fluorescent fixture. Cost: about $30. Result: more light and less draw on electricity.

Alterations beyond this or adding new fixtures demand electrical know-how. And, of course, what you do must be to code, not just because you must abide by the regulations, but for the safety of your family.

Surprisingly, the local building inspector may be one of your best sources of help. Since he must OK the finished job, he knows the answer to such questions as: What kind of cable? Can I splice off existing cable? How do I tie into the electric entry? Can I put a light in the ceiling over the shower? (Yes, on that last one, and a good idea for ladies who shave their legs in the shower. Nutone offers a UL listed, vaporproof showerlight/ventilator combo.)

Snaking new cable from the entry through existing walls is easier if the bath is above open joists in the basement. A second-floor bath over a finished ceiling presents a bigger problem. At some point, the walls and ceiling will need to be opened, and later, repatched.

Since time equals money for the electrician, his charge for the replacement of an existing fixture (if you can get him for that small a job) would be low. For rewiring through existing walls and ceilings for new fixtures, fans, or heating devices, you can expect a big bill.

Ventilation

A power ventilator is a welcome addition, even for a bath on an outside wall with a window. Few people open a bath window in winter. And a power vent carries away more moisture and odors than a cracked window any time of the year.

Optimum ventilator location is centered in the ceiling. The device operates on 115-V current, costs around $20 to $25, plus roughly $5 to $8 for each 5 feet of duct, and another $15 to $20 for an exterior wall or roof louver. While the parts are relatively low in cost, installing the vent is tough, and

even tougher if there is no wiring now in the ceiling. What's needed in the latter case is to break through the ceiling; snake new wire to opening; install the outside louver, sealing the flange; run duct between joists from louver to ceiling opening; make connections; secure vent frame; and—finally—repatch the ceiling.

Or, while you're at it, you might consider combinations: a vent fan and ceiling light (about $45); a vent fan with a fixture mounting two infra-red heat lamps (about $55).

Bath fixtures

Of the three regulars—toilet, tub, basin—the drop-in or wall-hung basin is least costly and the easiest to install. China lavs start at around $40 and run to more than $150. (For the most part, size determines price.) A pedestal lav runs higher, as much as $250.

Hole positions for fittings are standard and match single- or dual-lever faucets. Replacing a basin involves turning off water supply beneath lav; removing the fittings; removing old and putting in new basin; replacing fittings; and turning on the water. There are variations—for example, a new vanity with built-in basin. Such an alteration presents no unusual problems and it gives you a

chance to switch to new fittings, which generally fall in the $40 to $80 category per set.

Replacing a toilet demands more work, and unit cost is higher than for most basins. Prices for a simple, rim-flush, water-saving toilet, with seat, begin at about $75. At the top of the bracket are elegant, low-profile, quiet-flush closets, some of which top $350.

The steps you must take to lift out your old toilet and put in a new one are not especially difficult. But an error in setting the flange or leveling the bowl is far more critical than canting a basin a bit.

Here is a quick summary of the procedure: cut off water supply; flush residual water; unhook supply pipe; remove tank; unbolt bowl; remove bowl; take out old flange (clean or replace); clean the floor; replace flange; fix wax gasket to new bowl; putty the new bowl rim; install flange bolts; carefully lower bowl over bolts; tighten nuts; check bowl level; fit washer to tank outlet (if a separate tank); set and fasten tank; cover the bolts; and, finally, install seat.

Size and weight of the tub are the biggest hurdles you face in attempting replacement. Prices for a normal 5-footer start at about $150 and go up to $500. Enameled steel and reinforced plastic tubs tend to be toward the low, and cast iron toward the high end of the range.

The moves necessary to replace a tub are not very difficult: shut off water supply; remove faucet and drain flanges; break wall seal and grout lines at floor; and carefully work out tub. Once it's out, check beneath for signs of rot. Make any repairs. Then backtrack to put in new tub. One often overlooked problem: Some of the new tub/shower combos won't fit through the bathroom door. Better measure before buying.

It's possible for a plumber and one helper to replace all three of the fixtures in one working day, assuming no hidden problems appear. The convenience of a one-day job is worth considering. It might be better to spend an extra $250 or so for the pros than to struggle with the job for the first time yourself.

Once you decide that the toilet should be moved from one wall of the bathroom to another, both labor time and overall costs begin to climb. The extensions for the supply and waste piping go in, and patches must be made at the site from which the fixture was moved. Also, as in the case of

electrical work, such plumbing jobs must meet local code requirements.

Many a do-it-yourselfer has taken on a plumbing project and come off with a grin of satisfaction and money in his pocket. Just as many have started the job and then been forced to call in the plumber when the work got out of hand. Whether or not you take on this kind of project is a decision you had best make realistically. In fact, once you move fixtures to new locations, you're into major remodeling, and you might as well go the route and replace the finish materials to create a totally new bathroom.

Moving walls

Gaining more space is a perfectly reasonable goal in a cramped bath. But it's costly. Rarely is there ever a wall in an existing bath that does not have piping, wiring, or, in some cases, heat duct or risers in it. That means there's nothing simple about moving a "wet wall"—whatever is inside the wall must be redirected. In any area with harsh winters, piping in the outside wall of the bathroom must be re-

directed to the inside walls. Even a well-insulated outer wall is generally too cold for the supply piping. Yes—an outside wall can carry drain pipe, but not traps.

One alternative to moving walls to gain space is creating a separate dressing area for the master bath. If the piping is conveniently located, and there is extra space in the bedroom, a vanity/dressing table/lavatory combination could be built on the bedroom side of the wall separating bedroom and bath.

When you consider it, there are plenty of ways to make changes in your bathroom on your own and save a bundle, even though you've never held a paintbrush. Once the work graduates to plumbing or electrical changes, however, you would be wise to move ahead very cautiously.

Average bath remodeling costs, when the contractor handles all the work, begin at around $900 for fixture replacement, and rise to the neighborhood of $6,000 for a major remake of the bathroom—*John H. Ingersoll.*

two ways to insulate basement walls

You've been wanting to finish off that basement for years. Maybe you need a den or a workshop. But how do you justify the cost?

The answer is to do it yourself. Now there are rigid foam panels that not only help you get the job done quickly but will eventually save you money. It's estimated that nearly 20 percent of all home heat loss occurs through uninsulated basement walls. Little wonder—an 8-inch-thick concrete foundation is only slightly better at insulating you from the cold than a single pane of window glass. That not only makes your home more expensive to heat, but it accounts for the cold, damp environment of your basement.

In the past, the solution has been lots of work: You'd build a conventional 2×4-studded wall against the masonry, fill it in with fiberglass insulation, and finally cover it with drywall or paneling. It's expensive, provides only limited insulation value by high-efficiency standards, gobbles up floor space, and is time-consuming to do.

There are several ways to install insulating panels, including the two shown here. But any method is easier and more effective than the old way.

The most commonly installed rigid insulation is extruded polystyrene sheathing, such as Dow Chemical tongue-and-groove (TG) Styrofoam panels (next page). These are applied directly to the wall with adhesive, but you've got to apply your own drywall layer, and, since foam will burn, most codes require the finish wall to be nonflammable. The paneling in our photo of the finished basement was given a thorough flame-retardant treatment.

The newer insulating panel is Rmax Thermawall. It's

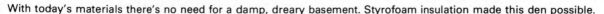

With today's materials there's no need for a damp, dreary basement. Styrofoam insulation made this den possible.

Styrofoam polystyrene sheathing is applied directly to the foundation wall. The panels may be cut by scoring and snapping. Application steps are shown in top row of photos. First, mastic adhesive is applied down panel every 8 to 12 inches. For economy, 3-inch-long beads, spaced 3 inches apart, would do. To prevent dissolving the Styrofoam, Dow recommends its No. 11 adhesive in caulking-gun cartridges. Prepare only one panel at a time and place against wall (second photo). Press every square foot uniformly with your hands to ensure a permanent bond. Don't insulate over water or drain pipes — they may freeze. Butt panels against pipes, and, if possible, wedge fibrous insulation material behind them. (You can bridge the pipes with finishing drywall.) Allow a full day for curing before installing the drywall (top right). Secure with mastic bond against insulation; nail top and bottom to furring. Joints may now be finished for painting, or paneling can be applied. Stud framing (bottom left) is still required around built-ins like this heat-circulating fireplace, faced with veneer brick (bottom right).

more than a foam board: It's a complete sandwich, with a foil backing, that gives you a rigid insulation panel (isosyanurate foam) and a gypsum-board finish wall in a single installation. I installed this in my home, using techniques shown in the photos.

Both of these products are easy to use and made for the do-it-yourselfer. Here's how they work.

Rmax Thermawall

Although it can be bonded directly to a masonry wall (the panels must be supported until the adhesive sets), I found it better to use the special Thermawall fastening system. The hangers (see photos next page) don't take up as much room as conventional wall studs yet allow enough space to run rear plumbing and wiring lines.

Working with Thermawall is much the same as handling ordinary drywall, except that it is much less fragile. A long-bladed knife is all you need; just score, cut through the insulation and paper backing, and snap off the piece you want. Taping and filling the joint are easier, too, since

there are no nail holes to fill. The only precaution: Be sure no foam is left exposed, since it is flammable.

My son and I installed and finished (except for painting) two 12- and 16-foot walls of our photo-lab area in three hours. The result was a drywall with an R-19 rating and a vapor barrier. Yet this finish wall is only 3¼ inches thick, compared with the 6½ inches necessary to obtain this much insulation by conventional methods.

Thermawall is manufactured in five thicknesses ranging (in ½-inch increments) from 1½ inches to 3½, including the ½-inch gypsum. It yields R-values of 11 to 25 when using the Thermawall fastening system. It's made by Rmax, Inc. (13524 Welch Road, Dallas, TX 75240), and is available through local building suppliers.

Styrofoam

Styrofoam TG polystyrene insulation comes as single sheets that are applied directly to the masonry walls. They are then covered with the wallboard or paneling of your choice.

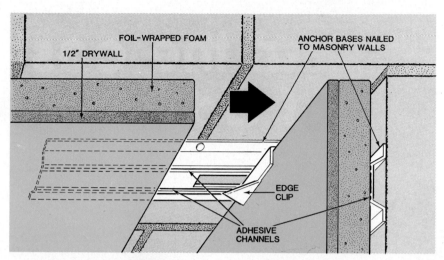

The procedure is simple: Apply beads of the adhesive to the back of the panel, press the panel in place, and apply uniform pressure across its face to ensure a firm bond with the masonry wall. (Many petroleum-based adhesives will dissolve polystyrene, so be sure to use a compatible type.)

Since the bond is fast and permanent, preparation is extremely important. Remove moldings and trim from all windows and doors. Attach horizontal wood nailers continuously along top and bottom edges of the walls and around the window and door openings. These strips should be 2 inches wide and the same thickness as the insulation panels you've chosen; they'll be used later to secure the covering wallboard.

All electrical wiring and plumbing must be in and secure—it will be extremely difficult to reroute lines once the panels are in place. In most cases, the electrical wiring should be run along the bottom of the wall so sockets may be easily installed. But, in a basement, most plumbing (if present) will come in from overhead.

Also, be sure the masonry wall surface is structurally sound, clean, smooth, and dry. It must be free of all grease and loose paint.

Water—the big enemy

Get water in an unfinished basement and you mop. Get it in your new den, and you could start building all over again. Naturally, *any* water problem must be repaired and sealed before walls go in place.

But there is yet another less obvious—and more serious—problem if you live in an area with water-retaining soil, such as expansive clays. When the foundation wall is insulated, the outside soil is deprived of the heat it once got from the house. Result: possible freezing. And with it comes soil expansion that, under severe conditions, could exert enough pressure to crack foundation walls.

In these areas, the standard cure is to install drainage tile or perforated plastic pipe covered with 6 inches of crushed stone outside at the base of the footings, so water will be drained away from the walls before it can freeze. This will not only prevent the expansion problem, but will also dry out a damp basement.

I should point out that this problem pertains mainly in cold climates. But it may be worth checking with local building inspectors before you buy insulating materials—*Evan Powell.*

Rmax Thermawall laminates a drywall finish to a foil-wrapped foam panel. System uses edge clips to hold panels while adhesive sets. Photos, from top left: Start in corner by installing anchor bases with concrete nails (into grout lines, here). Full vertical sections to right of corner are for adhesive only (no clips). Insert clips in slot of horizontal half sections to left of corner, and drive one point into face of glued-up panel. Apply adhesive to these channels (inset) and push left-hand panel into clip-points still exposed. This secures the butt-joint corner. Outer edges of each panel are now secured with clips while rest of bases are nailed up, on 48-inch centers (last photo) with top strip 18 inches from ceiling and bottom strip 18 inches from floor.

cut the cost of adding on

When you are adding on to your home, you have a constant enemy: the budget. It's not uncommon for square footage to shrink and accessories to be scratched from the list between initial planning and the completed project.

But there is a way to cut your costs and save a lot of time, without sacrificing what you want. By using a modular system to design and build your addition, you can minimize material and labor waste.

Planning. Planning on a modular basis means that your addition is designed to accommodate standard size construction materials. The result is that the work requires fewer cuts and less seaming, and there is less waste for both framing and finishing materials. Most of the material you purchase then goes into your home—it's not hauled to the dump as scrap—and that means you get maximum square footage with a minimum of building materials.

Also, the labor saved makes the job go much more quickly. And, if you are using a contractor, the time saved can substantially lower the price you have to pay.

Overall dimensions. Although construction materials are available in a wide variety of sizes, there is a system of commonality throughout. With few exceptions, building materials work best on a module of 4 feet.

The message here is that you should plan your addition so the length and width are in multiples of 4 feet. If you do, the work will go more smoothly and materials will go farther. Some additional savings are possible if the length of your room addition is planned in multiples of 8 feet; however, depending upon circumstances, the savings may not amount to much.

Floor framing. Generally, joists are designed to span the short dimension (width) of a house. In order to avoid using extremely large joists, one or more beams may be run the length of the house to reduce the span.

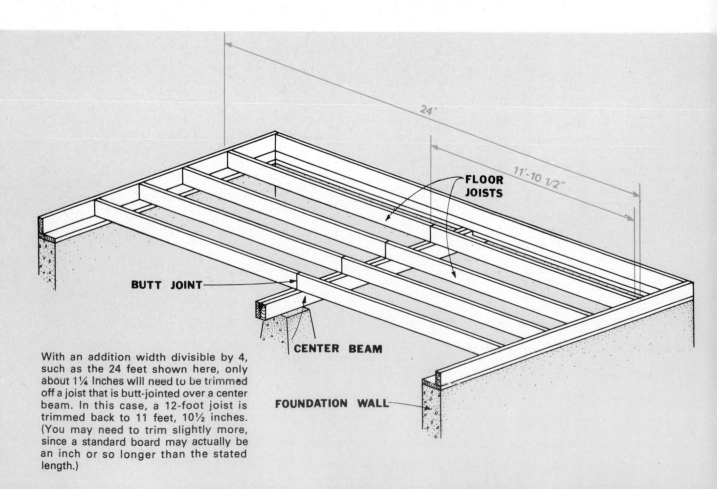

24'

11'-10 1/2"

FLOOR JOISTS

BUTT JOINT

CENTER BEAM

FOUNDATION WALL

With an addition width divisible by 4, such as the 24 feet shown here, only about 1¼ inches will need to be trimmed off a joist that is butt-jointed over a center beam. In this case, a 12-foot joist is trimmed back to 11 feet, 10½ inches. (You may need to trim slightly more, since a standard board may actually be an inch or so longer than the stated length.)

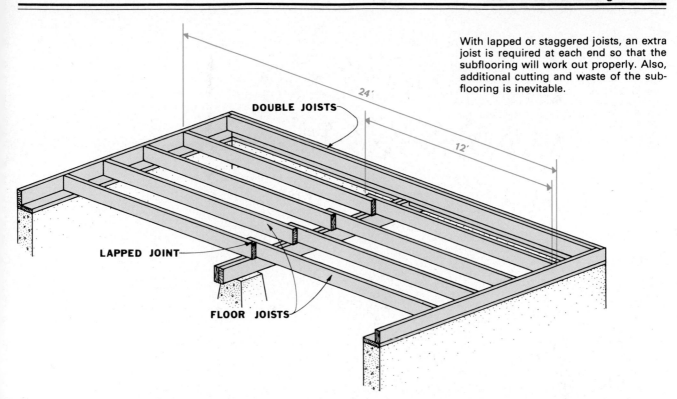

With lapped or staggered joists, an extra joist is required at each end so that the subflooring will work out properly. Also, additional cutting and waste of the subflooring is inevitable.

DOUBLE JOISTS

LAPPED JOINT

FLOOR JOISTS

Most additions will have either one center beam or none at all, depending upon the actual dimension. A 4-foot module works well for each. Since framing lumber is furnished in multiples of 2 feet, only a small piece must be trimmed from the end, as shown in an accompanying illustration.

Lapped or staggered joists may eliminate the need for cutting joists, but it requires double joists at the ends of the addition and additional work on the subfloor. "Butting" the joists is a better choice—it makes the overall job easier.

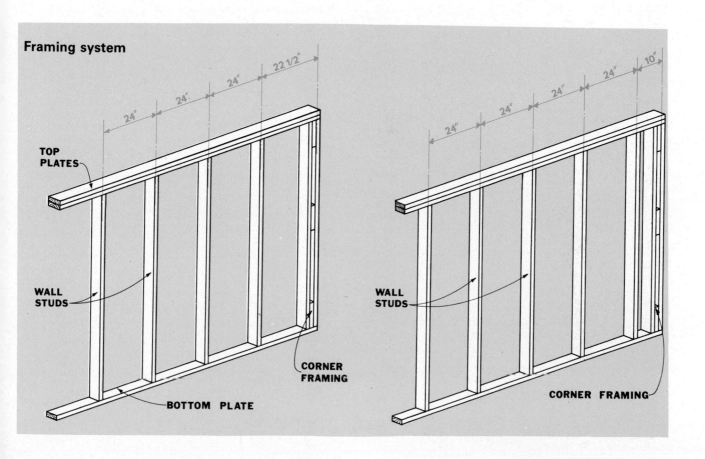

Framing system

TOP PLATES

WALL STUDS

BOTTOM PLATE

CORNER FRAMING

WALL STUDS

CORNER FRAMING

With a width in multiples of 4 feet and length in multiples of 8 feet, as shown, subfloor can be applied without any cutting or waste by allowing the seams to align along a single joist. Recent field tests have shown results of this technique to be equal in strength to a staggered subfloor.

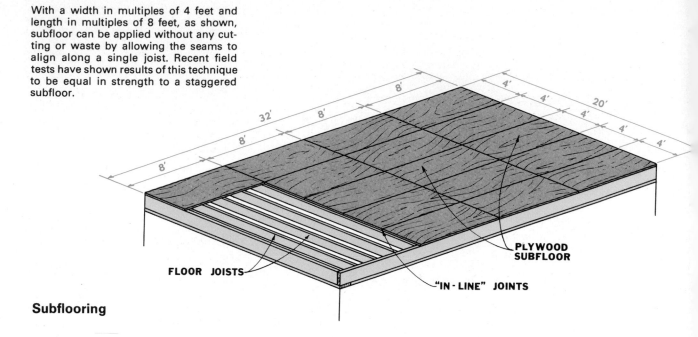

FLOOR JOISTS

PLYWOOD SUBFLOOR

"IN-LINE" JOINTS

Subflooring

The 4-foot module also works well for the length of the addition. Both 16-inch and 24-inch on center framing systems work out evenly in 4 feet. This helps maximize material usage by eliminating the need for an extra joist just a few odd inches from the end of the addition.

Subflooring. Most of the subflooring materials used today are manufactured in 4 × 8-foot sheets. The 8-foot dimension is placed at 90 degrees to the joists. When an addition's width is in multiples of 4 feet, and length is in multiples of 8 feet, the subfloor can be applied without any cutting or waste. This is accomplished by allowing the sheets to butt along the same joist. Field tests performed in recent years have shown that the common method of staggering plywood on subfloors and roof decking is no stronger than allowing the sheets to butt "in-line," along a single joist or rafter (check local codes).

Even if the length cannot be on an 8-foot module, adhere to a 4-foot module. The cutting will be at a minimum and waste may be eliminated or, at least, reduced.

Wall framing. As in floor framing, both 16-inch and

Windows

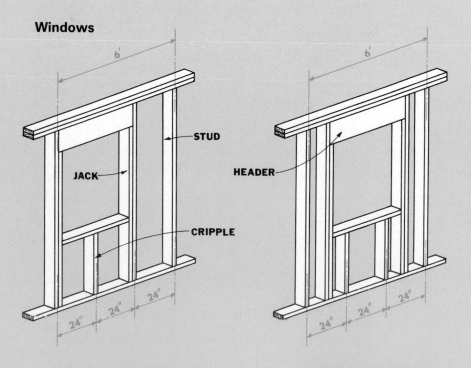

STUD

JACK

HEADER

CRIPPLE

WINDOW ON MODULE

WINDOW OFF MODULE

One advantage of modular construction can be seen in the accompanying drawings. When you use a 4-foot module, either the 16-inch or 24-inch (shown) framing system can be used with good results, and this applies to floor and roof framing as well as wall framing. Without a modular system, you can run into problems that cost time and extra material — you may, for example, be forced to place an extra stud or joist just inches from the end of your addition, as shown at the bottom of page 33. This page: Window at far left works with the framing system and will save one stud and cripple, compared to a window that works against the system, like the one near left. If, because of a window's width, only one side aligns, you still save cutting and placing one cripple.

24-inch stud framing work out evenly in a 4-foot module, eliminating odd sized stud spacing at the end of a wall. Today's sheathing materials and finish plywood and fiberboard panel siding all come in 4-foot widths. The only cutting for these materials, when using a modular system, will be for windows and doors.

There are many types of lapped siding, but most come in 8-, 12-, and 16-foot lengths. On a 4-foot module, there will also be less waste for this type of exterior finish.

For masonry or masonry-faced walls, both the standard 8-inch brick and 16-inch block course out evenly in 4 feet. This reduces the need for breakage and the over- or under-sized mortar joists sometimes required to fit odd wall lengths.

Design your windows and doors to work *with* the wall framing, instead of against it. By aligning at least one side of a window or door on the stud spacing pattern you will cut down on the number of studs you need to frame the opening.

Corners. If your plans call for your new addition to be something other than rectangularly shaped, continue the 4-foot module through the wall corners. Design the width of a corner and the distance from corner to corner in multiples of 4 feet, as is shown in the illustration below. This will allow the framing

and finishing materials to continue working out evenly, and so reduce the additional labor and extra materials usually associated with projects involving more than four corners.

Roofs. Both 16-inch and 24-inch framing and roof trusses work well in a 4-foot module. By observing a 2-foot overhang on both ends, the module will remain 4 feet in length for roof decking, though the width will vary because of the pitch of the roof. For flat (built-up) roofs, it will work out well in length and width.

As in floor framing, plywood decking may be seamed along a single rafter or truss, rather than staggered. If you use plywood clips on the roof decking, you eliminate the need for wood blocking underneath.

Roof trusses work particularly well with modular design. They provide strength equivalent to a conventionally framed roof, but at a much lower cost. Trusses are readily available from manufacturers in most areas, but can also be easily constructed on site.

Interior finish materials. The ideal room to finish is 12 × 12 feet, with a standard 8-foot ceiling. This allows walls to be covered evenly with two 4 × 12 sheets of gypsum board laid horizontally, or three sheets of 4 × 8 gypsum board or paneling laid vertically. The only cutting required would be for windows and doors. The floor could be covered with 12-foot-wide sheet vinyl or carpet, without seaming, and the ceiling would require three uncut 4 × 12 sheets of gypsum board. Such a room would waste virtually no materials and labor would be minimal.

But all rooms can't and shouldn't be 12 × 12 feet. Because of wall thickness, a home on a 4-foot module will have to have an odd-sized room.

Of course, you will want some rooms larger than 12 feet wide. Most carpets and sheet flooring also come in 15-foot widths. By observing 12 feet or 15 feet for one room dimension, the other dimension can be varied to make a larger or smaller room, but keep standard wall and ceiling material sizes in mind when setting the other dimensions. For a very large room, such as a recreation room, keep the width near, but not over, 24 feet. This allows laying two 12-foot widths of finish flooring side by side, requiring only one seam with little or no waste. The 24-foot width also works out well on walls and ceilings.

Interior finishing

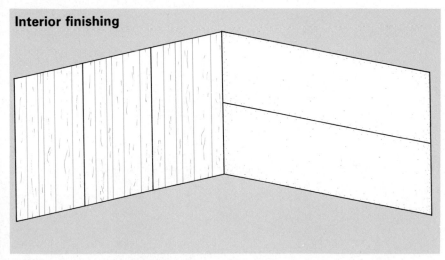

A 12-foot-wide interior wall with standard 8-foot ceiling can be conveniently covered with two 4 × 12-foot sheets of gypsum board laid horizontally (right) or three 4 × 8-foot sheets of gypsum board or paneling laid vertically (left). Only cutting required will be for windows and doors.

Areas that jut out

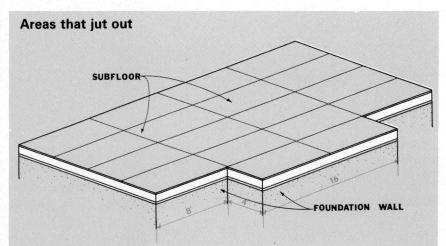

Are you planning an addition that is something other than rectangularly shaped? Even, for example, if your addition is to jut out from a main area, it's possible — and worthwhile — to keep everything on a modular system. To do that, make the jut width and length in multiples of 4 feet as shown.

In-line framing

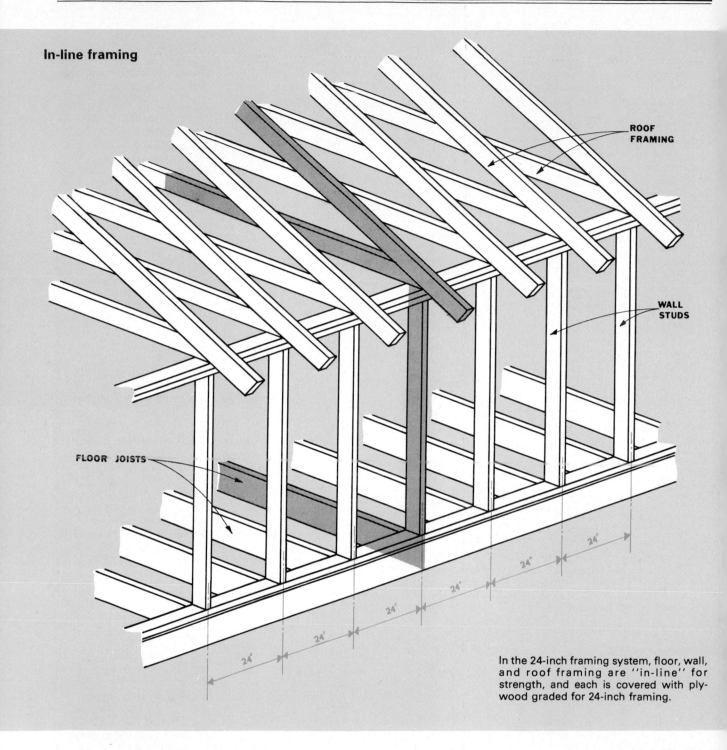

ROOF FRAMING

WALL STUDS

FLOOR JOISTS

24" 24" 24" 24" 24" 24" 24"

In the 24-inch framing system, floor, wall, and roof framing are ''in-line'' for strength, and each is covered with plywood graded for 24-inch framing.

Construction: 24-inch framing. Floors, walls, and conventionally framed roofs have been customarily built on a 16-inch framing system. But with the present day popularity of the money- and labor-saving roof truss, normally placed on 24-inch centers, many homes being built today are based on the 24-inch framing system throughout, with floor joist, wall stud, and roof truss in line for strength. Plywood sheathing is required for the 24-inch system, but this works nicely if you plan to use plywood siding as a finish material for walls.

The 24-inch framing system could save a lot of material and labor, but be careful. While accepted by national agencies and commissions, the system has not been approved by all municipalities. Check your local building department first. Also, the floor joists will need to be larger and the plywood subfloor thicker. The additional cost of these could offset other savings, so check material prices and compare.

Whether you use the 24-inch framing system or not, modular design can save substantially in material and labor. So before you pound the first nail, be sure you've planned carefully for a minimum-waste, low-labor addition—*Herb Hughes.*

remove a supporting wall

I f your house is conventionally built, the walls that run parallel to the roof ridge are usually supporting walls. Typically, these include the outer walls, supported by the foundation, and a central interior wall above the basement girder, which is supported by posts or Lally columns along its length.

The outside supporting walls carry the outer ends of the second floor or attic joists. The central interior wall carries the inner ends of the same joists. Thus, as it carries the inner ends of the joists on both sides, the interior wall supports approximately double the load of the outside walls, which carry only the outer ends of the joists on *one* side of the house.

If you want to remove a portion of a supporting wall, you must, of course, provide a means of support for the load the removed portion of wall originally carried.

First steps

However, before you even begin to remove the wall, you had better check it for plumbing that may be inside. This is usually easy to see in the basement. While wiring in a wall is fairly easy to relocate, major plumbing isn't so easy to shift. Be sure you know how you'll do it before removing any portion of the wall.

The first step in the actual removal job is opening the wall by removing the wallboard or other covering to expose the framing. Before you start removing the framing, it is necessary to place temporary supports at intervals (typically about 3 feet apart) between the studs. The supports should be long enough to jam at a *slight* angle between the 2 × 4 plate above the

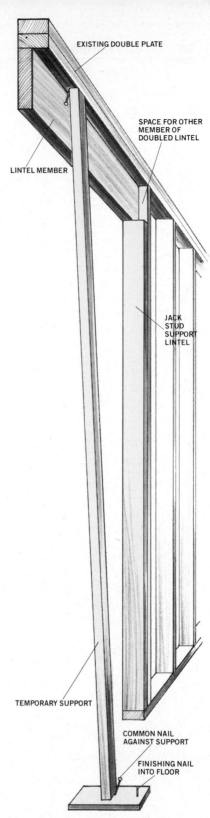

EXISTING DOUBLE PLATE

SPACE FOR OTHER MEMBER OF DOUBLED LINTEL

LINTEL MEMBER

JACK STUD SUPPORT LINTEL

TEMPORARY SUPPORT

COMMON NAIL AGAINST SUPPORT

FINISHING NAIL INTO FLOOR

After removing wallboard, remove studs by cutting near bottom after temporary supports have been put in place between floor and existing plate. Cut studs long enough so two can be used as jack studs at sides of wall opening.

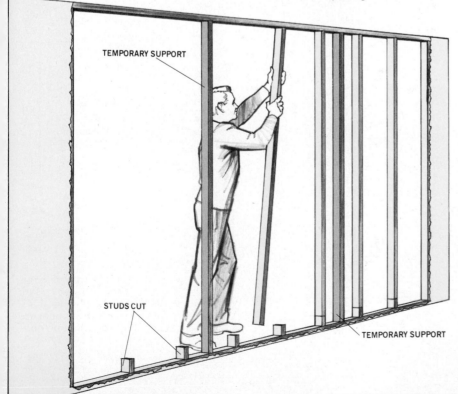

TEMPORARY SUPPORT

STUDS CUT

TEMPORARY SUPPORT

Temporary support here bears against existing plate, allowing one member of doubled lintel to be set in place. This supports plate while temporary supports are removed, so second member of lintel and spacer can be placed. A nail part way into underside of plate keeps upper end of support from slipping. At lower end, a wood pad keeps the temporary support from skidding on the floor. A common nail keeps support in place on pad, and a finishing nail into floor prevents skidding. The holding nails are removed with the support.

studs and the floor. A wood pad with a finishing nail driven part way into the floor at the base of each support will keep the lower end from skidding.

With the supports in place, you can remove the studs. This can be done by cutting through them near the bottom, so that the remaining upper pieces will be long enough to serve as the lintel-supporting member of the doubled stud at each side of the wall opening. (You need only two of these, but you might as well use the existing pieces of studding.) Hacksaw off any protruding nails left by stud removal.

The sole (2 × 4 at the base of the studs) is removed at this stage, allowing space for the doubled studs at each side of the wall opening. Since the sole is nailed to the subfloor, there will be a gap in the finished flooring where it is removed. The gap should be filled in with matching flooring, or covered with a shallow sill, depending on the finished appearance required by the individual job.

Extra studs

Nail the extra stud in place at each side of the opening, allowing just enough space to fit one of the lintel members snugly between the stud's upper end and the underside of the

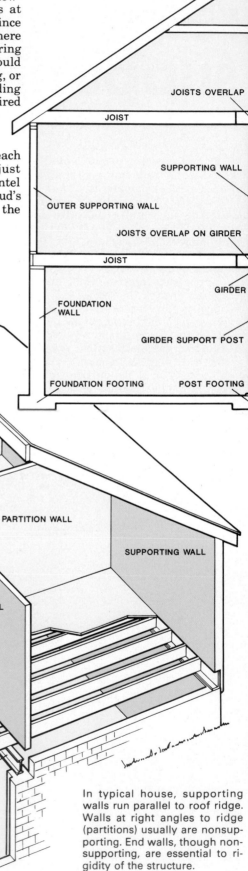

In typical house, supporting walls run parallel to roof ridge. Walls at right angles to ridge (partitions) usually are nonsupporting. End walls, though nonsupporting, are essential to rigidity of the structure.

Because girder, usually under centerline of house, supports ends of joists from both sides of house, it carries double the load of outer foundation walls, which support ends of joists from only one side.

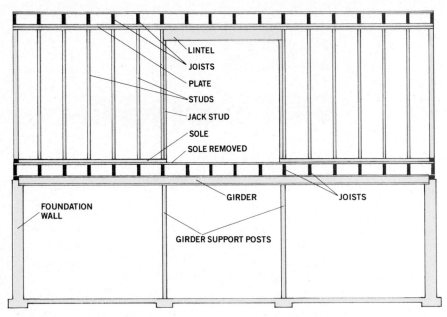

If removed wall section matches span between two girder support posts, the posts still carry the same load, because lintel above wall opening supports joists above it, and carries the load down doubled studs to the structure below.

plate. This calls for care. A small piece of the lumber size being used for the lintel can be helpful as a guide.

The temporary supports are left in place while the first member of the doubled lintel is set in place and nailed. After that, with the temporary supports removed, the first member of the doubled lintel provides support while you install the second member.

Spacers

As the doubled lintel doesn't add up to the same thickness as the 2 × 4 plate, spacer pieces must be used between the lintel members to avoid wall finishing complications. How thick the spacers must be depends on the age of the original lumber.

Today's 2 × 4 lumber is 1½ × 3½ inches. Older 2 ×4s were 1⅝ × 3⅝ inches. If the existing plate is the old size, and the doubled lintel is the modern size, you can use ⅝-inch plywood for the spacer. This can add a little strength if it's in fairly long strips the same width as the lintels.

If plate and lintel members are both modern size, you can use a strip of ½-inch lumber for a spacer.

Lintel width

As to lintel width, follow your local code if there is one. Otherwise, figure on doubled lintels of 2 × 4 lumber for spans less than 4 feet (like a doorway), doubled 2 × 6 for spans from 4 to 6 feet, doubled 2 × 8 for spans of 6 to 8 feet, and doubled 2 × 10 for spans of 8 to 10 feet. These are minimums.

If the opening is in the central supporting wall (above the basement girder), you can use the next larger lumber size for the spans, from 6 feet up if there's a second floor or occupied attic above. Beyond 10 feet, it's wise to use a truss with advice from your building inspector or an architect or professional builder. You can order the truss made to your required span through your lumberyard, but be exact in your dimensions and in describing the purpose of the truss—*George Daniels*.

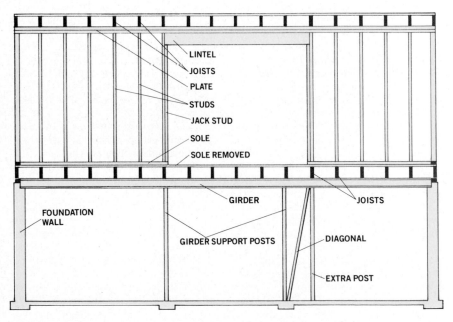

If wall opening exceeds span between posts below, extra post can be used to prevent sag beyond post. Diagonal may also be used. These extra posts—boxed or in partitions—may be needed in house of more than one story.

add a screened porch

"And the sliding doors open onto your patio!" the salesman said.

"Some patio," I muttered to myself. "A 10 × 14-foot slab of concrete."

Nevertheless, I bought the house. As the subdivision filled in, most of my neighbors contracted for screened aluminum porches. These give their owners a place in the shade and are fairly durable.

But they all look alike, and the prices are anywhere from $1,500 to $2,500. If I had wanted to spend that kind of money, I would have had the original house contractor add the porch so I could include it in the mortgage.

Just one hot and buggy Florida summer convinced me of the need to change my patio into a screened and covered porch. Since aluminum kits were expensive (and I could hear the rain's rat-a-tat on my neighbor's metal porch roofs from my own living room), I designed and built mine of wood. The total cost was about $500, even though I used expensive pressure-treated lumber.

Although it could have been enlarged, the size of the patio slab was the governing factor for the size of my porch. I made the walls tall enough to just fit under the overhang of the roof. Tying the 2 × 6 porch rafters into the house roof gave the slope needed for rain runoff.

The porch walls were made of 2 × 4s, with spacing of the studs and horizontal pieces varied for decorative effect. The vertical members of the long wall transfer the roof weight to the ground, and they must extend the full height of the wall.

Each wall was built on the ground

as a unit. I found that my neighbors still retained the pioneer "house raising" spirit: There were more than enough volunteers to assist me in raising the completed walls. As the walls were lifted into place, they were braced, nailed together at the corners, and anchored to the slab with ¼-inch bolts. I had previously drilled into the slab with a carbide masonry bit and installed lead anchors every 2 feet along the sill for the bolts. The frame walls were tied into the concrete-block house with the same technique.

The 2 × 6 rafters were cut to fit the pitch of the house roof (see drawing) and notched to rest on the long 2×4 wall. These rafters were secured to the house roof and the 2×4 wall with metal angles.

Sheathing for the roof was ½-inch exterior plywood, which was extended a foot at each end of the porch and supported by 2×4 "lookout" rafters. One-by-eight fascia capped the end of both the main rafters and these lookouts. One-by-tens were nailed on the underside of the rafters and lookouts, leaving a ventilation gap that was covered with screening.

The new roof was covered with tar paper and rolled roof shingles. At the joint between the old and new roof, the original roof shingles were laid back when the rafters, sheathing, and new shingles were added, then rebedded in a wide strip of roofing cement.

After being painted, the 2×4 walls had rolled plastic screen stapled over the outside. The excess was trimmed off, and a 1½-inch-wide lattice molding strip was tacked to the 2×4s over the screening. The 2×4 corners were

faced with 1×4s. I hung a standard screen door, brushed a color stain on the ceiling, and covered the slab with indoor/outdoor carpet.

The porch has proved comfortable, easy to maintain, and quite strong: It's withstood hurricanes. However, if you use this model in snow country, it will probably be necessary to use 2×8 rafters and heavier sheathing, either ⅝- or ¾-inch plywood—*Bob Gailor.*

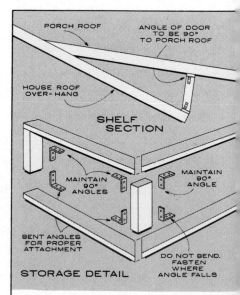

Horizontal members of the porch wall may be spaced as you like. Author Gailor fixed his at 17 inches up from the floor (in case he wants to add a built-in bench later) and at 30 inches (handy for a built-in table). The third horizontal can be located anywhere above. Gailor also added a simple frame and doors in the area between the new and old roofs (as shown) for storage.

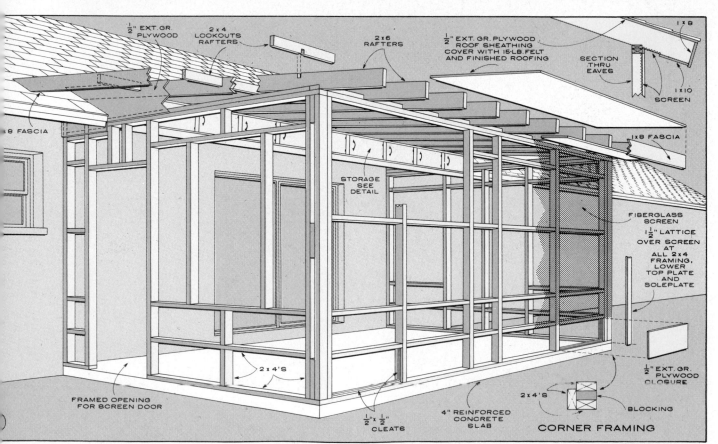

½" EXT. GR. PLYWOOD

2x4 LOOKOUTS RAFTERS

2x6 RAFTERS

½" EXT. GR. PLYWOOD ROOF SHEATHING COVER WITH 15-LB. FELT AND FINISHED ROOFING

1x8

SECTION THRU EAVES

1x10 SCREEN

8 FASCIA

1x8 FASCIA

STORAGE SEE DETAIL

FIBERGLASS SCREEN

1½" LATTICE OVER SCREEN AT ALL 2x4 FRAMING, LOWER TOP PLATE AND SOLEPLATE

2x4'S

FRAMED OPENING FOR SCREEN DOOR

½"x ½" CLEATS

4" REINFORCED CONCRETE SLAB

2x4'S

½" EXT. GR. PLYWOOD CLOSURE

BLOCKING

CORNER FRAMING

converting a garage to living space

Many homeowners would like a special-purpose room—an office or guest room, perhaps—but they can't find the space for it. One way to get the room you want is to convert an attached garage into, for example, a combination office/rec room like the one shown here, raising the floor level to that of the house and closing in the old garage door area. A project like this will add about 450 square feet of living space to your home—and over $10,000 to its value.

The garage conversion shown was left as one big room, with a half bath, but interior walls could have been used to divide it up into two or more rooms. To avoid overloading the existing heating system, and because this room will often be unused while heating is required in the house proper, radiant-heat ceiling panels were installed—a simple, more economical alternative than an additional forced-air or hydronic system. The conversion also features both track and recessed lighting and considerably

more convenience outlets than the code requires. Electricals are powered from a separate panel, with breakers installed in the room.

While such a project is no small undertaking, it is within the skill level of the average do-it-yourselfer (extra manpower is needed to lift heavier materials). The only special tools required are (1) a transit—to assure a level surface at the correct height—and (2) a concrete hammer (electric)—to break the floor in a couple of places for pier foots. Both are available at most tool rental outlets at nominal cost. Before starting the job, consult with your local building department to determine whether you're required to have additional car storage, such as a carport, and to make sure your design conforms to local codes.

This improvement will, of course, work with a one-car as well as a two-car garage, and whether or not there are Lally columns. If you have columns, just work around them and box them in later. The construction, basically the same in all these applications, should be done in the order below to eliminate unnecessary work. The game plan goes like this:

- Lay out and mark off garage for placement of structural members to support floor—ledgers, piers, girder, plates, and supporting block wall where the old garage doors were, and joists. Make foots for piers—and, if necessary, for the block wall—and allow these to cure.
- Install structural members listed above. Piers will support the girder center section, and ends are supported by existing masonry or new piers. Then the ledgers, plates, and girders combine to support the joists, bridging box header at front.
- With floor structure open, install rough plumbing and run necessary electrical cable under the structure. Rough-in electrical panel. Insulate the joist bays and nail on the complete subfloor.
- Erect exterior wall, including rough opening for door and any windows. If there's a girder in the center of the ceiling, gang several 2×4 studs to support the concen-

Conversion of this typical, two-car attached garage required minimal exterior construction. New door, left of former garage doors (drawings) gives new room its own entry. Efficient but homey office/study now fills spot where cars and garden tools once were parked. Comfortable conversational grouping lets home office double as family/guest room, and the versatile track lighting accommodates a variety of furniture arrangements. Ceiling made of gypsum radiant-heat panels provides zoned heating. Recessed lighting floods wall that is covered with durable vinyl "porcelain" basket-weave pattern (inset), used here to complement the rich, warm tones of the paneled walls.

Photos: Wayne Bukevicz

Half bath requires only about 30 square feet and is easily included at time of remodeling. Framed mirror and sidelights match oak bath cabinet. Washable vinyl wallcovering is cheerful, practical. Installation tip: With vinyl flooring in place, install toilet flange, wax seat, toilet, and its supply. Before fitting inside door casing and base molding, it's best to set vanity sink top and faucet in place and fasten them. Then connect P-trap to sink tailpipe and waste after hooking up hot and cold water supplies and their shut-off valves. Working in this order saves time and labor.

trated load. Sheath the wall and install door jamb and windows. After hanging exterior door, complete exterior wall with building paper and double course of siding shake or whatever other material matches the existing exterior finish of the house.

• If you're lacking ceiling joists, install them now, according to your local codes. Build up the interior wall for the bathroom and continue routing electrical cables into their boxes in the walls. Finish electrical roughing-in of ceiling by preparing the recess and track light boxes. Then insulate the ceiling.

• Get help to install radiant-heat panels, and route electrical supply cables down to the power supply/thermostat boxes. Fill open spaces between panels with plain gypsum board, integrate ceiling by taping and jointing. Paint.

• Insulate the exterior walls and finish the rough electric in the bathroom. Nail up the drywall. Set the bathroom door jamb and hang door.

• Install wall covering, panels, track lights, recessed lights, and cove moldings. Build out jambs flush with panels. Complete electrical work. Trim out windows. Finish the floor and install all molding.

Project participants

Paneling: Middleton Place™ "Hearthstone," Georgia-Pacific, 900 S.W. Fifth Ave., Portland, OR 97204. **Wall coverings:** Office/rec room—"Porcelain," Pattern B298, Reed Wallcovering, 979 Third Ave., New York, NY 10022; bath—"Chinese Dogwood/Slow Boat to China," Wall-Tex, Columbus Coated Fabrics Div. of Borden Chemical, Borden, Inc., Columbus, OH 43216. **Floorcovering:** Contempora "Seafoam Green," Congoleum Corp., 195 Belgrove Dr., Kearny, NJ 07032. **Lighting:** Pinch-back track lights and recessed wall washers, Halo Lighting Div. of McGraw-Edison, 400 Busse Rd., Elk Grove Village, IL 60007. **Furnishings:** JC Penney. **Heating:** Gold Bond Panelectric radiant heating panels, National Gypsum Co., 2001 Rexford Rd., Charlotte, NC 28211. **Bath:** Stratford Mirror, Bath Cabinet, NuTone Div. of Scovill, Madison & Red Bank Rds., Cincinnati, OH 45227. **Lumber:** Pressure-treated Wolmanized lumber, Koppers Co., Inc., 1900 Koppers Building, Pittsburgh, PA 15219.

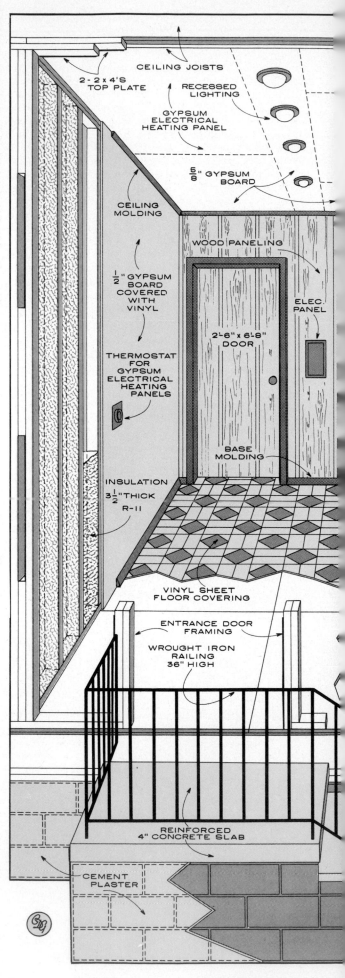

$\frac{5}{8}$" GYPSUM BOARD

GYPSUM ELECTRICAL HEATING PANELS

TRACK SPOT LIGHTING

GYPSUM ELECTRICAL HEATING PANEL

FAN LIGHT

$\frac{5}{8}$" GYPSUM BOARD

$\frac{5}{8}$" GYPSUM BOARD

$\frac{1}{2}$" GYPSUM BOARD

LOCATE THERMOSTAT FOR GYPSUM ELECTRICAL HEATING PANEL IN BATHROOM

FRAMING FOR 2'-6"x6'-8" DOOR

SOIL STACK

METAL JOIST HANGERS

CLOSET BEND

2 x 8 LEDGER

LAVATORY STUB-OUT

$\frac{1}{2}$" COLD WATER SUPPLY

$\frac{1}{2}$" HOT & COLD WATER SUPPLY

FINISH BATHROOM WITH DRYWALL AND VINYL INSIDE AND DRYWALL AND PANELING OUTSIDE

$\frac{5}{8}$" THICK UNDERLAYMENT

3-2x8'S GIRDER

CONCRETE BLOCK PIER

EXISTING 2 x 4 STUD WALL COMPLETE WITH $3\frac{1}{2}$" THICK R-11 INSULATION (FOIL FACING ROOM) FINISH WITH DRYWALL AND PANELING OUTSIDE

6" THICK R-19 INSULATION (FOIL FACE UP)

2 x 8 BLOCK BRIDGING

1/2" CDX PLYWOOD SUBFLOOR

2 x 4 SOLE PLATE

2 x 8 JOISTS

BOX HEADER

SILL

CAST STONE TREADS

SCREENED VENT

8" x 8" x 16" CONCRETE BLOCK FOUNDATION WALL

CONCRETE FOOTING DOWN TO FROST LINE

Recommendations for suspended wood joist floor, stud wall construction. For additional construction details see next pages.

RAISING THE GARAGE FLOOR LEVEL

To raise the level of a concrete garage floor, it is best to start by stripping out any existing door jambs and associated hardware. Then, with the aid of a transit (available at most tool rental outlets), determine the proper heights for the supporting structures (joists, girders, ledger, sill plates, and piers) that are necessary to bring the finish level of the garage floor even with the house floor.

If your garage has a girder and Lally columns that support over-the-garage living quarters, the out end of this girder (at the front) will need major support (several 2×8s spiked together and jammed between a wood pad and the girder) before you remove the center pier between the doors. If there is no living space over your garage, you may be able to get away with less support here. In any case, when you erect the exterior wall, it will carry the overhead load permanently.

Footings

Both the piers that will support the center girder and the block wall at the front will need footings. However, you may already have a footing at the front of your garage, so poke around under the slab, or using an electric concrete hammer, break a small hole through the slab to check.

If there is no footing at the front, break open a strip of concrete a couple of feet wide all the way across the front of the garage. Dig down to the frost line and pour a footing. The new footing should come up to the level of your original concrete floor.

In order to locate the pier footings, divide the garage in half from front to back and mark a chalk line across the width of the garage at this point. Then, for a two-car garage, divide the line into thirds. For a one-car garage, divide into halves and break out a two-foot square at these locations. You may have to chop through a little metal reinforcement, but it's no problem. You need dig down only about a foot (because you're inside a structure) and pour the concrete foots for the piers.

Bring these footings flush with the floor, but level—not at floor slope. One-yard capacity hopper-trailers with ready-mixed concrete are available at many tool rental facilities to help you in these short yardage jobs.

While you're doing the masonry work, check out the support at the side walls for girder ends. If you can't get a good purchase at the existing block ledges, erect auxiliary piers, similar in construction to those near the center.

Allow the footing to cure for two or three days. Then build up the piers from 8×8×16 concrete block. If the bottom of your existing house siding will be lower than the top of the block wall, use 6-inch wide block on top of a first course of 8-inch block, and when the mortar has cured, fir out the 6-inch block with 2×3s to bring the new sheathing

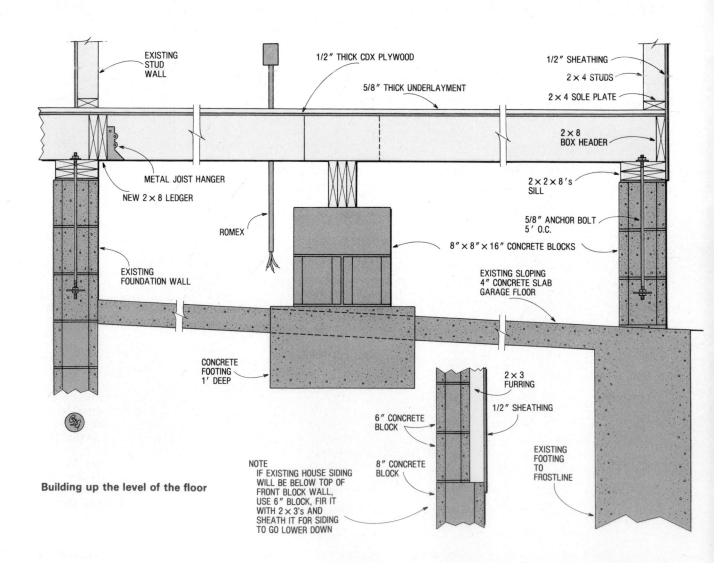

Building up the level of the floor

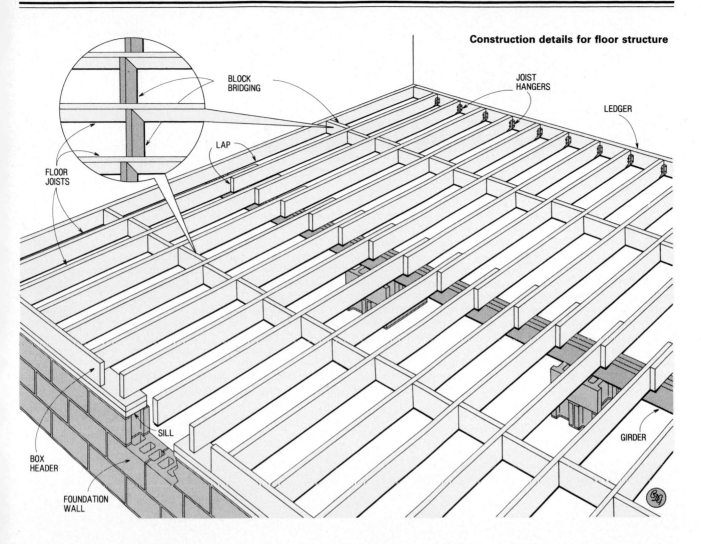

Construction details for floor structure

BLOCK BRIDGING

JOIST HANGERS

LEDGER

LAP

FLOOR JOISTS

SILL

GIRDER

BOX HEADER

FOUNDATION WALL

out so that it is flush with the existing sheathing adjacent to the garage.

Be sure to install enough foundation vents for adequate air circulation. Allow 1 square foot of ventilation area for every 300 square feet of floor area.

Starting the floor structure

With the masonry installed and cured, begin the floor structure by spiking three 2×8s together to form a girder. Then, set your girder on the piers in the center and the masonry overhangs or ledgers at the ends. Keep checking your work with a transit, and make any necessary corrections as you proceed.

Next, bolt up all the ledgers and set the sill plates on a thin mortar or concrete bed on top of the block wall. These plates should be locked down to the blocks with anchor bolts that are spaced every 4 feet or so.

Mark off the rear ledger (the one against the house), the girder, and the sill plates every 16 inches for placement of the joists. Remember that the marks on the sill plates should be offset to one side of the ledger and girder marks to account for the lapping of the joists. Fasten the joists to the rear ledger using metal joist hangers and to the girder and sill plates with nails.

Make sure that the joist overlap at the center is approximately a foot and that the joists are set back on the plates 1½ inches to allow installation of the box header. All joists should be crowned (checked for a slight belly) and the bow should face up.

Note that pressure-treated 2×8s were used throughout the structure pictured earlier. This wood provides maximum protection against damage from moisture and insects in the crawl space area that will be inaccessible once the work is finished.

Install the box header at the front and bridging between the joists. Two rows, spaced about 7 feet apart, should do.

Electrical cables, insulation

With floor structure still open, route the rough electrical cables under the floor from where the panel will be mounted to where they'll enter various walls. (This will be impossible to do later.)

Next step is to install insulation in the joist bays. (For our garage conversion project, we used 6-inch thick, R-19 insulation.) Use a light-duty hammer tacker or stapler for the job, and make sure the foil of the insulation faces up.

Fasten the subfloor by box-nailing 4×8-foot sheets of ½-inch CDX plywood. Top this off with ⅝-inch-thick sheets of underlayment. Do these in a staggered pattern so that the joints occur randomly over these joists.

Butt the joints tightly and make the cutouts for the plumbing studs and the electrical cables. All the nail heads must be flush, so the finish floor will not be damaged. Leave the temporary supports in place until the exterior wall studs are set up—*Bernard Price.*

add a spa wing

Spa tubs are not the sort of thing you just bring home and fill with water, like an above-ground pool. A spa takes planning. Sure, you could put one outside; but for all-weather use, nothing beats a spa solarium like this one I designed and added to a Pennsylvania home.

Double-glazed doors around the perimeter allow the sunlight to enter from east, south, and west, and trap the heat with a greenhouse effect. The walls between and above the glazing are insulated with 3½-inch Owens Corning foil-faced insulation; 6-inch insulation is tucked above the cathedral ceiling. A sidewall vent with fan keeps the accumulated heat and moisture under control.

As shown, the wing is built with conventional lumber, but, for appearance, all exposed interior members are faced with redwood. Redwood's natural resistance to rot makes it ideal for this humid area.

The spa—this one a 7-foot Caldera Aspen model—pierces a 4-inch concrete slab. Eight-inch American Olean Primitive tile surrounds the spa for a no-maintenance, no-slip apron. The tile is bedded in thin-set mortar and grouted with Acid-R grout.

For installation, an area is excavated that's at least one foot larger than the spa on all sides. This allows easy access for the plumbing and backfilling. An 8-inch overdig on the depth allows enough space for plumbing and the cement/sand base.

Plumbing is trenched to the pump-equipment location within an existing basement. If the trench must be back-

Passive solar room above was designed for active people. It has everything but privacy—but a big backyard ensures that.

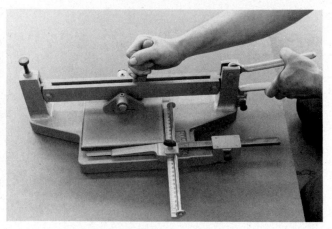

Tile cutter scribes surface for a clean break. No curved breaks are needed because spa rim's wide overlap masks edges.

filled before the spa is installed, a 6- to 8-inch-diameter plastic sewer pipe is laid in. The smaller water and air lines will slide through it when you're ready.

All plumbing should be connected to the spa before setting it in place, and a pressure test should be performed. All openings into the spa (jets, skimmer, return, and suction fittings) must be closed. The end of the air intake to the jets should be capped and tested with 30 to 40 pounds of pressure (check local codes).

Now the spa may be put into place. It must rest completely on temporary leveling braces and have clearance at all points between spa, plumbing, and the ground.

Backfilling under the bottom of the spa should be done with a sand and cement mixture (approximately 4:1). The mixture is just moistened (never flooded) and packed under and around the base for a firm support. The spa should be filled gradually with water as backfilling proceeds. The underside is checked for leaks.

Tapping the bottom of the spa with a piece of wood will assure that no hollow cavities exist. As backfilling continues, the mixture is packed under each seat contour. When finished, the mixture should be allowed to set overnight before braces are removed—*Douglas Gibson*.

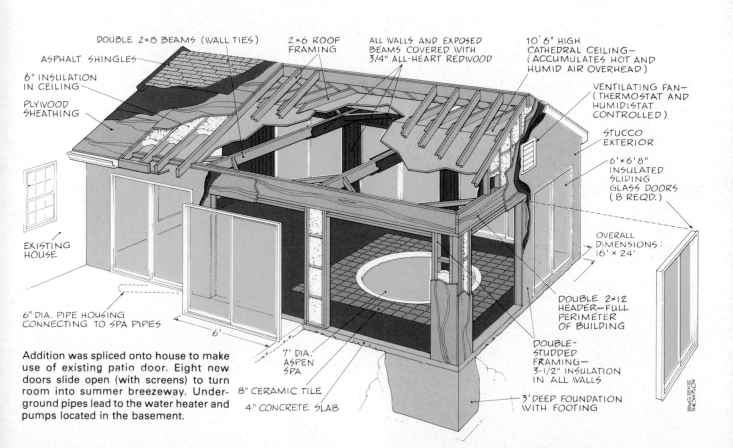

DOUBLE 2×8 BEAMS (WALL TIES)
2×6 ROOF FRAMING
ALL WALLS AND EXPOSED BEAMS COVERED WITH 3/4" ALL-HEART REDWOOD
10'6" HIGH CATHEDRAL CEILING—(ACCUMULATES HOT AND HUMID AIR OVERHEAD)
ASPHALT SHINGLES
6" INSULATION IN CEILING
PLYWOOD SHEATHING
VENTILATING FAN—(THERMOSTAT AND HUMIDISTAT CONTROLLED)
STUCCO EXTERIOR
6'×6'8" INSULATED SLIDING GLASS DOORS (8 REQD.)
EXISTING HOUSE
OVERALL DIMENSIONS: 16' × 24'
6" DIA. PIPE HOUSING CONNECTING TO SPA PIPES
6'
7' DIA. ASPEN SPA
8" CERAMIC TILE
4" CONCRETE SLAB
DOUBLE 2×12 HEADER—FULL PERIMETER OF BUILDING
DOUBLE-STUDDED FRAMING—3-1/2" INSULATION IN ALL WALLS
3' DEEP FOUNDATION WITH FOOTING

Addition was spliced onto house to make use of existing patio door. Eight new doors slide open (with screens) to turn room into summer breezeway. Underground pipes lead to the water heater and pumps located in the basement.

how to handle condensation problems

Condensation, a nagging problem for most homeowners, is simply the result of water in the air changing from a vapor to a liquid. Condensation occurs whenever warm, moist air meets a cooler, drier surface—a wall, window, whatever.

• Condensation problems run the gamut from minor to serious, such as decayed framing. Among the most common complaints: (1) Windows that drip condensed water onto sills, where paint peels and wood rots. (2) Damp basement walls that foster mildew and erode the joint between the wall and floor. (3) Sweating fixtures, particularly toilet tanks.

A home may also have hidden condensation problems that can cause structural decay and decrease the energy-saving effectiveness of wall insulation. Ironically, it is the tight, heavily insulated, newer house that is most susceptible to these hidden problems. In fact, severe condensation inside tight construction can produce so much water that the homeowner mistakes the sweating for a leaky roof.

Here's how a typical, hidden condensation cycle develops. First, the air inside the house accumulates moisture from cooking, washing, bathing, and other sources (estimates run from 7 to 10 gallons a day). This airborne moisture behaves like water—that is, it seeks its own level. Moisture-laden air doesn't bunch up in a corner; it distributes itself throughout the house and always moves toward drier air—particularly the cold, winter air outside.

During this equalizing process, the vaporized moisture penetrates interior surfaces, including wood, paint, and most wallpapers. This can contribute to such surface problems as bad paint adhesion and cracked wallboard joints, but the real trouble is inside the wall. There, the warm, moist air contacts studs, rafters, joists, pipes, and other surfaces that are absorbing cold from outdoors. The result? Seven to ten gallons of condensation, soaking and compressing fiberglass insulation and coating framing members, pipes, and sheathing with water. The dark, unventilated, thoroughly soaked cavity is a near perfect environment for the production of odors, mildew, and rot.

Even after the wall cavity surfaces are soaked, there may be enough moisture left to continue the equalizing path toward drier, outside air. When this happens, the moisture cracks and peels the exterior paint film as it passes through the siding. In other words, the moisture is going to get out one way or another—it's just a question of how much damage it does along the way.

In modern, tight, heavily insulated houses, it's not uncommon to have an extra duct to bring in enough outside air to support furnace combustion. If a duct is needed to bring in air, a duct is needed to move moisture-laden air out.

This leads to **Step 1** in the whole-house solution to condensation: *Duct out moisture from the source*. This means installing a bathroom vent fan; a kitchen vent fan or, better yet, a range hood; clothes-dryer vents.

Step 2 is an extension of the venting operation: *Ventilate attic and crawl spaces*. There are formulas for determining whether existing ventilation needs to be increased.

For attics, the overall rule is one square foot of vent for 300 square feet of attic floor. For greatest efficiency, continuous-strip or plug-type vents should be used in roof soffits in addition to conventional, gable-end, grill vents. If there is a vapor barrier, you should have 1 square foot of inlet (soffit type) and 1 square foot of outlet (gable type) per 600 square feet of attic floor. At least half the total vent area should be at the gable ends. Without a vapor barrier, about twice as much vent space is needed.

For crawl spaces, the rule is one square foot of vent per 150 square feet of bare ground. A complete vapor barrier (4-mil or thicker polyethylene or

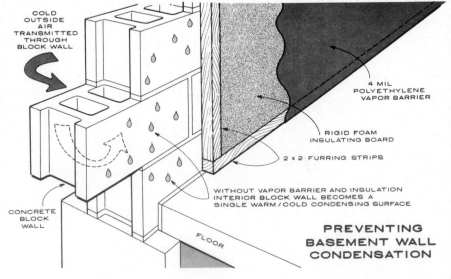

COLD OUTSIDE AIR TRANSMITTED THROUGH BLOCK WALL

CONCRETE BLOCK WALL

FLOOR

4 MIL POLYETHYLENE VAPOR BARRIER

RIGID FOAM INSULATING BOARD

2 x 2 FURRING STRIPS

WITHOUT VAPOR BARRIER AND INSULATION INTERIOR BLOCK WALL BECOMES A SINGLE WARM/COLD CONDENSING SURFACE

PREVENTING BASEMENT WALL CONDENSATION

Perm ratings for common materials

Brick, 4-inch-thick	0.80 – 1.10
Concrete block, 8-inch-thick	2.40
Plaster on gypsum lath	20.00
Gypsum wallboard, ⅜-inch	50.00
Hardboard, ⅛-inch	1.10
Fir sheathing, ¾-inch	2.90
Fir plywood, ¼-inch exterior	0.70
Mineral wool	29.00
Expanded polystyrene bead	2.00 – 5.80
Aluminum foil	0.00
Polyethylene, 4-mil	0.08
Polyethylene, 8-mil	0.04
Asphalt felt paper, 15-pound	5.60
Enamel, two coats on plaster	0.50 – 1.50

55-pound asphalt-impregnated paper, lapped at least 3 inches at the seams) reduces vent requirements to one foot per 1,500 square feet of crawl space.

Step 3 is as crucial as it is unknown to most homeowners: *Balance your perms.* What's a perm? It's the rating unit used to indicate the amount of moisture that can pass through building materials (permeability) at a given temperature and pressure. The lower the number, the greater the material's resistance to water-vapor transmission. Aluminum foil, for instance, is rated at 0.00; porous gypsum drywall, at 50.00. Every material in a wall has a perm rating, and the placement of materials, each with a different perm rating, determines whether or not moisture transmission will cause damage.

For example, consider how interior moisture would pass through a brick veneer exterior wall with these characteristics: The interior paint (primer and finish coat) has a perm rating of 4.00. Underneath it is drywall, rated at 50.00. These materials allow moisture to penetrate up to the 4-mil, polyethylene vapor barrier, which is rated at 0.08.

This nearly impervious barrier stops most of the moisture and, because the paint and drywall transmit the warm room temperature to the barrier surface, the moisture does not condense at this point. The low perm rating for polyethylene allows only small amounts of moisture through the barrier into the wall cavity—amounts that pass right through the kraft-backed insulation, rated at 29.00 for the insulation, 42.00 for the paper backing.

With the wall's insulation still dry and intact, the moisture, in very modest amounts, would then pass through the structural insulating board, rated at about 50.00, until it meets the cold, brick veneer (rated at about 1.00), where it would condense. An air space

between the sheathing and the brick is provided to ventilate this area. Similarly, aluminum siding has small vent holes placed to let air in, or, in severe conditions where no vapor barrier is used, to let condensation out.

The message is simple: A continuous vapor barrier (perm rating from 0.00 to 0.50) must be installed on the warm side of the wall to prevent interior moisture from entering the wall cavity, where it can cause structural damage and destroy the thermal resistance of insulation. Foil-backed insulation, sold as combined insulator/vapor barrier, works effectively only if the foil skin is continuous (lapped and securely stapled over studs).

Here's how to deal with some of the common condensation trouble spots.

First, let's take windows, where condensation blocks the view, rusts metal fittings, peels paint, and rots sills. The best solution: Storm windows. Single-thickness glass has a U-factor (heat-transmission rate) of 1.13 and loses heat ten times faster than an insulated wall. The high temperature variation from side to side makes it an ideal condensing surface. A second pane of glass cuts the U-factor to .50, gives you 40 to 50 percent more thermal resistance, and eliminates the single, warm/cold condensing sur-

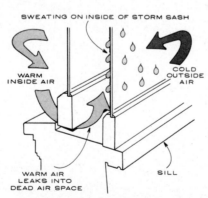

INTERIOR WINDOW SASH LEAKING

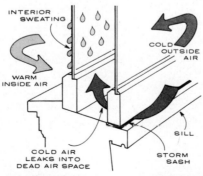

EXTERIOR STORM SASH LEAKING

face. Extra protection for wood components can be derived from coats of glossy, oil-based paints and, if necessary, a finish coat of marine-grade spar varnish.

The second common complaint is wet basement walls. In this case, you must distinguish between seepage and condensation. One test involves gluing a small pocket mirror or aluminum foil patch to the wall overnight. If the back is wet and the surface is clear, you've got a leak. If the surface is fogged and damp, you have condensation.

Combat condensation on masonry basement walls with insulation (eliminating the single, warm/cold condensing surface) and a vapor barrier (preventing moisture from getting to the masonry surface). This can be a complicated and costly process, although you will wind up with finished walls—an obvious and valuable improvement. The work involves (1) furring out the walls, (2) adding fiberglass batts or, to save space, rigid foam panels, (3) covering with a vapor barrier, and (4) finishing with drywall, over which you may panel.

Before you undertake the insulation and vapor barrier solution, there are two steps you should try. First, eliminate or duct out sources of moisture. This step should include a check of your clothes dryer's vent pipe, which can become clogged with lint. Second, check into the cost of a dehumidifier. They are rated by the pints of water they can remove from 80-degree air at 60 percent relative humidity in a twenty-four hour period. A serviceable unit should include a humidistat control, which you can adjust to maintain the relative humidity of basement air just below "wall-sweating" conditions. This moderate investment may be more than enough to control a variable and seasonal problem.

The third common condensation complaint, sweating toilet tanks, is more of a problem in summer. In this case, the porcelain tank acts as the single, warm/cold condensing surface. The inside is chilled by the cold water, while the outside is warmed by moist bathroom air. Two solutions are possible. First, if condensation is minor, improving ventilation may solve the problem. Second, where condensation is persistent, empty the tank, let it dry thoroughly, then apply a ½-inch-thick foam rubber lining with waterproof resin glue. This insulating layer (on the tank walls only) should last indefinitely—*Mike McClintock.*

basic workbench

When a homeowner is ready to graduate from a tool-box repair kit to a full-fledged home workshop, one of his first needs is a workbench. The bench shown here is one you can build yourself—with conventional tools, in a relatively short time and with no great expenditure.

The frame is made of 2 × 4s, solidly interlocked and secured with glue and ¼ × 3-inch FH wood screws as shown in the exploded drawing. The top is ⅛-inch hardboard, nailed to the top layer of plywood with finishing nails. And the shelf is also made of ¾-inch plywood—only one layer. For maximum rigidity, ⅜-inch plywood is

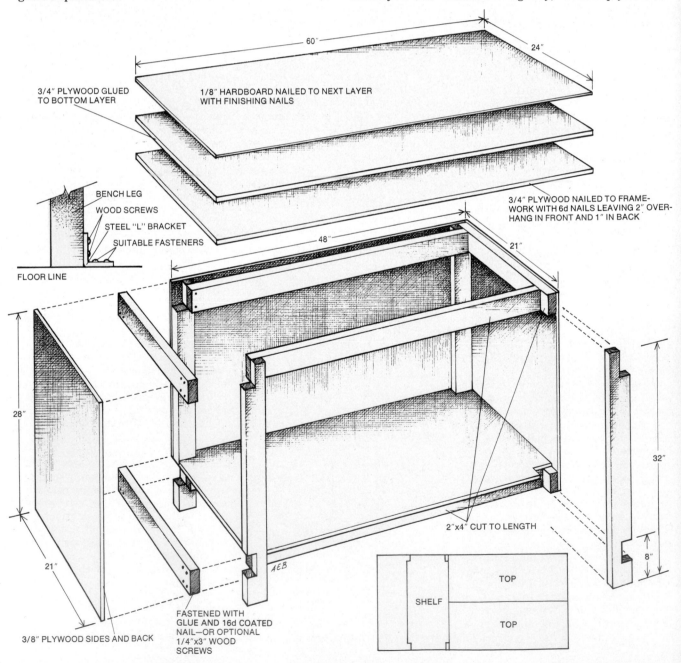

3/4" PLYWOOD GLUED TO BOTTOM LAYER

1/8" HARDBOARD NAILED TO NEXT LAYER WITH FINISHING NAILS

BENCH LEG
WOOD SCREWS
STEEL "L" BRACKET
SUITABLE FASTENERS

FLOOR LINE

3/4" PLYWOOD NAILED TO FRAME-WORK WITH 6d NAILS LEAVING 2" OVER-HANG IN FRONT AND 1" IN BACK

2"x4" CUT TO LENGTH

3/8" PLYWOOD SIDES AND BACK

FASTENED WITH GLUE AND 16d COATED NAIL—OR OPTIONAL 1/4"x3" WOOD SCREWS

SHELF

TOP

TOP

nailed to the backs and sides. With this arrangement, and with the legs anchored to the floor as shown, the table will not budge, even under the roughest treatment to which you are likely to subject it.

To begin work on your bench, lay out the diagram for the top pieces and shelf on a 4 × 8 piece of ¾-inch plywood. Use a straightedge and square for the lines, then cut out the various pieces with a hand saw.

Next cut all 2 × 4s, notching the legs as shown. Mark and drill screw holes as indicated, and then assemble the two end frames with glue and wood screws. You may want to countersink the screw holes for a neater appearance. Join the two end frames with the four long 2 × 4s, again using glue and wood screws.

Insert the lower shelf as indicated, after notching all

four corners to fit the bench legs. Nail and glue them into position.

Continue by marking the cutting diagram on the ⅜-inch plywood for the sides and back. Again, use a straightedge and square. Nail and glue these panels to the sides and back.

Now nail and glue the lower ¾-inch top panel to the frame top rails. Follow this with the next panel and the sheet of ⅛-inch hardboard. (Use only nails on the hardboard; that way, should it get stained, scratched, or damaged, you can easily replace it.) Keep all the panels under pressure until the glue dries.

Total cost of materials for the basic workbench is around $100—but more of course if you add any of the options shown—*John Traister*.

Optional features for your workbench

The basic workbench described above is complete in itself—you can use it as is, without further modification. However, there are many possible options that will prove useful. Those shown here:

Drawers. Two simple drawers are sure to prove handy. Center a 2×4 to the top-rail bottoms with lag screws or 8-inch carriage bolts, and attach the two 2×4s at the sides to the bench legs with 16d coated nails. Attach 2×3-inch strips to the 2×4s with ¼×1½-inch wood screws; these strips act as drawer supports.

The drawers may then be constructed with 1×3-inch lumber with hardboard bottoms.

Tool rack. A simple tool rack can be constructed of 2×4s and drilled to take screwdrivers, chisels, and other such tools.

Front doors. Doors may be added by ripping a 2×4 and installing the resulting 2×2 (minus thickness of plywood door) in a vertical position and centered. Cut ⅜-inch plywood panels to size and install hinges and latches.

Shelving unit. A shelving unit like the one shown can be hung on the wall or mounted to the basic bench. It's made of ¾-inch plywood and Peg-Board for tool hanging. The spacing of the shelves can be varied to suit your needs.

Shelving unit

Tool rack

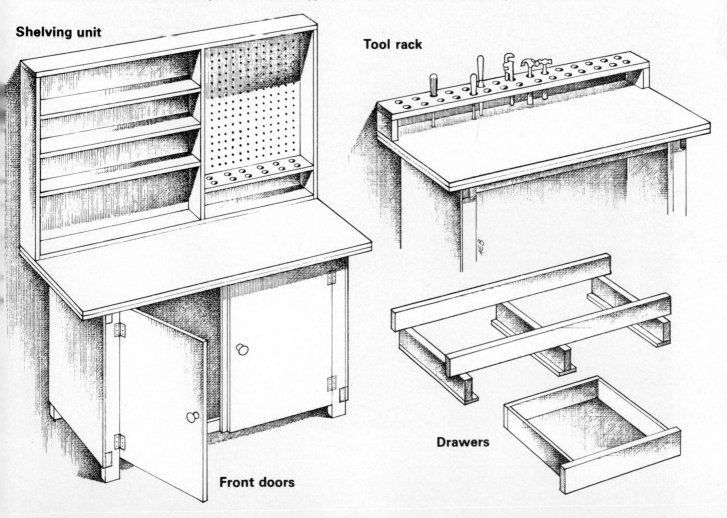

Front doors

Drawers

shop tool storage units

Here's a complete tool organizer for your home shop. The system consists of a 30 × 60-inch, wall-mounted cabinet above a cabinet with drawers. Some of its advantages:

1. The drawer section can be constructed small enough so it takes up no more room than a modest-sized workbench. But, if you have room, it can be made much larger.

2. Although, when it is closed, the box cabinet, uses only 10 square feet of wall space, when it is open, it provides 40 square feet of storage—and that's not even counting the front faces.

3. Either unit may be mounted separately.

4. Fold-out doors of the box cabinet (it is a modification of a tall kitchen cabinet) can be used to group tools according to the type of work for which they will be used. For example, I devote one entire section to router bits and accessories and another to woodwork measurement.

5. When the cabinet is open, tools are both visible and accessible. When it is closed, the tools are kept clean and dust-free.

6. Somewhat larger tools and bulkier supplies can be stored in the slide-mounted drawers of the lower section.

7. Neither piece is difficult to construct, and both use standard plywood as the basic material.

8. You may build both units at one time, or either unit at any time, depending upon your storage requirements and the time you have to devote to the project.

Drawer cabinets

The drawer sections may be built any length down to a minimum of two drawer widths. The 16-foot-long drawer unit shown—it was decided upon because enough space was available for it—took two full lengths of plywood.

Start by building the platform from 1 × 4 stock to provide a toe space and a level base for the cabinet. Assemble the box-frame platform, and level. You can do this either by scribing and trimming down the high spots, or by wedging up the low ones with undercourse shakes (these do the job as well as finish shake siding, and they cost a lot less).

Next, cut out the drawer section dividers, top and bot-

When top cabinet is open, tools are visible and easily accessible. Slide-mounted drawers of lower section are used for large tools. Both units are easy to construct and are primarily made of plywood. See the exploded view of cabinet.

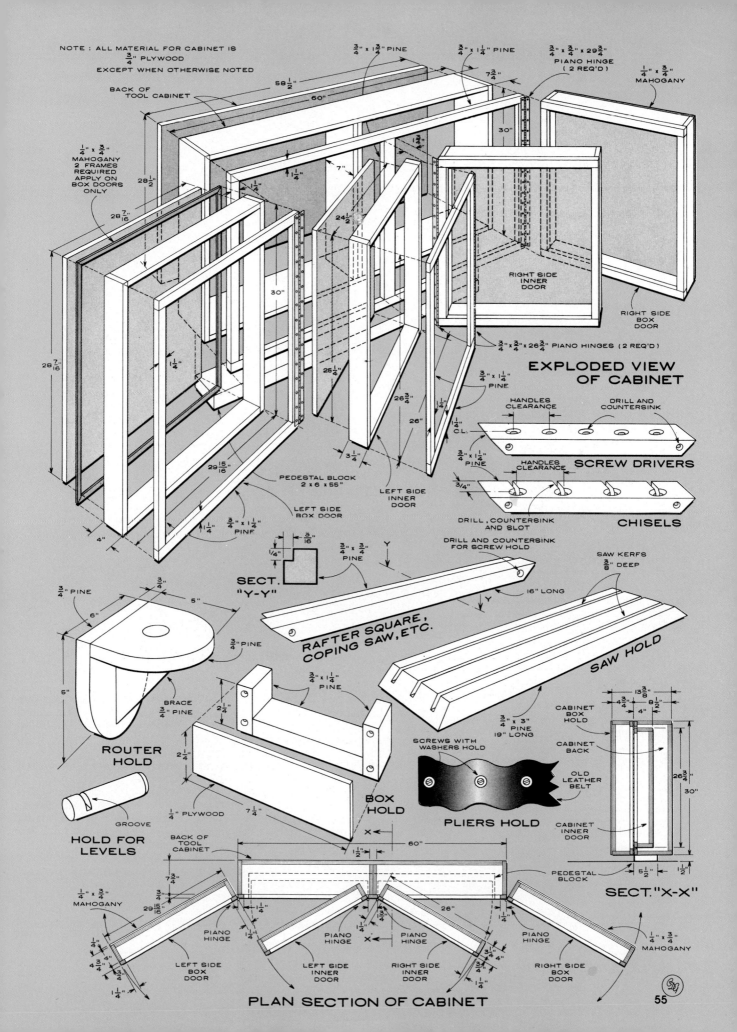

NOTE : ALL MATERIAL FOR CABINET IS ³/₄" PLYWOOD EXCEPT WHEN OTHERWISE NOTED

BACK OF TOOL CABINET

³/₄" x 1¼" PINE

³/₄" x 1¼" PINE

³/₄" x ³/₄" x 29¾" PIANO HINGE (2 REQ'D)

¼" x ³/₄" MAHOGANY

58½"

60"

7¾"

30"

28½"

¼" x ³/₄" MAHOGANY 2 FRAMES REQUIRED APPLY ON BOX DOORS ONLY

28⁷/₁₆"

7"

24½"

RIGHT SIDE INNER DOOR

RIGHT SIDE BOX DOOR

30"

25¼"

28⁷/₁₆"

26¾"

26"

3¼"

¼" C.L.

³/₄" x ³/₄" x 26¾" PIANO HINGES (2 REQ'D)

³/₄" x 1¼" PINE

EXPLODED VIEW OF CABINET

HANDLES CLEARANCE

DRILL AND COUNTERSINK

SCREW DRIVERS

29¹⁵/₁₆"

PEDESTAL BLOCK 2 x 6 x 55"

LEFT SIDE BOX DOOR

LEFT SIDE INNER DOOR

³/₄" x 1¼" PINE

HANDLES CLEARANCE

³/₄"

DRILL, COUNTERSINK AND SLOT

CHISELS

4"

³/₄" x 1¼" PINF

SECT. "Y-Y"

⁵/₁₆"

¼"

³/₄"

³/₄" x ³/₄" PINE

Y

DRILL AND COUNTERSINK FOR SCREW HOLD

Y

16" LONG

SAW KERFS ³/₈" DEEP

RAFTER SQUARE, COPING SAW, ETC.

SAW HOLD

³/₄" PINE

³/₄"

5"

6"

³/₄" PINE

5"

BRACE ³/₄" PINE

ROUTER HOLD

³/₄" x 1¼" PINE

2¼"

2¼"

³/₄" x 3" PINE 19" LONG

SCREWS WITH WASHERS HOLD

CABINET BOX HOLD

13³/₈"

4³/₄"

8½"

4"

CABINET BACK

OLD LEATHER BELT

26¾"

30"

GROOVE

HOLD FOR LEVELS

¼" PLYWOOD

7¼"

BOX HOLD

PLIERS HOLD

CABINET INNER DOOR

PEDESTAL BLOCK

5½"

1½"

SECT. "X-X"

BACK OF TOOL CABINET

X

1½"

60"

7¾"

³/₄"

29¹⁵/₁₆"

¼"

¼"

¼" x ³/₄" MAHOGANY

PIANO HINGE

PIANO HINGE

X

PIANO HINGE

26"

PIANO HINGE

¼" x ³/₄" MAHOGANY

4³/₄"

³/₄"

¼"

LEFT SIDE BOX DOOR

LEFT SIDE INNER DOOR

RIGHT SIDE INNER DOOR

³/₄"

¼"

RIGHT SIDE BOX DOOR

PLAN SECTION OF CABINET

55

tom. Then notch the dividers for the 1 × 3 and 1 × 4 horizontal stiffeners, but note that the front stiffeners are joined to the dividers with half laps (half the notch in the divider and half in the stiffener).

With a rafter square, carefully lay out the tops and bottoms to receive the dividers—when the drawers are installed with their slides, you should have a ½-inch space between each drawer side and its respective divider. This will ensure proper sliding action.

Mark off the half lap notches on the front stiffeners, using the top or bottom layout as a pattern. After cutting all notches, assemble the complete drawer sections and mount them to the platform. Apply border trim to the top to hide all raw edges.

Cut out all drawer parts and machine in the rabbets and grooves with a table saw or router. Assemble the box drawers, except for the face fronts, being careful to keep everything square. Next, lay out the drawer-pull screw holes and drill the large screw clearance holes in the front members. These will provide room for the screwheads, which mount the drawer pulls to the face fronts that will be installed shortly.

Now install the drawer sides according to the manufacturer's instructions. Then line up the face fronts on the drawers, mark their locations on the rear, and screw them in place. Mark and drill the face fronts for the No. 10 pull-mounting screws. Remove all hardware, identify the drawers and their respective openings, and apply your favorite finish. When the finish is dry, install all the hardware and the drawers in their proper places.

Wall-mounted cabinet

The wall-mounted cabinet is basically a divided box frame with both external and internal doors, continu-

Wall-mounted box cabinet requires only 10 square feet when it is closed; open, it provides 40 square feet of storage.

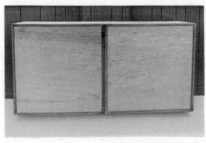

Each fold-out door can be used to group tools according to work they're used for.

ously hinged. The entire structure is made of ¾-inch plywood, with pine edging to cover the raw edges and provide solid screw-mounting surfaces for the doors. There's a little mahogany trim on the outer door edges for cosmetic purposes.

Cut out the pieces, assemble them, and add the pine edging. Sand these assemblies and apply your finish. Mount the divided box frame to the wall, using a bottom cleat if no drawer section is to be fitted beneath, or with a 2 × 4 or 2 × 6 to raise it off the top if a drawer cabinet is used.

Hinge all doors and mount magnetic latches for the outer doors only. Note that the inner doors can fold out to cover the opposite half of the divided box. Add the mahogany trim to the outer door edges.

Some of the devices shown for stor-

ing various tools may suit your purposes, but if not, here's a great chance to let your imagination run freely. Plan the tool panels according to the type of work you do most frequently. Just be careful to place the "thicker" tools where they won't conflict with anything else on the opposing surface when the doors are closed. Spring clips, leather pieces, dowels, slotted wood, ledges, and door sides and bottoms themselves can hold tools. For greatest efficiency, place the cabinet under an existing light or, if necessary, add one—*Bernard Price.*

Manufacturers

Cabinet material: Georgia Pacific plywood, ¾-inch AD Interior
Tools: Sears, Roebuck & Co.
Drawer slides: Grant Hardware
Drawer pulls, backing plates: Amerock Corp.

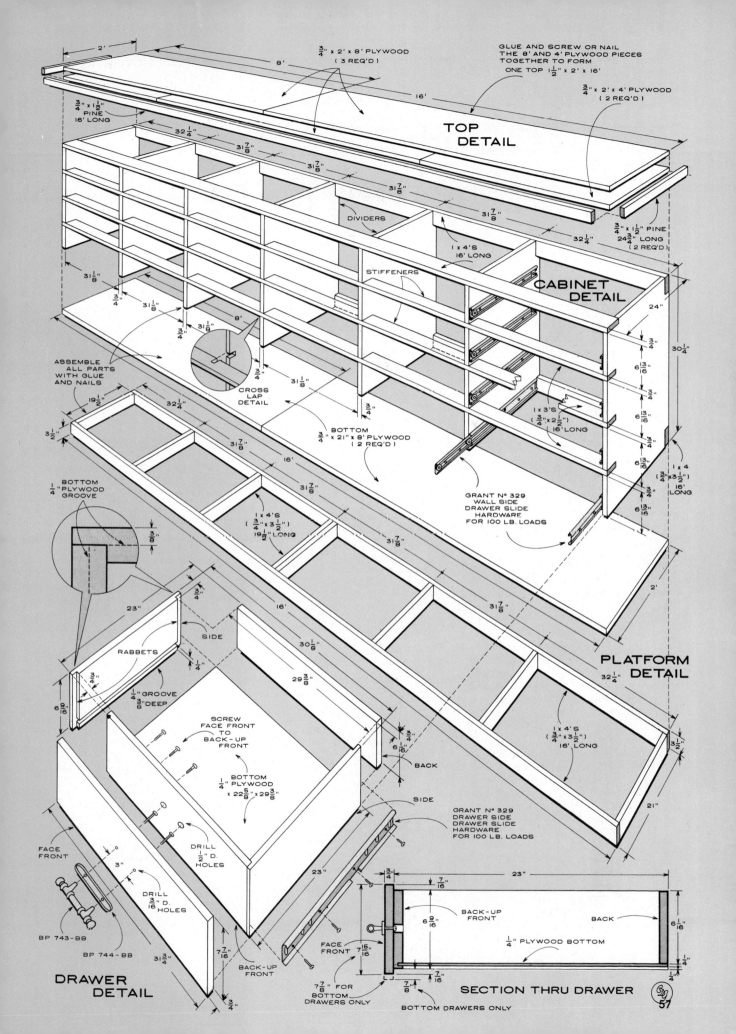

GLUE AND SCREW OR NAIL
THE 8' AND 4' PLYWOOD PIECES
TOGETHER TO FORM
ONE TOP 1½" x 2' x 16'

¾" x 2' x 8' PLYWOOD
(3 REQ'D)

¾" x 2' x 4' PLYWOOD
(2 REQ'D)

TOP DETAIL

¾" x 1½"
PINE
16' LONG

32¼"

31⅞"

31⅞"

31⅞"

31⅞"

DIVIDERS

¾" x 1½" PINE
24¾" LONG
(2 REQ'D)

32¼"

1 x 4'S
16' LONG

CABINET DETAIL

24"

30¼"

31⅛"

¾"

31⅛"

STIFFENERS

¾"

6 13/16"

¾"

31⅛"

¾"

8'

¾"

31⅛"

CROSS
LAP
DETAIL

ASSEMBLE
ALL PARTS
WITH GLUE
AND NAILS

6 13/16"

¾"

1 x 3'S
(¾" x 2½")
16' LONG

6 13/16"

¾"

1 x 4
(¾" x 3½")
16'
LONG

19½"

32¼"

31⅞"

16'

BOTTOM
¾" x 21" x 8' PLYWOOD
(2 REQ'D)

GRANT N° 329
WALL SIDE
DRAWER SLIDE
HARDWARE
FOR 100 LB. LOADS

6 13/16"

3½"

BOTTOM
¼" PLYWOOD
GROOVE

⅜"

1 x 4'S
(¾" x 3½")
19½" LONG

31⅞"

31⅞"

31⅞"

31⅞"

PLATFORM DETAIL

32¼"

23"

SIDE

RABBETS

¾"

¼"

¼" GROOVE
⅜" DEEP

16'

30⅛"

29⅜"

¾"

6 1/16"

BACK

¾"

SIDE

2'

21"

6 9/16"

SCREW
FACE FRONT
TO
BACK-UP
FRONT

BOTTOM
¼" PLYWOOD
x 22 5/8" x 29⅜"

1 x 4'S
(¾" x 3½")
16' LONG

3½"

GRANT N° 329
DRAWER SIDE
DRAWER SLIDE
HARDWARE
FOR 100 LB. LOADS

FACE
FRONT

3"

DRILL
½" D.
HOLES

DRILL
3/16" D.
HOLES

23"

BP 743-BB

BP 744-BB

31¾"

7 7/16"

¾"

BACK-UP
FRONT

DRAWER DETAIL

FACE
FRONT

7 15/16"

7 7/8" FOR
BOTTOM
DRAWERS ONLY

7 7/8"

7/16"

¾"

7/16"

23"

BACK-UP
FRONT

BACK

6 9/16"

¼" PLYWOOD BOTTOM

6 1/16"

¼"

BOTTOM DRAWERS ONLY

SECTION THRU DRAWER

57

table-saw alignment

Your table saw is one of the most versatile pieces of equipment in your shop. But modern assembly-line methods being what they are, it's very likely that not all the components of your saw are aligned properly. And in critical cutting situations, such as precisely cutting a frame with mitered corners, your saw's misalignment problems will be magnified.

By making the three jigs shown here and using them regularly, you can be sure that the parts on your table saw are as well aligned as it's possible to make them. Then, when you have a project that requires precision cuts you'll be able to make them with confidence.

One alignment factor you have no control of, however, is how the saw blade mounts on the arbor. Aside from making sure the saw blade, arbor, and collars (or washers) are clean, all you can do is correctly secure the blade, then make all alignment checks in relation to the blade's position. Cleanliness is important: Dirt or wood chips between blade and collars can throw the blade off and even make it work, to a small degree, like a wobble-dado cutter.

Is it worth making all this fuss about your table saw? If you're a craftsman, it is. Some plus-or-minus tolerances in woodworking are acceptable. But the closer you tune your saw, the better your projects will be —R. J. De Cristoforo.

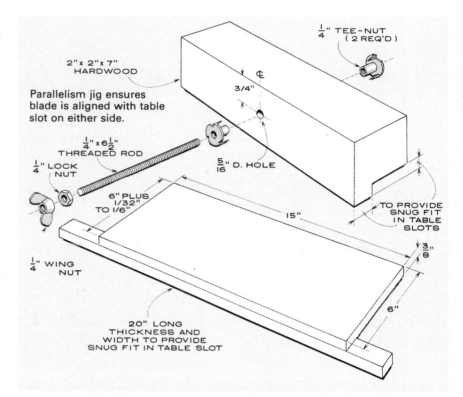

Rip-fence jig lets you align the fence parallel to the saw blade. Actually, many craftsmen prefer a slight offset. When the fence is parallel, the "back" teeth will be working in the kerf. This can cause binding and can also cause splintering and feathering when sawing plywood. Offsetting simply means that the distance between back teeth and rip fence is just a bit more than the distance between front teeth and rip fence. Offset should be minimal.

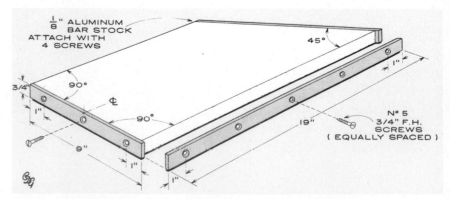

Square-and-angle jig is used to make important alignment checks.

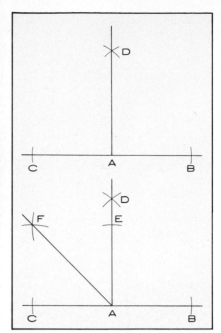

To see if blade is parallel with table's miter-gauge slots, insert parallelism jig in slot. Raise the blade to its maximum projection. Shaft of tool should just barely make contact with a blade tooth. If the blade has set teeth, be sure the tooth is angled toward the tool. Rotate the blade counterclockwise until that same tooth is in the position indicated by the arrow, slide jig along slot until its shaft is in the same relationship with the blade as it was previously. Shaft should slightly touch tooth as it did previously. If not, loosen the bolts that secure the saw table to the tub and lightly rap the table with your hand to rotate it slightly around the axis of the saw blade until blade and slot are parallel. Then, to guard against disturbing the setting, tighten each bolt in small increments until they are all tight. Make a last check with the jig.

Is your square really square? Is that a true 45-degree angle? These geometric constructions will tell you. To make a 90-degree angle (top), set compass for arbitrary radius. From A strike arcs B and C. Lengthen compass, and from B and C strike intersecting arcs D. A line from A through D forms a 90-degree angle with base line. To make a 45-degree angle, draw a perpendicular, then using distance AC, strike arc E. Strike arcs F using E and C as centers. A line from A through F will form a 45-degree angle between line AE and AC.

Setting the miter gauge at a 90-degree angle to the saw blade is easy with the square-and-angle jig. Hold the jig flush against the blade as shown at left. Loosen the locking knob on the miter gauge and advance it until its head sets flush against the jig. Tighten the miter gauge's locking knob. Adjust the pointer on the miter gauge, and, if the gauge is so equipped, adjust the auto-stop so you can return to this position after a change in miter-gauge angle.

For a 45-degree cut, follow the same procedure as when setting the miter gauge for a 90-degree cut, but position the square-and-angle jig so the miter-gauge head can be brought flush against the jig's 45-degree angle (left). Again, lock the head in place, adjust the pointer, and set the auto-stop (if any). For an opposite 45-degree setting, needed when making miter cuts on stock that can't be flipped, follow this procedure with the jig at the opposite side of the blade (right).

To check crosscut accuracy, flip the cut-off piece and place both pieces against the miter gauge. A V-shaped gap, exaggerated here, tells you the cut is not square. Check the miter gauge for correct adjustment and adjust as necessary.

To cut square edges, place the jig upright on the table and against the saw blade. If the blade has set teeth, be sure a tooth that is set toward the jig barely makes contact with it. Set the pointer on the saw's bevel scale, and adjust the auto-stop. To double-check your work, rotate the blade 180 degrees and recheck. For a 45-degree bevel cut, follow the same procedure, using the jig's 45-degree angle. Again, double-check by rotating the blade 180 degrees.

Arc marks occur when the rip fence is not aligned. These indicate that the back end of the fence is closer to the blade than the front end. Marks are more obvious when the blade has set teeth. Realign the fence to solve the problem.

To set rip fence, position jig as shown and move fence until it is flush against the jig. If your jig is 6 inches wide, adjust the rip-scale pointer to the 6-inch mark. Thereafter you can use the scale to set the fence for rip cuts. If it turns out that the rip-fence scale is not precise (and many aren't), then use the scale for approximate settings. Make the final critical adjustment by measuring between the blade and fence. If the blade has set teeth, measure from a tooth that is angled toward the fence. Remember, changing blades can affect the rip-scale setting. Some blades are thicker than others, and some have more set.

Jig used to set parallelism between the saw blade and table slots can also be used to align the rip fence. If you want to offset the rip fence, turn the threaded rod about a full turn before moving the jig to check the opposite end of the fence. Incidentally, the parallelism jig can also be used as a depth gauge.

tricks for a radial-arm saw

Like most power tools, the radial-arm saw has more going for it than its basic functions. Using the tool only for sawing and saw-related operations is like using a good portable drill just to bore holes.

Even when the manufacturer provides accessories that extend the tool's functions—for the radial saw, drill chucks and sanding equipment, for example—the saw owner must still "invent" jigs and fixtures that exploit these accessories and add to accuracy and operating convenience.

The ideas that follow are some of the ways you can make radial-arm saws into really multipurpose tools. All of the drawings are dimensioned for a DeWalt, but they should be easily adaptable to whatever make or model you own.

In a couple of cases (the fold-down extension table, for example), you may have to make an adjustment to adapt the plans to a particular table height. Check jig sizes against the tool before cutting and assembling parts. Teaching saws new tricks—mitering, horizontal boring, end drilling, or sanding—extends their usefulness and is worth the extra effort of making these jigs—*R. J. De Cristoforo.*

Fold-down extension table

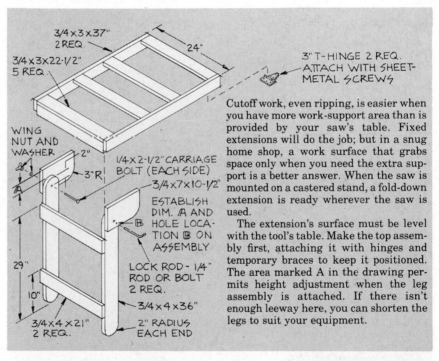

3/4 x 3 x 37"
2 REQ.

24"

3/4 x 3 x 22-1/2"
5 REQ.

3" T-HINGE 2 REQ.
ATTACH WITH SHEET-
METAL SCREWS

WING NUT AND WASHER

2"

3"R

1/4 x 2-1/2" CARRIAGE
BOLT (EACH SIDE)

3/4 x 7 x 10-1/2"

ESTABLISH
DIM. Ⓐ AND
HOLE LOCA-
TION Ⓑ ON
ASSEMBLY

29"

10"

LOCK ROD - 1/4"
ROD OR BOLT
2 REQ.

3/4 x 4 x 36"

3/4 x 4 x 21"
2 REQ.

2" RADIUS
EACH END

Cutoff work, even ripping, is easier when you have more work-support area than is provided by your saw's table. Fixed extensions will do the job; but in a snug home shop, a work surface that grabs space only when you need the extra support is a better answer. When the saw is mounted on a castered stand, a fold-down extension is ready wherever the saw is used.

The extension's surface must be level with the tool's table. Make the top assembly first, attaching it with hinges and temporary braces to keep it positioned. The area marked A in the drawing permits height adjustment when the leg assembly is attached. If there isn't enough leeway here, you can shorten the legs to suit your equipment.

Extension table can double the work-support surface, and it requires floor space only when it's in use. At other times the table folds down (far right). Holes for lock rods (one each for raised and lowered positions) are drilled after assembly's completed.

Two-piece mitering jig

This mitering jig can make miter cutting as simple as crosscutting: It reduces the possibility of human error. The design allows miter cuts on stock that's been precut to length as well as consecutive cuts on long pieces. Although the jig has two parts, it's easier to build if initially assembled as a single unit. First make the platform and its special fence and secure the assembly in the table so a crosscut will bisect the platform. Cut a shallow kerf across the jig. Position guide arms at 45 degrees with the kerf, then split the jig with a full-depth crosscut. Note that in sketch the right fence is longer.

Mitering jig above is used with frame parts that are precut to length. Use both guides when the work can't be flipped over.

Consecutive cuts on a single piece justifies the two-piece jig concept. Work piece passes through gap between two jig parts.

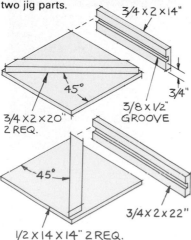

3/4 x 2 x 14"

45°

3/4"

3/8 x 1/2" GROOVE

3/4 x 2 x 20" 2 REQ.

45°

3/4 x 2 x 22"

1/2 x 14 x 14" 2 REQ.

Table for disc sanding and three special jigs

End sanding is square when you use this guide for the disc-sander table. Note that table is slotted to receive these accessories.

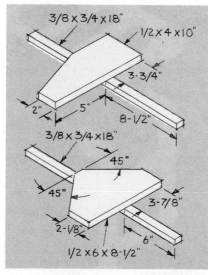

3/8 x 3/4 x 18"

1/2 x 4 x 10"

3-3/4"

2"   5"   8-1/2"

3/8 x 3/4 x 18"

45°

45°

3-7/8"

2-1/8"   6"

1/2 x 6 x 8-1/2"

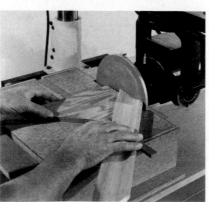

Miter joints require accurate sanding for a tight fit. The guide shown above can be used for left- or right-hand miter cuts.

The disc-sander table has one long leg that can be locked into your saw's guide-fence slot. A groove across the jig's table is for accessories used to position work. Table height should be level with the disc's horizontal center line or about 1/8 inch above it.

One of the accessories (below left, top drawing) is a right-angle guide. Although end sanding can be done freehand, a guide such as this ensures the end will be square with adjacent edges. Keep your work firmly against the guide as you move it forward. The 45-degree miter guide (below left, bottom drawing) has two bevels. You turn the guide end-forward to bring the correct one into play—especially with contoured moldings that can't be flopped.

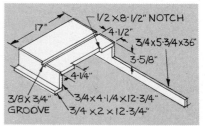

17"   1/2 x 8-1/2" NOTCH
4-1/2"
3/4 x 5-3/4 x 36"
3-5/8"
4-1/4"
3/8 x 3/4" GROOVE
3/4 x 4-1/4 x 12-3/4"
3/4 x 2 x 12-3/4"

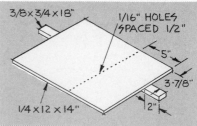

3/8 x 3/4 x 18"

1/16" HOLES SPACED 1/2"

5"

3-7/8"

1/4 x 12 x 14"

2"

Pivot guide is a piece of 1/4-inch plywood drilled for a small brad (drawing above). Distance from brad (photo above) to sanding disc equals radius of pivot circle. Work piece is impaled on the brad (top photo) and slowly rotated in finishing operation.

Jig for horizontal boring

The radial-arm saw makes a respectable horizontal-boring machine when it's equipped with a special table for work support. Our unit locks between the tool's removable table boards, as far back on the machine as possible. It has adjustable guides so spacing between holes can be accurate and automatic. (The pivot guide is for drilling radial holes in discs.)

Edge distance for holes is set by raising or lowering the tool's arm; drilling is accomplished by moving the motor toward the back of the machine. For holes of a specific depth, use a clamp on the arm as a motor stop. If you need holes at an angle, swing the radial arm to the left or right as you would for making miter cuts. Or tilt the motor head if you need a row of down-pitched holes—as for a peg-type coat rack.

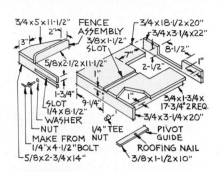

Special table makes accurate edge drilling easy. Table length matches that of the tool's regular table; fence aids support.

To drill, move the motor back toward the column. Use a clamp on the arm as a stop when the bore holes must be a specific depth.

Special guide above can automatically and accurately establish drill-hole spacing. Guide holes can be enlarged later, if needed.

Table for end drilling—and other jobs

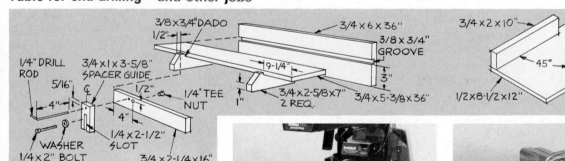

End drilling with the radial-arm saw is usually done by locating the drilling tool in a horizontal position, parallel to the fence. The work, placed on a height block that may have its own fence, is moved into the cutting tool. The table shown here provides a more flexible system.

The jig permits either the work or the tool to be fed, and many types of drilling operations are possible when you add guides. Examples of jobs: drilling into mitered edges, end drilling, boring radial holes in circular pieces, and concentric drilling with a V-block.

Set up the tool with the drill chuck facing the front of the table. Set the project so the drilling tool and table slot have a common center line—*R. J. DeCristoforo.*

Drawings by Gerhard W. Richter

Adapted by the author from his book The Magic of Your Radial Arm Saw, *Reston Publishing Co., $8.95.*

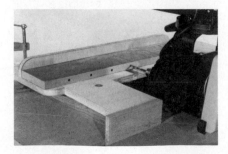

End-drilling table has an adjustable fence assembly to align tool and work. You can then feed either the work piece or the tool.

Custom guides can be clamped to the fence assembly to help drilling accuracy. The guide shown is for dowel holes in miter cuts.

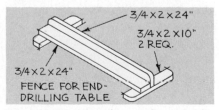

Special fence (above) made for end-drilling table enables you to use the table for edge drilling, as well (photo at left).

over-hood garage storage

Are paint cans, lawn furniture, garden fertilizer, and other such stuff eating up your garage floor space? You can clear the floor in a weekend's work by building an over-the-hood deck, shelves, and cabinet that will give you about 60 square feet of storage. The construction is basic and the required tools are minimal.

Drive your car into the garage in its normal parking location and measure: (1) the height of the engine hood (and possibly part of the windshield) at a point 6½ to 7 feet out from the wall facing your front bumper; (2) the location for a 2 × 4, which, when placed on the floor before the front wheels, will stop the car's forward progress; (3) the maximum width the storage deck can extend out from the garage side wall; (4) the width of your car. Make your deck 24 inches wider, so you can get in and out easily. The storage deck shown was installed in a two-car garage and extends from a side wall to the door that connects the house and garage.

Snap a chalk line a few inches above hood height on the wall in front of the car and on the adjacent side wall. This line marks the bottom edge of the wall ledgers. Next, locate the studs (this should be easy, since most builders don't hide the slightly recessed drywall nails under joint compound) and mark their locations just below the chalk lines.

The basic structure consists of wall ledgers, joists, joist headers, and a corner ladder. Start construction by trimming a ledger to 7 feet, 10½ inches and nailing or lag bolting it to the side wall so it butts against the front wall. Then trim another ledger 3 inches shorter than the actual long dimension of the deck (in our case, 9 feet, 3 inches) and fasten it to the front wall, butting it against the side wall ledger.

Set up a ladder at the external corner of the deck for a temporary support. Then, cut and toenail a joist header, the same length as the front wall ledger, to the side wall ledger, flush with its end, and rest the other end of the header on the ladder. Trim a joist, equal in length to the side wall ledger, and nail it to both the front wall ledger and the joist header. Now, nail the doubler to the header, making sure that it butts against the wall and is flush with the joist at the opposite end.

The ladder not only provides access to the deck, but also serves as permanent support for the external corner of the structure. Note that the garage floor slopes downward as it approaches the doors, so take this into consideration when you cut the ladder sides (the side nearest the garage doors may be slightly shorter than the other side). Therefore, measure and mark the spacing of the tread dadoes from the tops of the ladder sides so they'll be level.

Make the ½-inch deep tread dado crosscuts with your portable saw (adjust platen accordingly) and then knock out the waste between the cuts with a butt or firmer chisel. Cut the treads to length and nail the ladder together.

Erect the ladder temporarily at the corner and mark the notches on the sides to hold the deck joist. Place angle irons in position on the floor at the inside faces of the ladder sides and mark the hole locations on the floor and ladder sides. Remove the ladder and cut and chisel the notches. Drill the holes in the ladder side.

Set up your drill with a carbide-tipped bit and drill holes in the concrete for the lead anchors. While you have your drill in action, also make holes for the mounting bolts that will retain the 2×4 wheel stop. Insert the lead anchors into all holes, flush with the floor.

Attach the angle irons to the ladder sides with carriage bolts, nuts, and washers, then position the ladder over the angle iron lead anchors with the joist resting in the notches. Finish

the corner work by running lag bolts with washers through the angle irons into the anchors, and toenail the ladder to the joist.

Starting from the side wall, mark off the exposed faces of both the front ledger and the joist header at 16-inch intervals for placement of the remaining joists. Trim the joists to length at these marks and toenail them in place, keeping the 16 inches on center spacing.

Now nail on the plywood deck, making sure that all plywood joints parallel to the joists are squarely over the joist edges. You'll have to do a little fitting and notching around the ladder sides, but it's no problem. Complete the deck by nailing the fascias in place and painting it.

The shelves are built in two modules, then joined together on the deck to form an "ell" against the front and side walls. Cut the shelves, dividers, and ends for both the long and short legs of the "ell" from ¾-inch plywood. They should all be 9 inches deep, but the height depends on the distance between your deck and ceiling. Mark all cleat locations on the dividers and ends and nail or screw the cleats in place. Insert and fasten in the shelves, working from the bottom shelf up for ease of assembly.

Paint the shelf modules, and when they are dry, place them on the deck. Then join the ends together to form the "ell," nail the shelves to the deck, and fasten the upper parts to the walls with metal brackets.

Start the cabinet by making a box frame with a center shelf and lower divider. This should be sized so that it fits between the ladder side and the front wall of the garage, and high enough so that when the top touches the bottom edge of the joist, there's about a 6-inch clearance from the floor. This clearance will be handy later, when you sweep, hose, or paint the garage floor.

Add a plywood back to the box frame and then make up and install a face frame from 1×3 stock to hold the flap door and lower hinged doors. Cut all doors to size. Then fit a length of continuous hinge to the flap door and self-closing hinges and pulls to the lower doors. Paint the cabinet and doors. When everything's dry, mount the cabinet and install all doors. Provide screweyes and chains to support the door in a horizontal position and a gate hook and eye to hold it closed. Lag bolt the wheel stop in place and you're done—*Bernard Price.*

Plywood and dimensioned lumber:
Georgia Pacific

DETAIL C
1 × 3
3/4" PLY
DETAIL B
DETAIL A
2 × 8 LEDGER
1 × 2 CLEAT
1 × 3 FACIA
1 × 3 FACE FRAME
9'6"
3/4" PLY
TO SUIT CAR HOOD CLEARANCE
DOUBLED 2 × 8
2 × 8 JOIST
6'0"
3/4" PLY DOOR
DETAIL F
1 × 3 FACIA
DETAIL D
CONTINUOUS HINGE
DOORS HAVE SELF-CLOSING HINGES
FASTEN CABINET TO LADDER
DETAIL E
STANDARD, WALL, BOTTOM EDGE OF JOIST
2 × 6 LADDER AND TREADS

DETAIL A
2 × 8
2 × 8
2 × 8
1 × 3

DETAIL B
3/4" PLY DIVIDER
3/4" PLY SHELF
1 × 3
1 × 2 CLEAT

DETAIL C
LONG SIDE OF SHELF
TOP VIEW OF SHELF CORNER
SHORT SIDE OF SHELF

DETAIL D
2 × 6 LADDER STANDARD
3/4 × 1½"
2 × 6 TREAD

DETAIL E
1/4 × 2" CARRIAGE BOLT, NUT, WASHER
5/16 × 1-1/4" LAG BOLT AND WASHER
DRILL 1/2" HOLE FOR 5/16" LEAD ANCHOR

DETAIL F
1/4" PLY BACK
FACE FRAME 1 × 3
3/4" PLY TOP, BOTTOM, SIDES, DIVIDERS

home computer center

If you're like me, you probably have a space set aside somewhere that you call your home office. And if your home office is anything like mine was until recently, it may be a table containing heaps of papers, stapling machines, calculators, miscellaneous supplies, tools, and work in progress.

I've been meaning to build in a really efficient home office for years. And when I brought my new computer home recently, I decided the time had come. I wanted something handsome and useful. A place that would be pleasant to work in. A place in which everything I need—from the computer keyboard to a postage stamp—would be instantly available and convenient. It was a simple project; a few weekends of work and it was completed. You can see the result on the opposite page.

The main features are evident. The computer console sits on a typing wing where it is easy to operate. Most standard typing tables are 26 or 27 inches tall. That's slightly higher than I like, so I built this computer surface 25 inches from the floor. The main desk surface is at 28 inches—again 1 to 2 inches below standard. Adjust these figures to whatever you find most comfortable.

Just to the left of the computer console is the printer. My Epsom MX-80 sits on top of a box open at front and back. A 3-inch-thick supply of paper sits on the shelf below the printer. The box is mounted on standard nylon-roller drawer hardware, so the printer pulls out easily when needed, and disappears beneath the desk at other times.

The disc-drive mounting is straightforward. Disc drives are usually allowed to take up valuable desktop space. But mounted under the table the unit is even more convenient.

Construction is simple throughout. The horizontal desk-top surfaces are butt-joined to the vertical supports at the ends. I didn't want to drive screws through the visible surfaces, so I installed a 1×1 where the two panels came together and used 1¼-inch flathead screws and glue to make the joint secure. A 1×1 also serves as the shelf support at the right end of the typing wing. A ¾-inch plywood desk top always looks skimpy to me,

so I used screws and glue to attach a 1×3 to the underside of the front of each of the two desktop elements. Then I veneered the front edges, with 1-inch veneer on the vertical elements and 2-inch on horizontal exposed edges. It doesn't show in the drawings, but I used ¼-inch plywood gussets at the rear to stabilize the vertical members. The entire structure goes together easily and quickly with glue and screws.

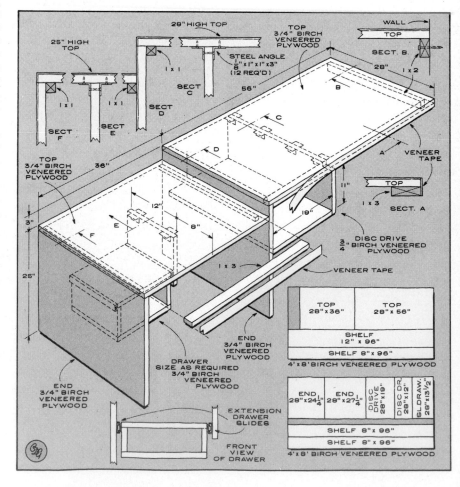

Several problems remain unsolved. The principal one is disc storage. I was unprepared for the fact that I would generate a lot of discs as I put my computer to work as a word processor, bookkeeper, and list retriever. But the discs are piling up. I now keep them in boxes on the shelf just above the computer. But this means that I am always shuffling through boxes of discs. I hope to build a filing system of some sort, although I don't have the design worked out as yet. I suspect that it may be built of Plexiglas, a versatile material that comes in many nice colors. And I think I'll design it to hang under the shelf behind or just to the left of the computer. It should let the discs slide out easily, and it should have some kind of tab identification system so that the de-

sired disc can be located quickly and easily.

My other storage problems have been solved in a conventional manner. While I was building the desk/computer stand, I also put four shelves on the wall above and behind it. The bottom one is 12 inches wide, convenient for holding the stationery cabinet you see in the picture, large books, and other outsized items. The three top shelves are 8 inches wide, suitable for all but the largest books. All shelves are mounted on conventional brackets and standards. Since I expected a heavy load of books, I mounted the standards on 20-inch centers and used heavy-duty brackets. The two plastic six-drawer units you see on the desk surface to the right of the computer hold bills that

need paying, stamps, address labels, letter openers, and a wide variety of other supplies.

I chose birch veneer with a tung-oil finish for the project because I like the color; the entire structure has a light, airy feeling. You can pick any material and finish, of course. Other furniture-grade plywood veneers would be handsome, as would a unit made of MDO plywood and painted.

My computer wing is 36 inches long, fine for most home computers. If your printer is larger, you may want to make this surface longer to leave room for the printer and your legs underneath. My main desk top is 56 inches—again a convenient length. Adjust dimensions to your equipment and to the wall you want to fit—*C. P. Gilmore*.

rolltop-desk kit

We've just finished building this classic rolltop desk from a kit manufactured by Heath. The company that's been marketing electronic kits for years has developed a quality line of furniture that's beautiful, functional, and reasonably priced. Here again, they've applied their usual meticulous approach—good components, compartmentalized packaging, parts identification drawings, and fully illustrated instructions with step-by-step checkoffs. There's a complete hardware package, including glue, sandpaper, and everything necessary to give you professional results.

The desk, made of select white oak, stands 49 inches high, 57 inches wide, and 28 inches deep, and weighs in at almost 400 pounds. There are seven drawers—one, a double-deep drawer—in the pedestals alone. In the pigeonhole section of the top, there are four more drawers, plus all kinds of slots and niches to help you organize household papers and stationery. The pigeonhole drawers, slideout writing table, and rolltop are fitted out with solid brass pulls, while the pedestal drawers have carved oak pulls. The kit is not inexpensive ($995 F.O.B. Benton Harbor, Michigan), but it's impossible to buy comparable quality for anywhere near that price.

Almost all component parts are machined and stroke-sanded down to #150 grit level, so the work boils down to some minor fitting, sanding, gluing and clamping, and fastening and finishing. What's more, you don't need an arsenal of tools—just a hammer, rule, drill, carpenter and combination squares, a common and a No. 2 Phillips

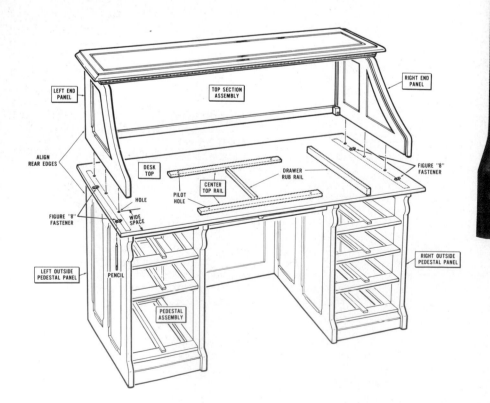

The heirloom styling of the desk has such modern refinements as pigeonholes designed to accept paper in the sizes available today and a file drawer for a suspension file frame. Many parts, such as the tambour and pedestal sides, are preassembled to reduce the time it takes to build the desk.

1. Drawer divider centers are marked for drawer guides.

2. Bar clamps and carpenter's square are needed for drawer assemblies.

3. Drawer divider subassemblies are glued to the pedestal side panels with mortise and tenon joints.

4. Before gluing pedestals to center rails and rear center panel, it's best to seat them on a pair of straight 2 × 4s, placed on edge. Checking across the pedestal tops with a level and shimming below assures flat fit with desk top.

5. End panels of top section are glued using bar and "C" clamps.

6. Top panel of top section is glued and clamped from rear.

7. Desk top and pedestal are screwed together. Screw pilot holes are located by punching through countersunk holes in top.

8. Best way to attach desk top to top section is to place section upside down on a flat surface, place desk top, also upside down, on the section, and drive screws. Tambour top has already been installed.

9. Pigeonhole assembly is placed on top of rear surface of the back and a pencil pattern marked out for nail locations.

10. Waxed paper prevents scratches on desk top when moving pigeonhole assembly into position.

11. Drawer front, sides, backs, and bottoms are assembled, glued, and clamped.

screwdriver, a small nailset, and some 4-inch "C" clamps and pipe clamps. (If your pipe clamps aren't long enough they can be quickly and inexpensively lengthened by inserting a plumbing coupling.) Included in the kit are a scribe to punchmark screwhole centers, a pair of twist drill bits, and a drill depth gauge that slides over the bits.

The kit arrives in five cartons, each coded to the pertinent part of the building sequence, which is totally covered in the instruction sheets. There's also an optional finishing kit (about $18), which contains stain and urethane, both in paste form. The paste is applied and rubbed off with a lint-free cloth and gives professional results.

While building the kit, we made notes—some general, some covering specific parts of the construction. The notes follow:

• Tape the sheets covering the work you're doing to a nearby wall so you can refer to them but don't have to handle them.

• Sand all parts down to #280 grit finish as you go along. That's better than trying to sand parts later, when they form a portion of an assembly.

• Always dry-fit parts before gluing. If there's a discrepancy, such as an overly tight joint, you can sand it to fit without worrying about the glue setting up.

• When gluing, have all clamps ready to go. Use scrap wood between clamp jaws and the work to prevent damage. Lay the glue down in beads on flat surfaces and screed it out over the area with a piece of rubber or felt. This will prevent most of the glue from oozing out of the joint.

• All glue that escapes the joint must be removed as quickly as possible, first with a damp, then a dry cloth. In sharp corners or tight places, use a screwdriver or awl tip covered with cloth. If you don't remove the glue, the wood under it won't take the stain.

- Raise assemblies to be glued up onto scrap wood for easier clamp installation.
- Any dent you get in the wood will probably come out if you place water over the area. Scratches or gouges that can't be sanded may be treated with special fillers.
- When assembling the pedestal sides to the drawer divider subassemblies and back panels, use eight clamps, instead of four (with pipe or web clamps on the two middle drawer dividers) for complete contact.
- In addition to prestaining the drawer fronts before assembly, try to balance out the wood grains for the most pleasing effect.
- When building the pigeonhole assembly, be careful to drive the brads in straight, and centered above the notches, to avoid a brad popping.
- Check the width of the pigeonhole back against the top section. If it fits too tightly, trim it to fit with about $3/32$- to $1/8$-inch gap before nailing it to the main pigeonhole assembly.
- With the top section built, sand, finish, and fit the rolltop to the groove. Generously wax both the ends of the tambour and the groove.
- To start the major assembly of the top section, desk top, and pedestal/center section, line up the desk top on the pedestals and, using the scribe, punchmark its bottom surface through the countersunk holes in the center section

rails. Now place the top section on the desk top, align it with the pedestals, and make pencil marks on the desk top around the rolltop stop blocks for reference. Then proceed to punchmark the bottom edges of the top section end panels through countersunk holes in the desk top from underneath. Do this with the desk top overhanging the pedestal ends. Be sure to use a scrap wood spreader between the fronts of the top section end panels to keep the section square.
- With the rolltop installed, place the top section upside down on a smooth surface. Then insert a couple of 8d finishing nails into the drilled holes in the bottom edges of the end panels. With a helper, hold the desk top, upside down, over the top section, and lower it while aligning its holes with nails. (This prevents damaging the desk top.) Then pull nails and drive all screws.
- Stain and finish the desk top before installing the pigeonhole assembly. Lay waxed paper on the desk top before moving the pigeonhole unit into position (avoids scratches).

Glue and clamp areas are marked on the plans to make the work easier. According to Heath, this project should take about one hundred hours. Satisfaction with the job grows as the desk takes shape, and the finished product will be prized as much for its practicality as for its charm—*Bernard Price.*

Other build-it-yourself kits

Heath Craft Woodworks butler table, right, is made of mahogany solids and fine wood veneers. Parquet top is of crotch mahogany with swirling grain. Table can be built for $250 — about half the price of the name-brand piece of comparable quality. Assembly time: a weekend. Kit, top, left, includes brass hinges, all necessary hardware, instruction manual, drill bit to start screws, depth and centering guide for drill bit, sandpaper, and glue. Turn-of-the-century octagonal dining table ($495), below, left, has 8-inch-thick pedestal, claw-and-ball footed legs, and oak-veneered top. It is $48 \times 48 \times 29$ inches high; with 16-inch leaf added it seats six. Other kits available include a grandfather clock, a child's cradle, and a line of embossed pressback oak chairs. For a free catalog of the entire Heath Craft Woodworks collection, write: The Heath Company, Department 432-015 (HT), Benton Harbor, MI 49022.

modular storage units

Those modular cabinets are smartly styled, allow quick room-design changes, and are easy to make. They are laminated inside and out with Wilsonart Union Maple pattern, and separated by spacers finished in Wilsonart black suede.

Cabinets are in three heights, but all are the same width and depth. Upper units have smoked Lucite doors; base units, laminated ones—all with invisible hinges. Center cabinets have movable shelves.

The cabinets can be set up as single, double, or triple stacks (3×3 array with nine spacers) to cover 7 feet

Standard 3½-inch-high spacers nest ¾ inch into adjoining units, securely interlock cabinet stacks.

of wall space. Other options: Combine two base cabinets, four spacers, and a slab top for a telephone nook with plenty of storage space. Or set up cabinet columns in varying heights by stacking three mid-size cabinets next to three base ones. Or separate two full-height stacks with a cabinet-width space and hang the third top cabinet between them. Or fit mid-size cabinets with flap doors to create a counter-height desk complex for household papers and bills.

Detailed instructions for applying the plastic laminate are given in an accompanying box. While you're making the cabinets, keep in mind that, until the laminate is applied to the core (Novoply or an equivalent high-density particleboard), it's brittle and subject to cracking—so handle it carefully. Also, leave the protective paper on Lucite doors until you drill the hinge holes and sand edges. To avoid scratches, rest these doors on a soft, nonabrasive surface when drilling pull holes. Finally, follow the game plan closely to take advantage of the assembly and finishing method.

First, laminate the *edges* of all core pieces. Then, laminate inside surfaces of the sides, the movable shelves on both sides, and the fixed shelves on one side. Laminate only inner surfaces of the large doors until the hinge bores are drilled, or the spade bit pilot will go through to the outer surface.

Now make the rabbets on the rear inner edge of each side piece—yes, right through the laminate. Cut the backs to size and prime and paint them. While the backs are drying, make up the shelf-stiffener assemblies and laminate stiffener fronts. Screw sides to the fixed shelves and nail in the backs with small brads. This squares up the cabinet.

Next, laminate outer surfaces of the sides this way: Set a straight cut laminate edge flush with the rear edge of the side and file or sand the edge (you can't use the laminate trimmer properly in this situation). This completes the cabinet boxes.

Saw the Lucite doors to size, sand the edges, and drill the hinge holes. Drill the bores for the hinges in the large plastic laminate doors ½-inch deep and apply laminate to the front surfaces of the doors.

Mount the hinges (self-closing) on all doors now (remove protective paper from Lucite ones first). All hinges screw into plates (wing-type for large hinges, straight-type for smaller

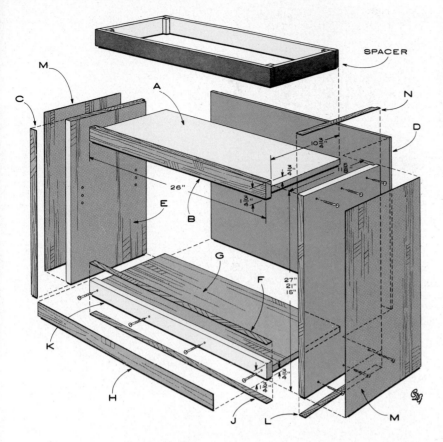

LAMINATE SCHEDULE

	INSIDE	OUTSIDE	TOP	BOTTOM	FRONT	BACK	LEFT	RIGHT
SIDES	✓	✓	✓	✓	✓	–	–	–
TOP FIXED SHELF	–	–	–	✓	–	–	–	–
MOV. SHELF	–	–	✓	✓	✓	–	–	–
STIFFENER	–	–	✓	✓	✓	–	–	–
BACK	–	–	–	–	–	–	–	–
LAM. DOOR	–	–	✓	✓	✓	✓	✓	✓
BOT. FIXED SHELF	–	–	✓	–	–	–	–	–

A – TOP FIXED SHELF WITH LAMINATE ON BOTTOM SURFACE
B – TOP SHELF STIFFENER
C – SIDE LAMINATE FRONT EDGE
D – MASONITE BACK (1/8")
E – SIDE PLUS SURFACE LAMINATE ON BOTH SIDES
F – STIFFENER LAMINATE TOP EDGE
G – BOTTOM FIXED SHELF WITH LAMINATE ON TOP SURFACE
H – STIFFENER LAMINATE FRONT EDGE
J – STIFFENER LAMINATE BOTTOM EDGE
K – STIFFENER
L – SIDE LAMINATE BOTTOM EDGE
M – SIDE LAMINATE SURFACE
N – SIDE LAMINATE TOP EDGE

ALL SUBSTRATES 3/4" NOVAPLY (R) OR EQUIVALENT
ALL PLASTIC LAMINATES 1/32"

To make cabinets. *Top row, below:* Combination bit as shown (left) will make pilot hole, shank clearance hole, and countersink in one drilling pass. Line up stiffener and fixed shelf by resting shelf on ¾-inch-thick spacer (center). Guide line locates assembly screw holes. Use soap or other lubricant to make driving screws easy (right). Drive four or five to lock pieces firmly. *Center row:* Run cabinet sides through the saw (left), face down, then at 90 degrees to machine rabbet that will hold the back. To assemble sides and fixed shelf (center), rest shelf, laminate side up, on a ¾-inch-thick spacer; then drill holes. Pump assembly screws in to lock

sides to shelves (right). Make sure the screwheads are below the surface. *Bottom row:* Drill the 26mm (1-inch) holes for the Lucite door hinges slowly (left), using a spade bit to avoid chipping and cracking. Smooth saw edges of doors by going from No. 120 to No. 400 grit with wet-or-dry paper used wet. Remove protective paper from doors and install hinges and cover plates. Mount hinges and make horizontal adjustment. Test for door-edge and door-to-door clearance and adjust gap. Tighten lock screw. Right: Make large hinge bores (35 mm), using 1⅜-inch diameter spade bit from door back (front laminate *off*).

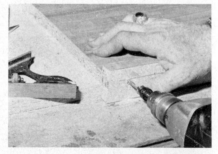

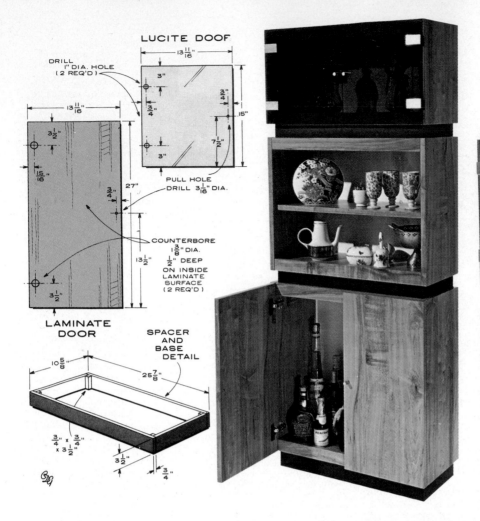

LUCITE DOOF

DRILL 1" DIA. HOLE (2 REQ'D)

13 11/16"

3"

3/4"
3/4"

.15"

7 1/2"

3"

PULL HOLE
DRILL 3 1/16" DIA.

13 11/16"

3 1/2"

15/16"

27"

3/4"

COUNTERBORE 1 3/8" DIA. 1/2" DEEP ON INSIDE LAMINATE SURFACE (2 REQ'D)

13 1/2"

3 1/2"

LAMINATE DOOR

10 5/8"

25 7/8"

SPACER AND BASE DETAIL

3/4" x 3/4" x 3 1/2"

3 1/2"

3/4"

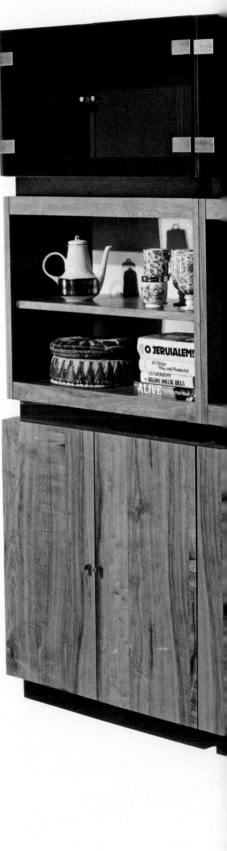

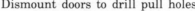

ones), which, in turn, mount to the inner surfaces of the sides.

To hang the doors, snap all hinges out to the "door open" position. (You'll feel the detent action of the self-closing hinges.) Screw the inner parts of the hinges to the plates, so the outer plate ends are as close as possible to the hinge fulcrums. Holding each door at the correct vertical position,

with the inner door edge just touching the front, mark the plate location.

Plates for large door hinges have slotted screw holes to allow vertical adjustment, but plates for smaller hinges can't be adjusted after mounting. Separate plates and hinges. Then, punch-mark plate-mount holes, screw plates in place, and remount hinges. All hinges will adjust the doors both horizontally and out from the cabinets, so provide inner-door-edge and door-to-door clearance before locking hinges to plates.

Dismount doors to drill pull holes

1. Upper units are 15 inches high, have smoked Lucite doors, and self-closing hinges.

2. Inter-cabinet spacers nest ¾ inch into each adjoining unit.

3. Back is ⅛-inch painted Masonite panel.

4. Mid-size unit is 21 inches high and has adjustable shelves.

5. Base, 27 inches high, has wood-grain plastic laminate over Novoply door, with hidden self-closing hinge.

Several stacking arrangements are shown on these pages. Two 27-inch-high base cabinets and a slab top make a desk, shown at bottom, far left, which complements the rich wood grain of the wall units. Single stack of wall units and construction details are at the top, far left, and, near left, a combination setup. Many variations are possible.

Materials

Plastic laminates: Wilsonart Union Maple (No. 7901 13), 1/32 inch, 4x8 feet; Black (No. 1595, 6 Vel), 1/32 inch, 4x8 feet. **Hardware** (available at Albert Constantine & Co.): hinges, full overlay wood door (HC8V2X/OB); wing mounting plates (HBOV3Z/2); pull, satin brass, with ½-inch screws for Lucite doors and with 1-inch screws for laminate doors (T-7050 R); hinges, full overlay glass (HC10533/OW); cover plate, satin brass for glass-door hinges (HB80102 R); flathead screws to mount plates and large hinges (No. 8x⅝ or ¾ inch).

and, in mid-size cabinet sides, drill ¼-inch diameter holes for shelf-support clips. Assemble and laminate black spacers, and laminate a flush door (1 foot by 6 feet, 8 inches) for a slab-top telephone table.

Any slight tilt discrepancy in spacer-to-cabinet fit is easily shimmed with a dry laminate scrap. If you're using cabinets full height against a wall, fasten the back of the top cabinet with a screw, nails, or Molly—*Bernard Price.*

Steps in lamination process: (1) Apply water-base latex contact cement to back side of laminate and edge of the substrate (core). After drying for thirty minutes, it will appear "flat." Place laminate on edge and lock it down with scrap and hammer. (2) Roller guide on special router base can be adjusted to control depth of cut made by combination carbide tipped bit. (3) First, test cut on scrap. Then hold router flat on surface to trim laminate. Move router counterclockwise. (4) To prepare edge surface for adjacent pieces, smooth slight laminate overhang with #120 grit sanding belt. (5) With all edges trimmed, hand file all corners to a smooth bevel. Expose only minimum "dark inner" laminate. (6) Before laminating main surface, belt sand all edges on both sides, working from outer edge inward on surface. Apply cement to backside of surface and main core surface. Go for a thin, but complete, coat. (7) Place the laminate down accurately, using waxed paper or dowels to prevent it from sticking in the wrong places. Then lock it down. (8) Trim surface edge in two steps—first, make a straight cut; then, a bevel cut. Be very careful not to cut too deeply. (9) Finishing the edge is also done in two stages—first, with a plastic file; then make it perfectly smooth with a fine scraper or sanding block.

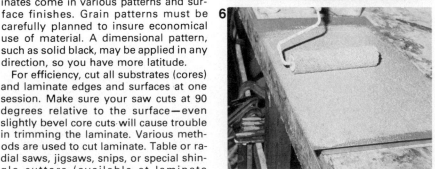

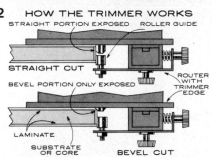

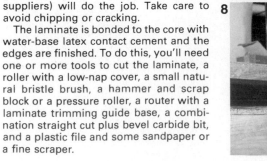

Tips on applying plastic lamination

For vertical applications and cabinet work, ¹⁄₃₂-inch-thick laminate is best. Laminates come in various patterns and surface finishes. Grain patterns must be carefully planned to insure economical use of material. A dimensional pattern, such as solid black, may be applied in any direction, so you have more latitude.

For efficiency, cut all substrates (cores) and laminate edges and surfaces at one session. Make sure your saw cuts at 90 degrees relative to the surface—even slightly bevel core cuts will cause trouble in trimming the laminate. Various methods are used to cut laminate. Table or radial saws, jigsaws, snips, or special shingle cutters (available at laminate suppliers) will do the job. Take care to avoid chipping or cracking.

The laminate is bonded to the core with water-base latex contact cement and the edges are finished. To do this, you'll need one or more tools to cut the laminate, a roller with a low-nap cover, a small natural bristle brush, a hammer and scrap block or a pressure roller, a router with a laminate trimming guide base, a combination straight cut plus bevel carbide bit, and a plastic file and some sandpaper or a fine scraper.

HOW THE TRIMMER WORKS

STRAIGHT PORTION EXPOSED   ROLLER GUIDE

STRAIGHT CUT

ROUTER WITH TRIMMER EDGE

BEVEL PORTION ONLY EXPOSED

LAMINATE

SUBSTRATE OR CORE   BEVEL CUT

fold-up stool

Ideal for sitting on at a fireworks display or marshmallow roast and sturdy enough to stand on while searching the upper closet shelf, this collapsible stool folds up for compact storage or travel.

A table saw, jointer, and drill press speed things up, but hand tools will do. No special hinges or fittings are needed. Wood may be either clear pine or hardwood. To prevent pivot nuts from loosening, use ¼-20 self-locking nuts with a plastic or fiber insert. I used full 1⅛-inch stock for the seat halves, but if you use 1-inch stock, you'll have a stool that folds flush and easily slides under a car seat.

Construction tips

● Rip, plane, and sand 1×1¼-inch stock and cut to length.
● Pivot holes are for ¼×1¼-inch stove or hex-head bolts. A ⁵⁄₁₆-inch counterbore will drop bolt head below surface, but doesn't allow extension above surface on opposite side. Nuts must be self-locking type. A ⅜-inch deep counterbore will permit nut to clear surface, so folding parts slide past.
● Don't try to predrill counterbores. Start assembly and counterbore to screwhead or nut depth as you go. Best tool is piloted ¼ inch to align in ¼-inch bolt holes. Alternate way is to counterbore first with spade bit and follow with ¼-inch drill.
● Install seats and leg braces last. Pilot drill ⁹⁄₆₄ inch or ⅛ inch (depending on wood hardness) for 1¾-inch #8 screws. During assembly, space pass-

ing surfaces of legs with thin cardboard (calling card or matchbook) while drilling seat and brace pilot holes. Otherwise stool will be too snug to open and close easily.
● Chamfer or round seat edges and ends. Oil or wax finish is recommended—*E. F. Lindsley.*

Stool makes a good gift. Little people, and big ones, love a handy little seat that collapses for lugging around or for storage. Folded stool will slide under car seat or slip into closet. Seat can be made of 1-inch stock.

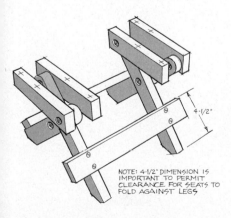

NOTE: 4-1/2" DIMENSION IS IMPORTANT TO PERMIT CLEARANCE FOR SEATS TO FOLD AGAINST LEGS

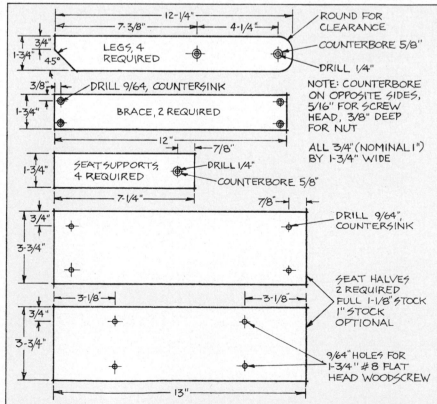

appliance and wine rack

Those Mondrianlike doors on that colorful kitchen closet, facing page, aren't what you think. Only the two skinny ones are conventional hinged panels; the other two are spring-roller window shades—and one of them is mounted upside down (see drawing for installation tips).

My kitchen needed utility storage in a hurry, and because it's all very crisp and white I designed the simplest shelf unit I could, keeping the lines clean, but introducing panels of bold color. A honeycomb sheet-metal wine rack set the dimensions for the lower-left compartment—but posed a problem: This wall faces a sunny window, so the stored wine would have to be protected from the light and heat of direct exposure. Rigid panel doors on compartments of this size are clumsy—and cut off cooling air flow.

Besides, racked wine makes a fine display when solar protection isn't required, so I wanted a cover I could quickly dispense with. A colorful shade, mounted backwards to minimize the roller, proved ideal.

It then seemed logical to give the upper compartment the same treatment—except that my shelf unit stands 8 feet tall, lifting a top-mounted roller out of reach. I contacted Joanna Western Mills (a manufacturer of quality window shades) for advice, and learned of its special kit that would let me mount this shade low and raise it with cords and pulleys, as I'm shown doing in the second color photo. So the two Joanna shades you see are: for the wine rack, a translucent custom shade called Viking (the color is "tan"); the Bottom Up shade is also Viking cloth in light gold.

The problem with most built-in compartmentalized storage is complexity of construction. Here, I've kept the shelf assembly so simple you can do the whole job with hand tools. I used ¾-inch panels (particleboard for the uprights, plywood for the shelves), assembled with glued-and-screwed butt joints—no rabbets or grooves; and the structure is tied into the end wall by means of metal L-brackets anchored with expansion fasteners (Molly bolts).

The ⅝-inch-plywood doors for the two skinny compartments shouldn't be cut until the shelving unit is in place—you want a neat fit against that end wall. To avoid cutting hinge gains, I surface-mounted with brass flathead screws—1½-inch No. 6 for attaching the leaves to the edge of the particleboard upright. Note that the broom-closet door has no stop strip. It simply closes against two wall-mounted magnetic catches—*Al Lees*.

Closetless kitchen offered ample cabinet space but no place to store mops and brooms, bulky appliances, cookbooks—or author's growing wine collection. Tucking super-simple rack in wall niche solved all problems. Note window-shade doors.

Butt joints, fastened with glue and screws, simplified assembly of rack's ten panels. Note that when shelves and uprights were painted, joint lines and edges to be glued were skipped (left). Plywood doors for right-hand sections use magnetic catches.

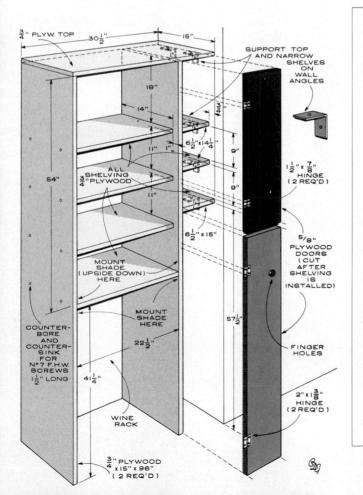

Mounting an upside-down shade

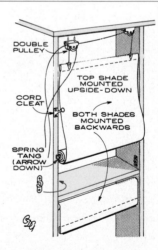

The appliance rack calls for a special shade since you can't mount a regular one upside down. The shade must be under constant tension, since it has only two positions—all the way up or down. Constant-tension rollers are available in custom lines, such as Joanna Western Mills Viking; Joanna calls this mounting a Bottom Up shade and offers a kit with brackets, pulleys, cord, cord cleat, and instructions. (If you can't find a local dealer, write Joanna at 2141 S. Jefferson Street, Chicago, IL 60616.) Two metal clips snap onto the shade slat for attaching the cords. Cords pass up over their respective pulleys, screwed under the top shelf. One cord is long enough to pass across to the second pulley, to join the first on its way down to the cord cleat where they're both secured.

kitchen island

This island is my kitchen's centerpiece. Topped by a massive 3×7-foot chunk of butcher block, it holds a lot of cooking gear in two standard kitchen base cabinets; one has slide-out shelves (lower photo, facing page) for handy storage of pots and pans next to the island's drop-in range. (We used custom-built cabinets; you could substitute knockdown versions, sized to fit.)

The range is positioned slightly off-center to provide generous space for food preparation to one side. There's a 6-inch overhang on one side of the island; with bar stools it doubles as an eating area. The island's sleek, off-white enameled sides face the dining area, screening the unfinished sides and backs of the cabinets within.

Since the island divides the kitchen from our dining area, the chef isn't left out when dinner guests arrive. In keeping with the "stage center" aspect of the island, the work top is lighted by three track-mounted floodlights, controlled by a dimmer.

Putting it together

Construction begins with the 2×4 framing: We built it in three sections, shimmed and nailed *square* to the floor (see drawing). Next, we attached the butcher-block top; our supplier cut the range opening for us—highly recommended since rock-hard maple is no joy to saw. Shim and level the top if necessary; this is especially important when you're installing a range that hangs from the counter top (you don't want your omelets to slip to one side of the pan!). Predrill holes for screws and attach the butcher-block top from the underside of the upper framing members. A power screwdriver such as Skil's Boar Gun makes this task a lot easier.

We faced both sides of the 2×4 framing with ½-inch-thick drywall. We reinforced outside corners with metal beading before we taped the drywall. (Tip: If you're not an experienced taper, a damp sponge helps to even the joint compound.)

Next we pulled up old flooring and ran gas and electric service between floor joists. The two base cabinets and filler strips needed for the range go in next; we placed an electric outlet in one filler strip, convenient to the work area. The drop-in range really does—once it's hooked up to the gas line and plugged into a second electric outlet inside the island—*Richard Stepler.*

Photos by John Keating

closet-door pantry

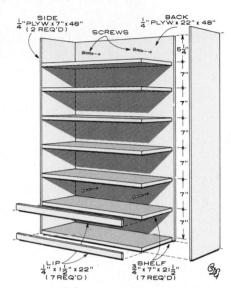

In today's compact homes, the old-time pantry has been eliminated. So canned and packaged goods must be stored in deep cabinets below and above counters and appliances, often forcing the hapless cook to crouch uncomfortably or climb a precarious step stool to reach needed items.

Yet if you have a closet near the kitchen—or even a basement stair—you can convert the door into a serviceable mini-pantry by adding this shelf unit to the back surface.

Mine has seven shelves spaced 6¼ inches apart and is simply attached to the door with four wood screws through the back panel of ¼-inch plywood. Narrow plywood strips, nailed across the front edges of the shelves, create a lip that keeps stored items from being jostled off when the door is opened and closed.

For easy cleaning with a damp cloth or sponge, you'll want to seal all surfaces with varnish or a quality enamel before the unit is mounted.

A major advantage of this type of shallow-shelf storage is that your supplies can be inventoried at a glance. Since everything shows, you can tell at once exactly what needs replenishing.

You might even want to add smaller units to the backs of some of your cabinet doors. And because the shelf is detachable, you can take it with you should you move—*Louis Hochman.*

Sleek sides of this island face a dining area (left photo); the business side (below) shows off its generous and handy storage. Drawing at right shows construction.

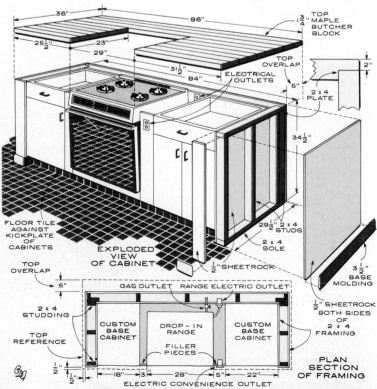

stereo tower

The latest piece of gear your hi-fi store wants to sell you doesn't make a sound. It's a rack that enables you to stack stereo components in a storage unit. You save lots of space in your listening room, cables don't show, and controls are easier to see and use. The drawback: you must already own rack-mountable stereo gear.

But there's a way to get the same effect with standard shelf-type components—build your own stereo tower. The one shown here is made from furniture-quality oak-veneer plywood. Price: $165 and a few hours of your time.

Naturally, my stereo tower may differ from yours. Cutouts will vary, depending on the equipment you own, and even the overall design may be changed to conform with your style of furniture. But the basics of building your own unit are all here, and each deserves special attention.

Equipment placement. Ideally, components with meters should be placed at or slightly below eye level for easy viewing. Power amplifiers and other heat producers should be located toward the top. Other gear should be placed with an eye to operating and adjustment requirements. Equalizers, for example, can be near the bottom (once set, you forget them), and turntables should be near waist height for easy use.

Equipment mounting. This, of course, depends on your gear. In general, though, the tighter the front-panel cutout around the box, the neater the appearance and the better

All components are within reach; tapes and records are within sight. Oak veneer gives cabinet a professional appearance.

the seal—keeping inside dust to a minimum. To allow for future changes, use screws to hold the front panel in place.

Concealed wiring. False backs (such as behind my open turntable area) nicely hide component wiring. The 1-inch air space helps to ventilate the tower, and double shear bracing gives it additional strength.

Lighting. Use standard incandescent lights; fluorescent fixtures emit radio frequencies that can interfere with your equipment. China-cabinet fixtures work well, but night-light sockets are cheaper and easier to find.

If the lights are too bright, wire them in series (like Christmas-tree lights). Use only two bulbs per circuit. The lights—along with the other components—are plugged into the AC socket on the amplifier.

Ventilation. The life of your equipment is at stake. Be sure there is adequate ventilation for each component. Brackets and shelving within the compartments must be cut out or perforated under the vented portions of the equipment chassis. If the temperature of the compartment consistently runs 10 degrees above room temperature, try more rear holes or

install a small fan. (Small, quiet fans designed for this purpose are available in many hi-fi stores.)

Storage. Records must be stored vertically to prevent warping. Placed at the bottom of the tower, they remain cool, and their weight helps stabilize the unit. Cassette and reel-to-reel tapes may be in any position—as long as you can easily read the labels.

Construction notes

Edge all shelves and dividers by gluing and nailing ¼-inch hardwood-strip shelf edges. Use ¾-inch mounting cleats on rear edges of false backs.

Drill several 1-inch-diameter vent holes in back, and cut a 12-inch-square hole for external wires (antenna, AC power, speaker leads, etc.).

Assemble toe kicks and side cleats into the subassembly frame as shown. Center, glue, and nail to the underside of the bottom shelf. Predrill shelf cleats for future mounting, then glue and nail each to its respective shelf.

A record stop-block is set 14 inches back from the front edge of the bottom shelf. (This keeps record jackets from sliding back into the cabinet, out of reach.)

Both end panels are cut at once; securely tape them together with good faces in. Carefully lay out tapers and 2½-inch radii. Cut tapers on a table saw, radii with a scroll saw. Be sure all edges are perfectly square to the front face; otherwise, veneer edging will not line up properly. If out of square, sand with a belt sander. Separate panels and glue veneer strips to the top and front edges using contact cement. After bonding, rub the edges with a wood block to ensure complete adhesion. Use tape to support the critical places around the radii and let set overnight. Sand flush with end panels.

Glue and nail cassette dividers into dadoes in top shelf.

Fill and sand all nail holes. Sand all subassemblies (120 paper is best), apply stain, and let dry overnight. Spray or brush on several coats of Deft lacquer, rubbing down each coat with 0000 steel wool before applying the next. Don't rub the finish coat—*Carl W. Spencer.*

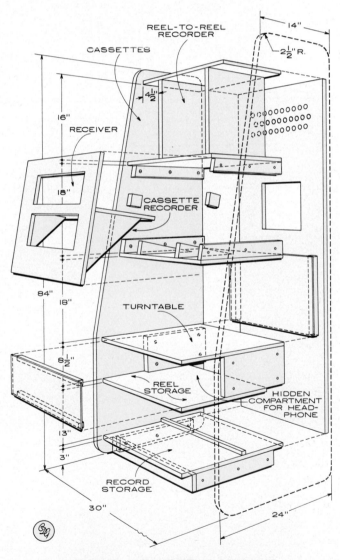

REEL-TO-REEL RECORDER

CASSETTES

14"

2½" R.

4½"

16"

RECEIVER

18"

84"   18"

CASSETTE RECORDER

TURNTABLE

8½"

REEL STORAGE

HIDDEN COMPARTMENT FOR HEADPHONE

13"

3"

RECORD STORAGE

30"

24"

MUSIC-CENTER CABINET ASSEMBLY DETAILS

False backs let air and cables pass through all sections of tower. Rear cutout is for external wiring. Measure components carefully for proper front-cutout sizes. Use night lights for indirect lighting where necessary.

COMPONENTS USED IN TOWER

Kenwood KR-5010 receiver, Kenwood KD-3100 turntable, Teac A-55ORX cassette deck, Teac X-7R reel-to-reel.

The author owns Presidential Industries (PO Box 2531, Riverside, CA 92516), a cabinet shop specializing in custom hi-fi cabinets.

free-standing closet

Think *your* home is short of closets? Pity the poor buyer of loft space in any major city: He gets *no* storage because what he's buying is open space. At best, kitchen and bath have been partitioned off, as in my loft pictured below. But the rest of the floor is as naked as a basketball court—not even a place to hang a hat.

Solving that problem was the first task I set for myself, designing a sturdy closet that's a spacious wardrobe. (Line it with cedar and it would be an ideal out-of-season storage-partition for family room or den.)

My structure makes economic use of its 4×8 plywood and particleboard panels. Two uncut ¾-inch panels are butted edge-to-edge to form the back, with the joint glued and screwed along a 2×4. Another ¾-inch sheet is cut down the center to form two end panels—each framed in 2×2s, which, with the grooved 4×4 base, create a structural trim.

I used particleboard for the back panel and two end doors. The center door is ⅝-inch plywood; since each door is 33 inches wide, you'll have scrap strips for shelving. I used a 5-inch strip of the ⅝-inch panel for the cornice that hides the door track.

The doors were hung with an 8-foot sliding-door set (Stanley 2850) that features dial-alignment hangers. Since the outer edges of two doors complete the frame around the end panels, alignment is critical—the hangers simplify adjustment.

Three different colors of enamel complete the project. The end panels are MDO plywood for a smooth face to contrast with the particleboard textures on back and outer doors—*Al Lees.*

Ratchet driver with extension socket will sink bolt heads below groove bottom.

Compartmentalizing helps in meeting special storage needs.

Also handy to exit: grocery cart. Extra leaves for dining table go in slot, right.

Storage from scratch: an innovative built-in that can be adapted to any home that's short on closet space.

In the unpartitioned loft above we designed an island closet (tucked under a structural beam here, though it's designed to stand free); it masks the entry door from the living space, screens off the bathroom door to the right, and provides ample storage for outerwear and bulky items that must be handy to the exit.

The plywood-particleboard case is assembled on a simple frame, most of which is external and treated as a design element. Hung within the recessed end panel shown are vulnerable artworks: a silver plaque and a Jon Baugh glass assemblage.

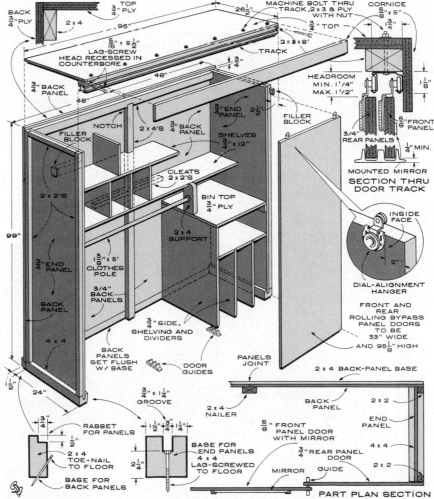

darkroom work cabinet

A darkroom area must, above all, be functional. This means it must serve as a storage area for most, if not all, your photographic equipment. The compact worktable-storage area shown here will adequately store such items as chemical bottles, mixing bucket, contact printer, print dryer, film washer, trays, developing tanks, filters, enlarging lenses, paper-mounting press, and timers, as well as provide a comfortable work area—*Claudia* and *John Caruana.*

Above right, measurements, for components. They are coded (A, B, etc.) to drawing. In parentheses: how many of same size pieces are needed.

Measurements in inches

A = ½ × 60 × 17	(1)	L = ¾ × 1½ × 13 (1)
B = ½ × 59 × 16¾	(1)	M = ¾ × 1½ × 12½ (3)
C = ½ × 38 × 17	(2)	N = ½ × 13½ × 7½ (2)
D = ½ × 34½ × 16¾	(3)	O = ½ × 11⁷⁄₁₆ × 6⁷⁄₁₆ (2)
E = ½ × 14 × 16¾	(3)	P = ½ × 17¼ × 6⁷⁄₁₆ (4)
F = ¼ × 35¾ × 59	(1)	Q = ½ × 11⁷⁄₁₆ × 6⁷⁄₁₆ (2)
Masonite	(1)	R = ¼ × 11⁷⁄₁₆ × 16¼
G = ½ × 3 × 59	(1)	
Ha = ½ × 13½ × 15	(1)	Masonite (2)
Hb = ½ × 14 × 15	(1)	S = ½ × 2 × 59 (1)
Ia = ½ × 13½ × 18	(2)	T = ½ × 2 × 17¾ (2)
Ib = ½ × 14 × 18	(1)	U = ½ × 8 × 16¾ (1)
J = ¾ × 1½ × 32½	(4)	V = ½ × ¾ × 16¾ (16)
K = ¾ × 1½ × 60	(2)	W = ½ × ¾ × 14¼ (2)

It takes about thirty hours, including cutting the pieces, to make this darkroom cabinet (twenty hours, if the pieces are precut). Equipment needed: tablesaw, handsaws (rip, crosscut), sandpaper (medium, fine), hammer, plane, 6-foot ruler, pencil, level, angle, miter box and saw, chisel, files (medium, fine, coarse), router, screwdriver, 6d finishing nails, brush (medium size), and glue.

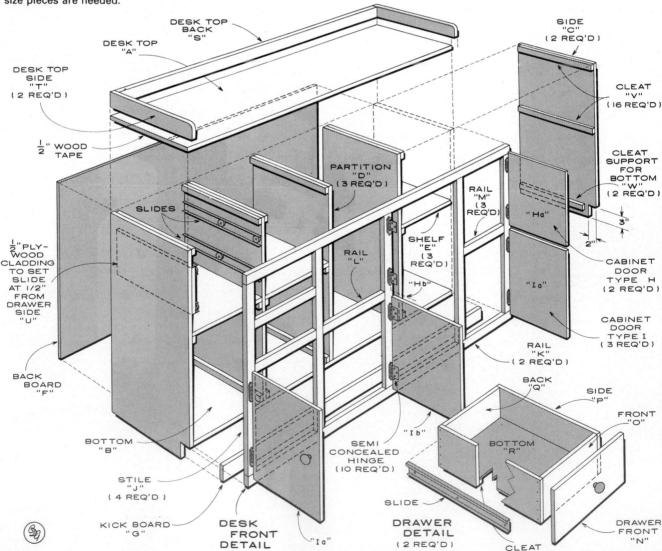

DESK TOP BACK "S"

DESK TOP "A"

DESK TOP SIDE "T" (2 REQ'D)

½" WOOD TAPE

SIDE "C" (2 REQ'D)

CLEAT "V" (16 REQ'D)

CLEAT SUPPORT FOR BOTTOM "W" (2 REQ'D)

PARTITION "D" (3 REQ'D)

SLIDES

RAIL "M" (3 REQ'D)

"Ha"

3"

2"

CABINET DOOR TYPE H (2 REQ'D)

½"PLY-WOOD CLADDING TO SET SLIDE AT 1/2" FROM DRAWER SIDE "U"

RAIL "L"

SHELF "E" (3 REQ'D)

"Hb"

"Ia"

CABINET DOOR TYPE I (3 REQ'D)

BACK BOARD "F"

RAIL "K" (2 REQ'D)

BACK "Q"

SIDE "P"

FRONT "O"

BOTTOM "B"

BOTTOM "R"

STILE "J" (4 REQ'D)

SEMI CONCEALED HINGE (10 REQ'D)

"Ib"

KICK BOARD "G"

DESK FRONT DETAIL

"Ia"

SLIDE

DRAWER DETAIL (2 REQ'D)

CLEAT

DRAWER FRONT "N"

magazine cradle

This dowel-and-redwood rack displays a selection of magazines of varying size for easy access. And it's quickly made with hand tools and a power drill.

Begin by gathering all materials and cutting pieces to length (see table). Next, cut the lap joints in the side pieces (the width of the redwood and halfway through each piece). Mark the crosspieces for the dowel holes: Place the first mark 1⅛ inch from the end and the rest 1¼ inch on center. Use a ½-inch drill; make holes slightly deeper than ¼ inch. Sand all pieces.

Drill and counterbore holes in the four sides for screws and ½-inch plugs. Tap one row of dowels into the center crosspiece, then set the dowel tops into a top crosspiece. Tap lightly on the crosspiece to secure the dowels. Repeat for the other row of dowels. Glue and screw the sides to the crosspieces. Glue the dowel plugs in place and sand them flush when the glue is dry. Apply a clear finish—*V. E. Smay.*

LUMBER	CUT TO	FOR
Redwood		
2 6' 2×2's	4 22" lengths	Sides
	3 21" lengths	Crosspieces
DOWELS		
8 4' ½" dia.	32 10½" lengths	Supports
HARDWARE AND MISCELLANEOUS		
6 2¼" #10 flat-head wood screws		
Wood glue		

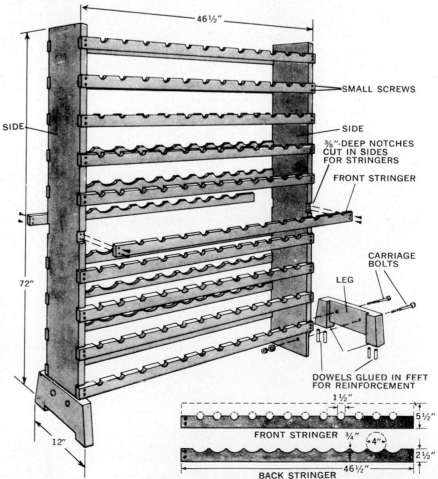

SIDE
CROSSPIECES
22"
24"
11½"
SIDE
SCREWS AND DOWEL PLUGS

wine rack

Front stringers of rack are fashioned by boring holes in 1×6s, then rip-sawing the boards in half. Scallops for the back stringers must be cut individually.

This redwood rack survives damp storage. The design calls for two sturdy 2×8s, half-lapped to the base of the uprights and reinforced with glued-in dowels for extra strength. But if the joists in your basement ceiling are exposed, just make the rack's sides tall enough to tie into them for greater stability—*Paul Bolon.*

46½"
SMALL SCREWS
SIDE
SIDE
⅜"-DEEP NOTCHES CUT IN SIDES FOR STRINGERS
FRONT STRINGER
CARRIAGE BOLTS
LEG
72"
DOWELS GLUED IN FEET FOR REINFORCEMENT
12"
1½"
5½"
FRONT STRINGER
¾"
4"
2½"
46½"
BACK STRINGER

one-wall vanitory

There's a lot more than the plumbing in a bathroom. In addition, there usually are a vanitory cabinet, medicine chest, mirror, some electrical convenience outlets, and lighting. Knowing how to build, finish, and install such items can be a real money-saver in the remodeling of what amounts to the most expensive area of your home (on cost per square foot basis).

We took a partly finished bath and finished it, continuing with the same materials and colors. Since the floor and some walls already were tiled, the same American Olean Siena putty shade was used for the vanitory top. The vanitory base, the medicine chests, and the light enclosures we laminated with Wilsonart's Natural Almond, a color that matched existing fixtures.

The work began with building the vanitory cabinet and top, medicine chests, and light enclosure. These pieces are of simple, but strong construction. For the chest and light enclosure, butt-joining was used only in developing the box structure, while the vanitory was butt-joined everywhere except the face-frame, which requires mortises and tenons. All doors are slab overlays and all drawers, simple boxes with separate laminated faces. The mirror arrangement lets the user see the back of his head. (There is one mirror on the back of each medicine chest door, and another, larger one mounted between the chests.)

All the cabinet work, assembly, lamination, and tiling procedures are covered in accompanying photos and drawings, but here are some suggestions that could be helpful:

- Mount medicine chest doors with Stanley No. 131 pin hinges. The hinges allow the door at the internal corner to open properly.
- Silicone caulking—for example, Phenoseal—can be used to mount the mirrors on the backs of doors.
- A GFCI (Ground Fault Circuit Interrupter) outlet should be used in the area of the vanitory or lavatory.
- Use only noncombustible, water-base latex contact cement.
- Once the drawers have been assembled, they should be mounted on the three-point suspensions and adjusted. Then the prelaminated fronts should be aligned and marked for mounting. The screw hole for the drawer pull should be drilled completely through front and slightly into the drawer as a pilot. The pilot hole may be countersunk or enlarged for screwhead clearance.

(Text continues next page.)

1. **Location** for the new vanitory cabinet, with the old medicine chest cut out and the plumbing stubs showing.
2. **Mortise is** made with drill press and hollow chisel adapter. With workpiece in a clamp or vise, bore a continuous row of overlapping square holes.
3. **Tenon is made** on a table saw. The shoulders are first cut to the correct depth with aid of miter head and rip fence.
4. **Second step** in making tenon is the cutting away of waste. Blade height and fence adjustment are left as before. Flanks of tenon are cut away by rapid back and forth motion across the blade, gradually advancing toward output end.
5. **The components** are glued and then bar-clamped together as shown here.
6. **After assembly** has dried and been sanded, it's glued to cabinet sides.
7. **The drawer** members are butt-joined with glue and nails. Quarter-inch dadoes support bottom shelf.
8. **Contact cement** is brushed on the front surface of the piece to be covered with laminate and on the back surface of the matching piece of laminate.

9. **After the cement** dries, laminate is positioned and pressure is applied—here, by means of a wood block scrap and a hammer—in order to lock the laminate down in the proper position.
10. **Laminate** edges are trimmed with a small router/trimmer and solid carbide bit. Use the flat cutting edge as opposed to the bevel part. Setup shown uses the guide on the router itself.
11. **The trimmed** edges are belt-sanded with #120 grit; the motion of belt is from outer to inner part of the panel. This motion helps you avoid chipping or otherwise damaging the laminate.
12. **Edge corners**—and wherever two laminated surfaces join at 90-degree angles—are carefully worked with file.
13. **Whenever two** laminate edges meet, the overlap is trimmed with the router.
14. **Here, the** front face of chest is being jigsawed as a "picture frame."
15. **Feed direction** for the router when trimming the inside and outside edges.
16. **With completed** cabinet in position and level, drill the holes for screws through face-frame and into wall studs.

(Steps continued on page 91.)

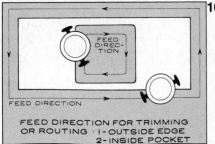

FEED DIRECTION FOR TRIMMING
OR ROUTING : 1-OUTSIDE EDGE
2-INSIDE POCKET

• When you begin to mount the medicine chests and the large mirror and its retainers, exercise care to keep everything square. Otherwise gaps are likely to develop between the components.

• The baseboard bullnose tile—it probably would prevent the vanitory cabinet from seating flush against the wall—should be removed as necessary. Later, the tile can be retrimmed at the ends—*Bernard Price*.

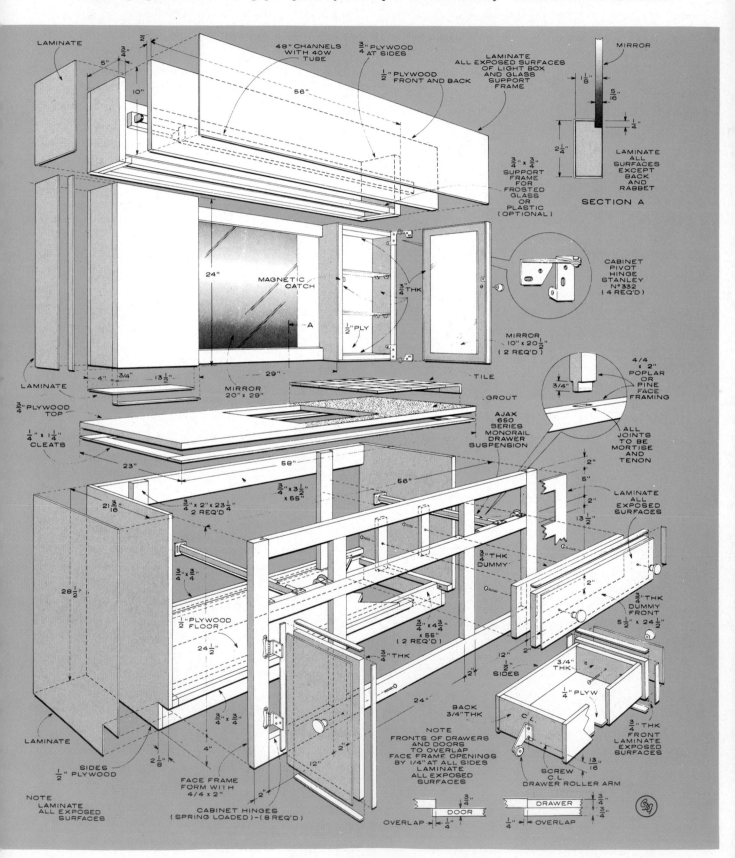

17. The cabinet top is scribed in order to ensure proper fit against the wall.

18. A template and star-wheel tracer are used for marking the location of the cut-out for installation of the lavatory.

19. Jigsaw is used to make the cutout.

20. Dry-fit all the tiles before applying any mortar to the vanity top. Tiles are then removed and placed close at hand in the order of application.

21. The trowel used to apply the mortar has ¼-inch-square notches.

22. Border tiles are set first and spaced,

as they generally lack spacing projections found on most flat tiles.

23. The tiles are locked in mortar by striking over them in several directions with a hammer and scrap of plywood.

24. The grout is applied with a rubber-bottomed float to fill all cracks.

25. While grout is still wet, excess is removed with a squeegee pulled over the tiles in a dragging motion.

26. As the grout dries, a dry haze will form over the tiles. This should be removed by polishing with burlap.

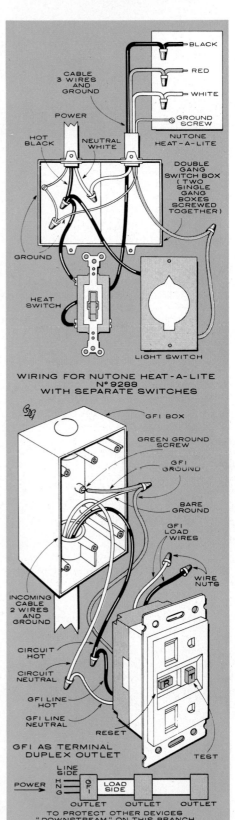

WIRING FOR NUTONE HEAT-A-LITE Nº 9288 WITH SEPARATE SWITCHES

GFI AS TERMINAL DUPLEX OUTLET

TO PROTECT OTHER DEVICES "DOWNSTREAM" ON THIS BRANCH POWER THEM FROM LOAD LINES ON GFI DUPLEX

Project participants

Laminate (Natural Almond D30-6): Wilsonart, 600 General Bruce Drive, Temple, TX 76501. Tile (Siena): American Olean, 2743 Cannon Avenue, Lansdale, PA 19446. Wallcovering: Reed Wall Covering, Atlanta, GA 30349. Ceiling fixture (Model 9288 Heat-A-Lite): Nutone, Madison and Red Bank Rds., Cincinnati, OH 45227. Faucet (FA 102 washerless): Nibco, Inc., 500 Simpson Street, Elkhart, IN 46515. Epoxy, grout: L and M Surco Mfg., Inc., Whitehead Avenue, South River, NJ 08882.

bathroom built-ins

I f you have a bathroom the size of a gym, remodeling it is no problem. All the home magazines are full of ideas on where to put your his-and-hers sinks and toilets, hot tub, and steeping bath. Fine, but what can you do with a real-world bathroom like mine—one that measures just 5×6 feet?

I soon discovered that if I wanted a good-looking vanity that wasn't so large that it blocked the door to the room, I'd have to make it myself. And as long as I was going to make the vanity, I decided to make the rest of the furnishings as well. That way they would all match and I could use a few ideas to make the room look and function like a larger one.

Medicine chest is sized to fit the narrow wall at the left end of the vanity. This frees the area over the counter for the large mirror, which gives the room a feeling of depth. Chest construction is simple: Make an oak frame with a hardboard back, sized to fit between studs. Fasten on the oak trim and secure the unit in place. The back edge of the door is rabbeted to give a thinner look. Be sure to rout the front of the door with a rounding-over bit *before* cutting the rabbet, or the bit pilot will have no surface to follow.

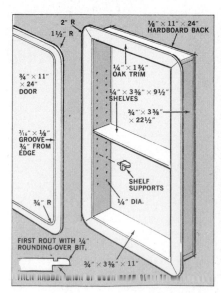

2" R
1½" R
¾" × 11" × 24" HARDBOARD BACK
¾" × 11" × 24" DOOR
¼" × 1¾" OAK TRIM
¼" × 3⅜" × 9½" SHELVES
¾" × 3⅜" × 22½"
³⁄₁₆" × ⅛" GROOVE ¾" FROM EDGE
SHELF SUPPORTS
¼" DIA.
¾" R
FIRST ROUT WITH ¼" ROUNDING-OVER BIT.
¾" × 3⅜" × 11"

The photos and sketches show what was done using $120 worth of solid oak and $100 worth of stock oak butcher block. Other materials and fixtures used are as follows:

The walls and floor are finished with American Olean's Tanbark Siena ceramic tile and Tuscany Malt grout. The tub is Kohler's Villager; the toilet, Kohler's Wellworth Water Guard—both in Mexican Sand finish. The sink is a tiny 12-inch-round bowl from Mayfair China, hand paint-ed at the factory with trim bands to match the wallpaper. With Kohler's Antique brushed-chrome faucets, it creates an old-fashioned dry-sink look.

My remodeling raised one practical problem: The position of the vanity blocked the bath's hot-air register. Solution: I fed the duct in under the bottom of the vanity and cut louver slits in the front of the toe board to let the hot air out—A. J. Hand.

Photos by the author
Drawings by Gerhard Richter

Vanity, made from solid oak, is designed to fit into a corner of the room. The counter and leaf were cut from a single piece of 16×60-inch oak butcher block. The leaf section makes good use of the normally wasted space over the toilet, but can be removed to allow access to the tank. The rounded corner of the vanity looks difficult to make but is really quite simple. Start by making an ordinary butt joint, backed up by a 1×1 oak cleat. Trace an arc with a 2-inch radius on the top and bottom edges of the joint. (I just traced around a coffee can.) Then plane the corner down to match the curve. The back-splash is made from resawn oak: Using thin oak provided clearance for the faucet handles. Even so, the position of the faucets pushed the sink out slightly, so the rear surface of the vanity's top rail had to be routed to clear it. The vanity, counter, and back-splash were sealed with Watco oil, then given three coats of satin varnish. The mirror is also framed in oak. Its floral design was etched into the rear surface of the mirror, then hand painted.

Towel-and-magazine rack is built in be-tween wall studs to create extra space. In the original bathroom a conventional double-hung window occupied this posi-tion. I removed it and placed a Pella awn-ing window up high, making space for the rack. To build the rack, you cement foam insulation to the sheathing between studs. Then cement hardboard over the foam. Paint or paper the hardboard, then cut oak frame and trim parts to fit. Thin oak for the trim and face of the magazine rack was made by resawing ¾-inch oak.

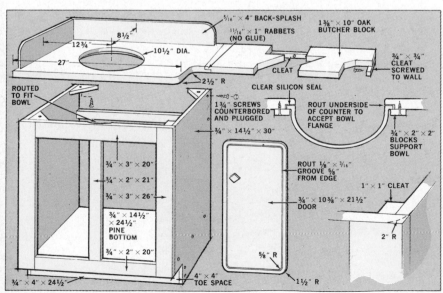

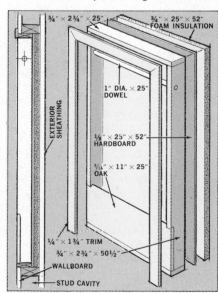

early american medicine chest

Your bath or powder room doesn't have to be all chromium plate and porcelain enamel. Take, for example, the medicine cabinet shown here. It's made entirely of lumberyard pine and styled Early American. It does everything today's cabinet does, but with a lot more warmth. You can build it at little cost (most expensive element is the mirror), and with only a small investment of your time.

This cabinet is made entirely of ½-inch pine, with brads and glue joinery. Cut and shape pieces as illustrated. Then follow these steps.

● Spread glue along a side edge and drive brads through the back into the edge. Keep the back and side edges flush. Do the same with the other side.

● Measure the distance between the sides and cut the top and bottom to fit. Glue and nail these two pieces in place. Sink brads that go through the sides and fill holes, preferably with slivers of wood that you sand smooth, although any wood filler will work.

● Cut shelves ¹/₁₆ inch shorter than the top and bottom pieces, but do not rip them to width yet. (Our cabinet has two shelves; you may want three, depending on what you'll keep on them.)

● Measure the opening between top and bottom of the two sides. Put the mirror-frame door together as shown, making it barely smaller than the opening. The corners are mitered, and the mirror and backing are held in place with thin strips ripped off the edge of ½-inch pine.

● Rip the shelves to proper width by removing an edge exactly equal to the thickness of the door, including the strips that hold the mirror in place. Thus, the shelves become the stops that let the door close properly.

● Determine shelf positions and fasten cleats in place with ½-inch brads and glue. Cleats can be "off-fall" from the strips on the back of the door.

All that's left now is finishing and hinging. Choose an Early American pine stain in the color you want for the outside. Give the interior two

Drawing below, right, shows how cabinet goes together after pieces are cut to shape and size. Shelf width is determined by door thickness. Rip ½-inch stock 1½ inches wide and cut rabbet from back as shown below, left; miter corners for good fit. Buy mirror to fit frame; back it up with hardboard and fasten in place with a thin strip fastened to frame with brads.

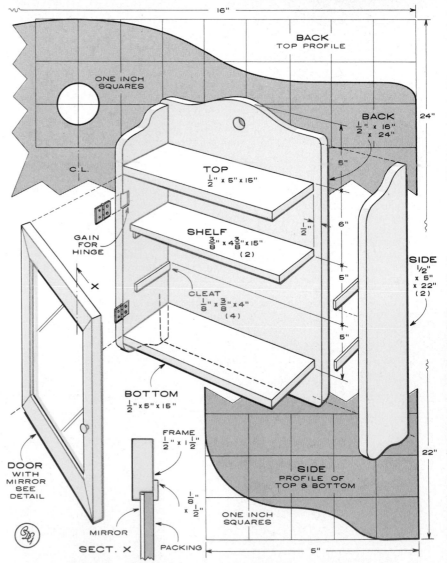

The back is 16 inches wide—two ½×10s edge-glued and ripped to size. To cut the shape at the top, draw 1-inch squares on the back as shown in the drawing above, or draw the shape on cardboard and trace it on both top corners. Follow the same technique for cutting the sides to shape (drawing at right). The top and bottom curves are identical. After cutting the sides, sand the cut edges.

coats of glossy enamel to make cleaning easy.

Your hardware store carries small brass butt hinges and brass knobs. Buy the ½-inch size. Mount them about 2 inches from the top and bottom of the door. Mortising the edge of the door deep enough to accept the entire hinge is easier than mortising both the edge and the cabinet side.

In keeping with Early American style, the cabinet back has a hole at the top. It provides you with an easy mounting method—*if there is a stud* behind the hole. If not, mount the cabinet with two toggle bolts through the back into the wall—*Jackson Hand.*

Lay out curves as indicated in the drawings; then clamp two pieces of pine together (top) and saw them both at once for perfect uniformity. Construction is entirely brad-and-glue (center). Sink brads, then insert wooden plug in hole; break it off at surface and sand smooth. Cut into door edge with a mortise deep enough to accept both wings of hinges—simpler than mortising both cabinet edge and side—as shown (bottom).

airtight attic door

A pull-down staircase makes it easy to get things up into an attic, but it also lets cold air spill down into the living areas of the home. When all the weatherstripping and sealants I tried didn't keep the cold wind from cascading down my hallway, I devised the "airlock"—an airtight double door that permits easy access to the attic, but keeps cold drafts out.

No more than a bottomless box with a hinged lid, the airlock is easily built with under $20 worth of materials and installs in minutes without altering the ceiling. The parts can be cut from plywood, particleboard, or 1-inch lumber. I made mine with 1×12 sides and a scrap of underlayment for the door. Also needed: a pair of 2-inch strap hinges; a roll of adhesive foam insulating tape; a screen-door handle; a hook-and-eye latch; a few nails, screws, and stove bolts.

Cut the sides of your airlock to form a box with outside dimensions a half-inch smaller in length and width than the opening in the ceiling. Make certain the box depth will accommodate the folded stairway. Butt join the sides, using glue, screws, or nails. Use 2×2 corner cleats for an easier and stronger assembly, but make sure the hardware doesn't interfere with the ladder or folding mechanism. Attach the door with strap hinges secured with wood screws or stove bolts and washers. Seal door edge with foam tape or felt weatherstripping.

A helper stationed in the attic simplifies installation. Slide the box up to him, then lower it into place. Fasten it to a header with nails or screws, square it with shims, and secure the remaining sides. Fill any gaps between the box and ceiling frame with insulation and pull the fiberglass batts snugly against the sides. Mound shredded cellulose fill around the airlock to eliminate cold spots and gaps. Staple a batt to the top of the door for an added R-value or two, and screw on the door handle. Bumps on the head can be avoided by supporting the trap door with a friction lid prop or pneumatic door closer. Letting the door swing open to rest on the joists will, however, create a firm landing and loading platform.

To prevent attic winds from lifting the door and vacuuming warm air from the house, install a hook-and-eye latch to help hold the weatherseal—*Joel Hamm.*

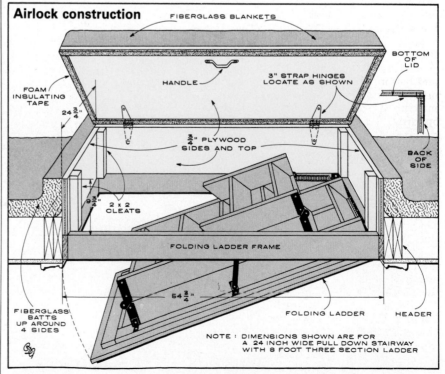

Airlock construction

FIBERGLASS BLANKETS

HANDLE

3" STRAP HINGES LOCATE AS SHOWN

BOTTOM OF LID

FOAM INSULATING TAPE

24¾"

¾" PLYWOOD SIDES AND TOP

BACK OF SIDE

9¾"

2×2 CLEATS

FOLDING LADDER FRAME

FIBERGLASS BATTS UP AROUND 4 SIDES

54¾"

FOLDING LADDER

HEADER

NOTE: DIMENSIONS SHOWN ARE FOR A 24 INCH WIDE PULL DOWN STAIRWAY WITH 8 FOOT THREE SECTION LADDER

sewing center

Here's a convenient and efficient sewing center you can build. Even though the unit is better than most of the expensive commercial models, it was built a few years ago for only about $80.

The main section of the unit holds a fold-down table to which a portable sewing head is bolted; four storage compartments; a sixty-spool thread rack; a recessed fluorescent lighting fixture; and a triple-slot electrical outlet for the machine, light, and electric scissors. There are large top and bottom storage compartments.

The unit is constructed of ½-inch particleboard. Dimensions of the unit—81 inches high, 31 inches wide, and 19 inches deep—allowed most efficient use of available material, but you can vary them. The basic cabinet, including doors, is cut from two 4×8-foot sheets. Sections cut out as door openings are used for doors themselves; to compensate for size difference, ½-inch half-round is used on inside edges of door openings and all door edges. This allows for a strong, attractive, one-piece cabinet front.

After drawing the sections on par-

Materials

Two 4×8 sheets particleboard
Ten 10-foot lengths ½-inch half-round
Four 10-foot 1×2 pine
One 5-foot 1⅜-inch dowel
2 feet ½-inch dowel
12 feet ³/₁₆-inch dowel
One 30×78-inch ⅛-inch hardboard
One 7½×31-inch Peg-Board (³/₁₆-inch holes)
6 feet decorative molding
29-inch piece 2×4 (table mount)
5 feet particleboard shelving (8-inch)
Two pair 2-inch strap hinges
Six pair 2-inch self-closing hinges
Six door pulls
Four 1¼-inch flathead screws
18-inch fluorescent fixture
12-foot electrical cord
Three-slot receptacle
As required: eighteen ⅝-inch brads, seventeen 1-inch brads, 4d and 6d finishing nails, carpenter's glue, spackling paste, paint, and/or stain.

ticleboard sheets as shown in diagrams 1 and 2, drill ½-inch holes in diagonal corners of each door opening and use them as starter holes for your saber saw to cut out doors. Cut remaining parts as shown.

To assemble the cabinet:

1. Using 4d finishing nails and carpenter's glue, assemble so each compartment bottom is flush with lower edge of its door opening. Top piece should be flush with top edge of front and sides.

2. Cut 1×2-inch stock to length for vertical corner supports (twelve required) and fasten in place.

3. For small shelves, cut 1×2-inch stock in 6-inch lengths (six required).

Fasten three to inside of left side of cabinet, spaced to suit needs, and the others to one side of small-shelf vertical support in corresponding positions.

4. Install small-shelf vertical support flush with back edge of compartment bottoms. Glue in shelves.

5. Using a little glue, install the 7½×7½-inch shelf supports in upper and lower compartments.

6. Put 4½×29-inch base front in place.

7. Place table mount (29-inch 2×4) flat on main compartment bottom, snug against small-shelf vertical support. Nail through cabinet sides into ends with 6d finishing nails.

8. Close cabinet back using tempered

hardboard and eighteen ⅝-inch brads.

9. Cut and install ⅝-inch shelving in top and bottom compartments.

10. Install molding around top. With ½-inch half-round and eighteen 1-inch brads, add decorative touch to each side (see photo).

11. Using ½-inch half-round and seventeen 1-inch brads, cover exposed particleboard edges, including inside of door openings and six doors.

12. Spackle as required and sand.

To construct the spool rack:

1. Fasten the 3×30-inch triangular supports to a 7½×31-inch piece of Peg-Board (³/₁₆-inch holes) using eighteen ⅝-inch brads.

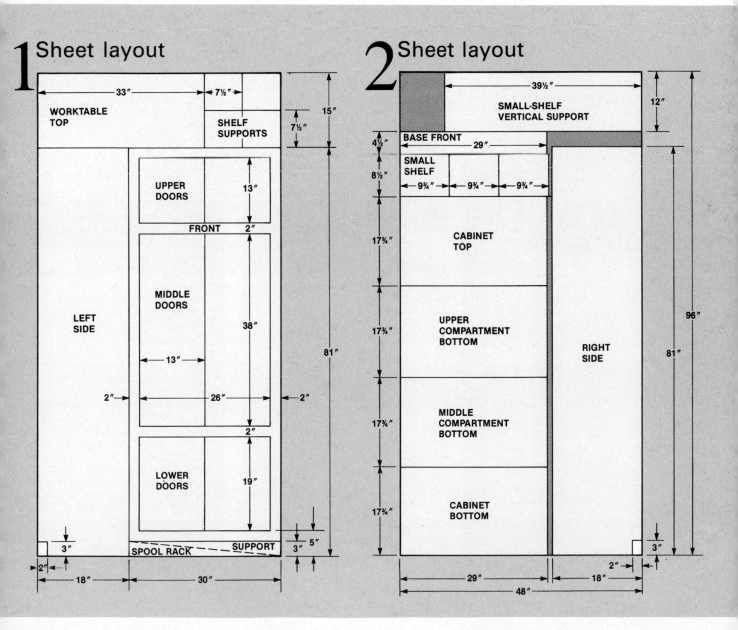

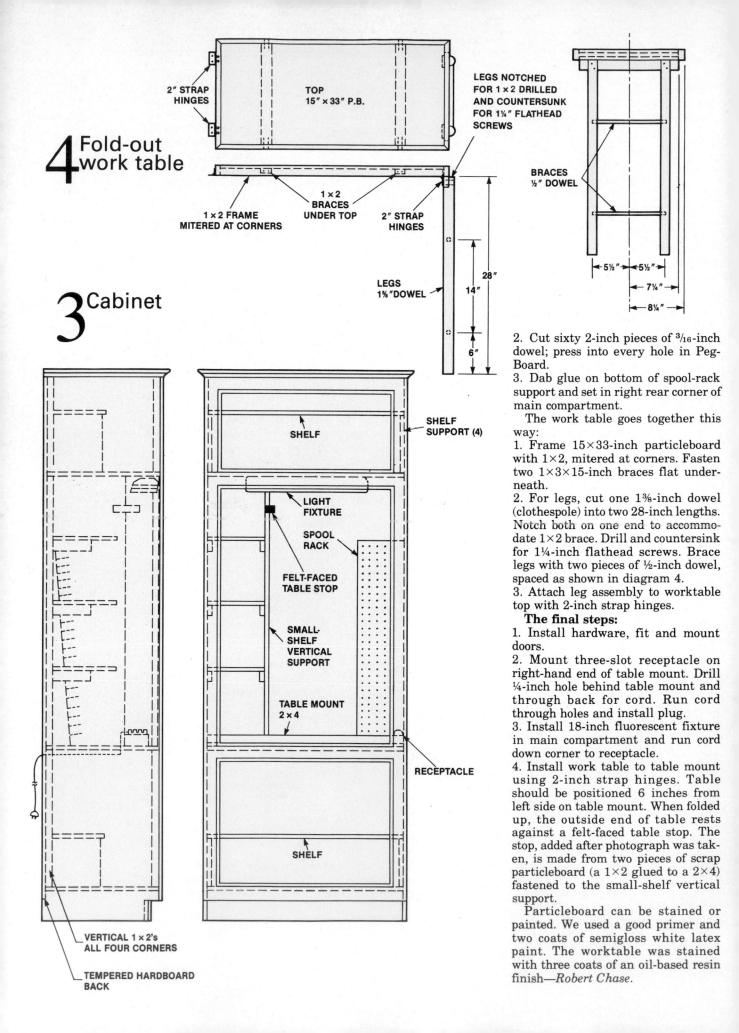

4 Fold-out work table

2" STRAP HINGES

TOP
15" × 33" P.B.

LEGS NOTCHED FOR 1 × 2 DRILLED AND COUNTERSUNK FOR 1¼" FLATHEAD SCREWS

1 × 2 FRAME MITERED AT CORNERS

1 × 2 BRACES UNDER TOP

2" STRAP HINGES

LEGS 1⅜" DOWEL

BRACES ½" DOWEL

28"

14"

6"

5½" 5½"

7¼"

8¼"

3 Cabinet

SHELF

SHELF SUPPORT (4)

LIGHT FIXTURE

SPOOL RACK

FELT-FACED TABLE STOP

SMALL-SHELF VERTICAL SUPPORT

TABLE MOUNT 2 × 4

RECEPTACLE

SHELF

VERTICAL 1 × 2's ALL FOUR CORNERS

TEMPERED HARDBOARD BACK

2. Cut sixty 2-inch pieces of ³/₁₆-inch dowel; press into every hole in Peg-Board.

3. Dab glue on bottom of spool-rack support and set in right rear corner of main compartment.

The work table goes together this way:

1. Frame 15×33-inch particleboard with 1×2, mitered at corners. Fasten two 1×3×15-inch braces flat underneath.

2. For legs, cut one 1⅜-inch dowel (clothespole) into two 28-inch lengths. Notch both on one end to accommodate 1×2 brace. Drill and countersink for 1¼-inch flathead screws. Brace legs with two pieces of ½-inch dowel, spaced as shown in diagram 4.

3. Attach leg assembly to worktable top with 2-inch strap hinges.

The final steps:

1. Install hardware, fit and mount doors.

2. Mount three-slot receptacle on right-hand end of table mount. Drill ¼-inch hole behind table mount and through back for cord. Run cord through holes and install plug.

3. Install 18-inch fluorescent fixture in main compartment and run cord down corner to receptacle.

4. Install work table to table mount using 2-inch strap hinges. Table should be positioned 6 inches from left side on table mount. When folded up, the outside end of table rests against a felt-faced table stop. The stop, added after photograph was taken, is made from two pieces of scrap particleboard (a 1×2 glued to a 2×4) fastened to the small-shelf vertical support.

Particleboard can be stained or painted. We used a good primer and two coats of semigloss white latex paint. The worktable was stained with three coats of an oil-based resin finish—*Robert Chase.*

yarn box

Here's an attractive, useful gift you can make—at almost no cost. The base and center frame of the box are made of wood salvaged from wine crates; the trays, from fruit boxes. The hinges are made of ¼-inch shock cord. Other supplies needed are: elastic strips (used across the trays to keep yarn from falling out), scrap wood for thumb grips and handle, white glue, Duco cement, ½-inch brads, plastic wood, and a finish of your choice.

If you live in a city you can probably obtain boxes discarded by wine merchants, supermarkets, or grocers. Ask your local merchant to save them for you. Select crates 3/16 to 3/8 inch thick; under 1/8 inch will not be strong enough.

The wood should be stored in a dry place for two or three months before use, since it will probably be green. After the crates are broken apart, the seasoned wood should be planed to a uniform thickness. Measure and cut your pieces; dado the edges for gluing. Sand all inside surfaces before assembly.

Use white glue for assembly and wipe carefully if a natural finish is to be applied. Use thin, ½-inch brads; set and fill holes with plastic wood to match the finish you plan to use. (I chose a dull gloss varnish and used two coats, sanding lightly between. When second coat was dry, I rubbed with 0000 steel wool and polished with terry cloth.)

The toggle action of the shock cord hinges locks the two trays open or closed. Allow about 12 inches of shock cord (available at camping equipment stores) for each hinge. Ends can be single knotted, trimmed, and coated with Duco cement to prevent raveling. But *don't trim knots until you're sure the tension is correct.* If it's too tight, the trays will bind; if too loose, they will sag open.

Hand carve the handle from pine, or use a commercial handle for easy carrying—*Earl Chapin.*

Box dimensions can be varied to suit needs. Best way to tie hinges is with trays out of frame, placed flat with bottom sides together. Experiment to get right tension; it should require a rather firm pull to separate trays enough to slip over and down frame to position. Elastic strips are held in place by two ½-inch brads (see drawing). Don't stretch elastic tight and predrill ¼-inch pilot holes for brads.

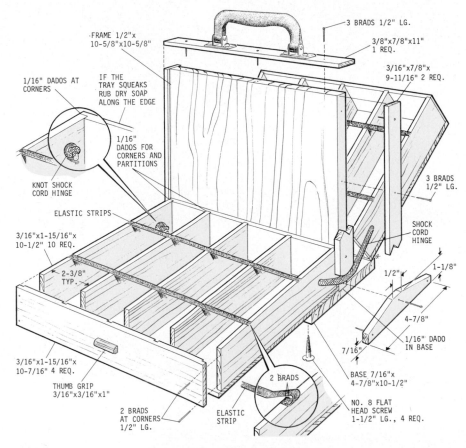

FRAME 1/2"x 10-5/8"x10-5/8"

3 BRADS 1/2" LG.

3/8"x7/8"x11" 1 REQ.

3/16"x7/8"x 9-11/16" 2 REQ.

1/16" DADOS AT CORNERS

IF THE TRAY SQUEAKS RUB DRY SOAP ALONG THE EDGE

1/16" DADOS FOR CORNERS AND PARTITIONS

KNOT SHOCK CORD HINGE

3 BRADS 1/2" LG.

SHOCK CORD HINGE

ELASTIC STRIPS

3/16"x1-15/16"x 10-1/2" 10 REQ.

2-3/8" TYP.

1/2"

1-1/8"

4-7/8"

1/16" DADO IN BASE

7/16"

3/16"x1-15/16"x 10-7/16" 4 REQ.

THUMB GRIP 3/16"x3/16"x1"

2 BRADS AT CORNERS 1/2" LG.

2 BRADS

ELASTIC STRIP

BASE 7/16"x 4-7/8"x10-1/2"

NO. 8 FLAT HEAD SCREW 1-1/2" LG., 4 REQ.

hot-tub deck

On most patio decks you have a choice between sitting and standing. This one, you can jump into.

It has a built-in hot tub. After a summer soak, your dip into the pool will be that much more refreshing. And at the end of the season—when it's too cool for the pool—the tub extends your outdoor fun.

The L-shaped all-redwood deck, designed by Larry and Florence Regular, is approximately 150 square feet supplemented by an adjoining 50-square-foot deck containing a gas-fed

brick-lined firepit. The built-in butcher-block benches and steps were adapted from the Design-a-Deck plans kit described on the next page. The kit is available for $5 from California Redwood Assn., 1 Lombard St., San Francisco, CA 94111.

All decking, stairs, and benches are made with knot-textured construction-heart redwood. Deck boards are 2×6s; the understructure is made from 4×4s anchored to concrete footings and flanked by 2×6s, forming the main structural beams at the deck's perimeter; joists are 2×6s; and

benches and stairs are made from 2×4s and 2×6s.

The main deck encircles a 6-foot-wide, 4-foot-deep tub made of kiln-dried, vertical-grain, clear all-heart-grade redwood. The tub shown comes as a kit, but tubs are available preassembled as well. The tub is recessed 18 inches into the ground, resting on a 1-foot layer of gravel to dampen any ground shifts. Blocking supports the deck boards, which are trimmed to match the tub's contour (see drawing). No ledgers should be attached to the tub itself, and you'll want to leave

breathing space between tub and deck boards.

A variety of tub sizes and shapes are available from manufacturers. A list of sources is available from the California Redwood Association. The tub you choose should meet or exceed the standards set by the International Association of Plumbing and Mechanical Officials. Also, before installation check all local plumbing and electrical codes. In most cases electrical and gas hookups must be done by a licensed electrician and plumber— *William J. Hawkins.*

Drawings by Gene Thompson

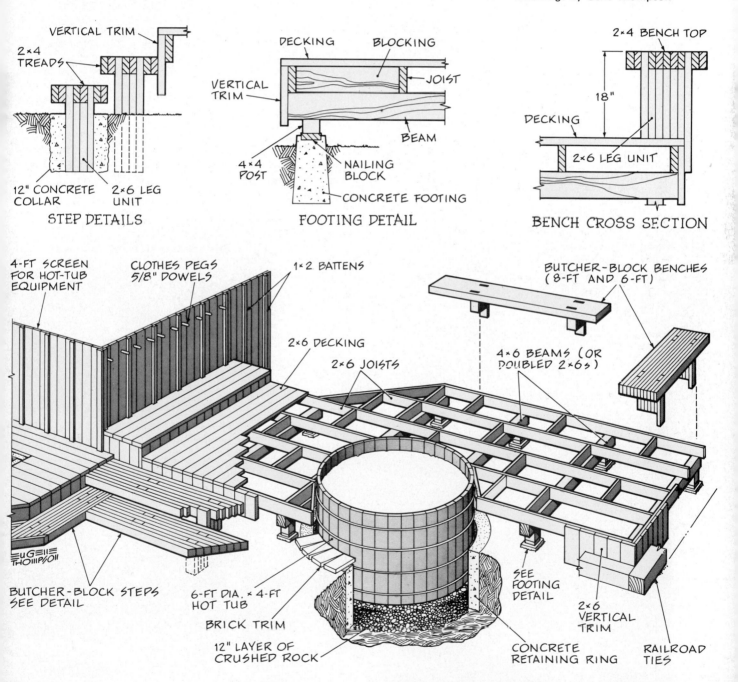

butcher-block construction

Simple hammer-and-saw construction is at its best when you think butcher block: Rugged, handsome projects can be built in just a few hours and, if you use redwood, they'll last through years of abuse from weather or people.

Shown here are two similarly fabricated backyard projects: a deck bench for the patio, and butcher-block steps for the entrance to your house or patio. Since they were designed for the California Redwood Association, it's not hard to believe that redwood is the suggested lumber. CRA says to apply a water repellent containing a mildewcide before assembly, plus a second coat after it's nailed together. To avoid corrosion stains, use hot-dipped galvanized 16d nails throughout the projects.

The butcher-block is 18 inches high, 18 inches wide, and can be 4, 6, or 8 feet long. Use construction-heart grade lumber for bench legs that come in contact with the ground; construction common redwood can be used elsewhere. See photos and table for construction details.

Butcher-block steps are not recommended for more than four risers. To fit landscaping and ground contours, the steps can be staggered or varied in length; the materials list covers the same three lengths as for the bench.

If connected to a deck, usually the top step can be nailed to the deck skirtboard. Step legs should be placed in 1-foot-deep holes and—with the steps propped level—embedded in concrete.

Left natural, redwood weathers to an attractive driftwood gray. If you wish to apply a stain or bleach, let the wood weather for a month, then brush on two coats of semitransparent oil-based deck stain diluted fifty-fifty with water repellent containing a mildewcide. (Should mildew ever form, scrub the wood with a detergent and rinse with liquid bleach and water.)—*William J. Hawkins.*

BUTCHER-BLOCK BENCH — your choice of three lengths, and 2×4 or 2×6 construction

	2×6s needed:	Pieces cut to:		
Bench legs:	(2) 12 ft.	(4) 18 in. (12) 12⅜ in.		
Bench:	Length	Long pcs.	Short pcs.	Inserts
4 ft.	(6) 8 ft.	(10) 4 ft.	(4) 9 in.	(2) 18¾ in.
6 ft.	(12) 6 ft.	(10) 6 ft.	(4) 12 in.	(2) 36¾ in.
8 ft.	(12) 8 ft.	(10) 8 ft.	(4) 16 in.	(2) 52¾ in.
	2×4s needed:	Pieces cut to:		
Bench legs:	(2) 14 ft.	(4) 23⅞ in. (12) 20 5/6 in.		
Bench:	Length	Long pcs.	Short pcs.	Inserts
4 ft.	(6) 8 ft.	(10) 4 ft.	(4) 9 in.	(2) 22⅞ in.
6 ft.	(12) 6 ft.	(10) 6 ft.	(4) 12 in.	(2) 40⅞ in.
8 ft.	(12) 8 ft.	(10) 8 ft.	(4) 16 in.	(2) 56⅞ in.

Simple but handsome pieces are easy to build with butcher-block construction. This bench can be built from construction-heart or common 2×6 redwood lumber.

Bench legs are made of five 12⅜-inch pieces sandwiched between two 18-inch outer supports. To start, nail just one support to stack; second nails on later.

Open end of leg support is nailed to edge of bench top. Fill spaces between legs, and from legs to sides, with 2×6s. Be sure top edges are splinter-free.

Nail two 2×6s on outside of bench legs to complete first side. Flip over, nail second outer support to legs. Complete with 2×6 fillers and two last top pieces.

Butcher-block steps are built in the same way—but lower, and of 2×4s, not 2×6s.

BUTCHER-BLOCK STEP — your choice of three lengths

Materials lists:
Legs — all 2×4s

Vertical drop	Steps	2×4s	Cut to
12 in.	One	(2) 10 ft.	(4) 18 in. (6) 14⅞ in.
18 in.	Two	(2) 14 ft.	(2) 23⅞ in. (6) 20⁵⁄₆ in.
24 in.	Three	(1) 10 ft. (2) 16 ft.	(4) 30 in. (6) 26⁷⁄₁₆ in.
30 in.	Four	(1) 12 ft. (2) 18 ft.	(4) 35⅞ in. (6) 32⁵⁄₁₆ in.

Treads — all 2×4s (per tread)

Tread length	2×4s	Pieces cut to
4 ft.	(6) 8 ft.	(10) 4 ft.
6 ft.	(12) 6 ft.	(10) 6 ft. (4) 12 in. (2) 40⅞ in.
8 ft.	(12) 8 ft.	(10) 8 ft. (4) 16 in. (2) 56⅞ in.

DECK PLANS AVAILABLE

If you need help designing a deck for your backyard, there's a planning kit you can buy. The California Redwood Association (1 Lombard St., San Francisco, CA 94111) is offering a Redwood Design-a-Deck plans packet: a clever array of plan sheets, and punch-out cardboard modules that help you prepare a custom deck. Created by Richard K. O'Grady, the kit is available from CRA for $5.

solar concentrator

Masonite and aluminum foil—that's all Rick Steenblik, a research engineer at the Georgia Institute of Technology, needs to bring the sun into focus. Conventional point-focusing solar concentrators are paraboloid dish types. Made of metal, these complex-shape reflectors must be precisely molded and machined—therefore, they're expensive.

Steenblik's simple design begins with a computer program that prints a spiral pattern. This pattern is transferred onto a flat material already covered with a reflective medium, then cut out on a band saw. By lining up mounting points (also printed by the program) along a straight frame member, the proper twist is given to each segment of the spiral to concentrate sunlight at the selected focal point. The computer program can vary the focal length of the spiral or even alter the design to focus light behind the reflector.

Nine Georgia Tech Spiral Concentrators have been built thus far. For such simple applications as solar cookers Steenblik has used as materials aluminum foil and hardboard. Other models have been made with sheet aluminum. Steenblik believes his reflector can replace parabolic concentrators in some present applications at a much lower cost.

For the Spiral Concentrator Experimenter's Kit with 4-foot-square spiral pattern and instructions on cooking and other applications, send $10 to the Suntwist Company, Box 342, Stone Mountain, GA 30086—*Paul Bolon.*

Focal point of the spiral concentrator reaches 2,000°F—hot enough to ignite wood or to cook on. With more twist it can focus light behind itself, too.

4-in-1 backyard center

Versatility is the key to our multipurpose backyard center—a unique concept for organizing outdoor activities. The modular design offers flexibility so you can adapt the unit to your family's needs.

The unit we built and photographed has four separate work areas: a cold frame/mini-greenhouse, a barbecue, a potting bench with sink, and a storage cabinet for outdoor equipment. You can copy our design by building one of each of the four units, or you could double up on some and omit others—for example, join two storage areas, a barbecue, and a cold frame. Each module could also be an independent structure, stood against a fence or wall if you don't

have enough yard space for the full assembly. Each of the counters has a generous 30×42-inch work area.

The potting area has a latticework surface that simplifies collection of spilled potting soil—just put a tray or basin on the shelf underneath for a neat catch of any overflow. Water from the sink next to the lattice counter makes potting easier (it's also handy for watering seedlings in the cold frame). Two large storage cabinets below complete this module.

The mansard equipment shed has room for large implements, such as mowers, as well as bulky yard supplies. The unique hinging of the top and side allows easy access to all the storage space.

The easy-opening wing-shape roofs of the cold frame/greenhouse make tending seedlings a snap. The tops are made with inexpensive polyethylene stretched over pine frames.

The adjacent barbecue counter is designed to hold everything you need for cooking and serving. A 27-inch-diameter hole in the center is ringed with aluminum and takes a standard grill. There's also a storage area underneath for charcoal and cooking utensils. When not in use, a cover fits over the barbecue opening to keep it out of the weather (and out of sight).

Construction is easy; the caption below gives details and tells how to order a plans packet—*Susanne Stevenson.*

Design by Peter Stevenson

Complete plans let you build full assembly or separate modules

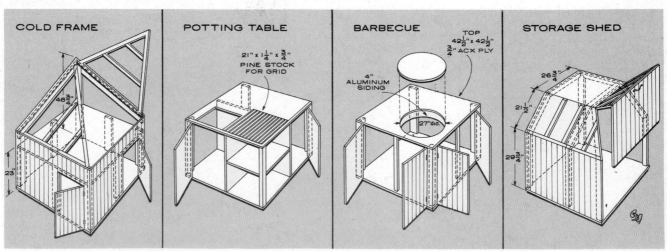

COLD FRAME   POTTING TABLE   BARBECUE   STORAGE SHED

Sections of backyard center measure 30×42½ inches with T 1-11 exterior plywood as siding and doors. Horizontal work surfaces are ¾-inch ACX (exterior) plywood. Wing-shape tops of the cold frame are made of ¾-inch-×-1¼-inch pine strips with 6-mil polyethylene stapled on the underside. The "mansard-roof"

storage area has a double-hinged side and roof of ½-inch ACX ply with 1¼-inch-wide decorative strips tacked on. The cruciform center frame is built of 2×4s, covered with ½-inch ply and capped with redwood 1×6s. For detailed plans send $7 check to Stevenson Projects, P.O. Box 584, Del Mar, CA 92014.

Backyard center in action: planting at the potting bench (top), broiling on the barbecue (left), and cultivating in the cold frame (above). Sloped-roof storage cabinet stands to right of the cold frame. Water for the potting table's sink can be plumbed underground or supplied via a garden hose. The drain can simply empty into a gravel-filled hole in the yard. A concrete slab, mortar blocks, or just gravel will provide an adequate foundation.

weatherproof chairs

This simple, clean-lined chair of select heart redwood is used both indoors and at an outdoor dining table at the William L. Russell residence in San Diego, California. It has a framework of 2×2s with 2×2-inch slats for the seat and a 2×6-inch backrest. The seat is 18×21 inches. Height to top of backrest is 28½ inches. Seat support members are routed ½ inch to accept slats. The backrest is slightly canted for comfort. The chair is finished with polyurethane sealer. Mortise and tenon joints are used for all main structural members, and all edges are beveled and sanded. Proper joinery is one evidence of fine cabinet work, and the mortise (rectangular broach) and tenon (tongue that fits mortise) used here is one of the strongest and most popular. Four of the many ways to make this joint are shown here—*George Lyons* and *Bernard Price.*

Design by Designplace, El Cajon, Cal.
Photo by George Lyons

1 Hand Method

After laying out the four-shouldered tenon with a square and marking gauge (near right), cut shoulder stop lines with a back or other fine-toothed saw. Finish tenon by removing waste wood stock from all four sides, down to the shoulder cut (far right), again using a fine-toothed saw. Make square cuts.

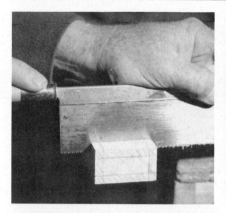 

2 Table Saw Method

If you own a table saw, make shoulder stop cuts with blade raised to correct height (near right). Keep piece square with miter head and shoulder cut at the correct depth against the rip fence. To remove waste stock from all four sides (far right), remove miter head and pass stock over blade transversely very rapidly in a reciprocating motion (left and right). Keep blade at same height and the fence acts as a stop.

3 Hand Chisel Method

To make the mortise by hand, lay it out first and, using a mortising chisel (near right), break rectangle into segments. Strike down on the chisel with a wooden mallet and pop out waste in the middle. Let the ends go until last; clean these by striking down on chisel, but with flat side facing end. Mortise should fit tenon with reasonable pressure (far right), but not so tight as to squeeze out assembly glue and leave dry joint.

4 Drilling and Shearing Method

First lay out mortise. Then drill a series of holes along centerline of the rectangle to required depth (near right). This method may be done with bit and brace or a drill guided by Portalign jig. With most waste removed by drilling (far right), clean ends of mortise with a chisel, flat face to end. Clean mortise by shearing long walls down with a broader chisel, flat face toward walls.

projects for fiberglass-reinforced plastic

ere are ten innovative, good-looking projects in which fiberglass-reinforced plastic (FRP) is the dominant construction material. This lightweight panel is clean and easy to cut, drill, and install over minimal framing; and FRP now comes in a variety of types, styles, and colors, from flat translucent sheets to square-ribbed panels with awninglike stripes. It isn't just the "green banana" any more, though FRP manufacturers still make those vivid corrugated patio-cover sheets that once identified the product.

The following thumbnail sketches are only meant to suggest the construction, so you can judge whether the project is one you'd like to undertake. If you choose to go ahead, you can order construction plans directly from Filon Marketing Services, 12333 S. Van Ness Avenue, Hawthorne, CA 90250. Send $1 for each plan you want, specifying by name (for example: Pool-side Cabana). All ten of the projects are within the skills of the average do-it-yourselfer, and all are practical, attractive uses of a material more homeowners should get to know—*Al Lees*.

Pool-side Cabana   GARY KERR, San Diego, Calif.

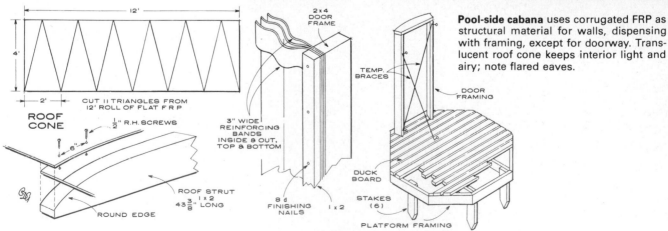

ROOF CONE

CUT 11 TRIANGLES FROM 12' ROLL OF FLAT F R P

½" R.H. SCREWS

ROOF STRUT 1 x 2 43⅜" LONG

ROUND EDGE

2 x 4 DOOR FRAME

3" WIDE REINFORCING BANDS INSIDE & OUT, TOP & BOTTOM

8 d FINISHING NAILS

1 x 2

TEMP. BRACES

DOOR FRAMING

DUCK BOARD

STAKES (6)

PLATFORM FRAMING

Pool-side cabana uses corrugated FRP as structural material for walls, dispensing with framing, except for doorway. Translucent roof cone keeps interior light and airy; note flared eaves.

Collector Wall

GARLAND MILLER, Oxon Hill, Md.

Collector wall runs air past racks of water-filled plastic jugs and back into garage behind, keeping workshop at comfortable temperature without backup heater. Each stud space has separate tambour-type Styrofoam shutter operable from inside; these move on aluminum track to retain heat by masking FRP when sun's not shining on it.

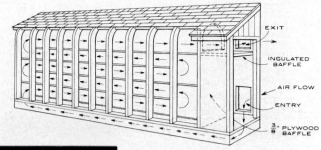

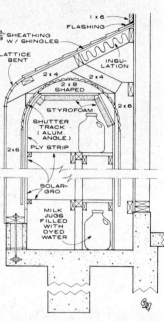

Outdoor Room

RICHARD SPENCER, Irvine, Calif.

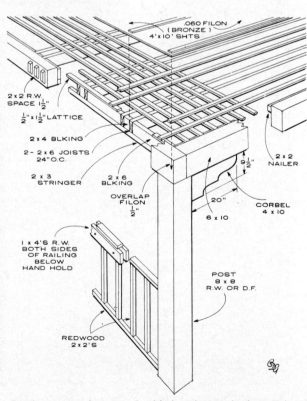

Outdoor room is created with handsome lattice-work ceiling supported by massive posts, beams, and paired joists, and railing of 2×2s—all redwood here. Bronze Filon sheets overhead give sunny glow to space, even on overcast days, and keep the parrot dry.

Greenhouse HAROLD HONER, Conifer, Colo.

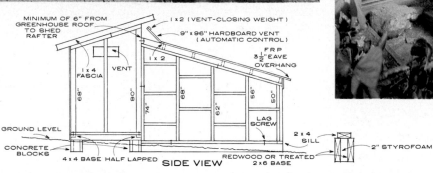

Double shed couples greenhouse of clear, corrugated FRP to plywood structure that stores potting and yard tools. Floor of latter bridges simple block footing; greenhouse is floorless.

Diagram labels:
MINIMUM OF 6" FROM GREENHOUSE ROOF TO SHED RAFTER
1 x 2 (VENT-CLOSING WEIGHT)
9" x 96" HARDBOARD VENT (AUTOMATIC CONTROL)
FRP 3½" EAVE OVERHANG
1 x 4 FASCIA
VENT
1 x 2
68"
80"
74"
68"
62"
56"
50"
LAG SCREW
GROUND LEVEL
CONCRETE BLOCKS
4 x 4 BASE HALF LAPPED
SIDE VIEW
REDWOOD OR TREATED 2 x 6 BASE
2 x 4 SILL
2" STYROFOAM

Privacy Enclosure ANDY BERGLUND, Seattle, Wash.

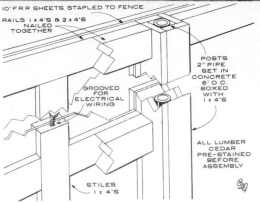

Diagram labels:
10' F R P SHEETS STAPLED TO FENCE
RAILS 1 x 4'S & 2 x 4'S NAILED TOGETHER
GROOVED FOR ELECTRICAL WIRING
POSTS 2" PIPE SET IN CONCRETE 6' O.C. BOXED WITH 1 x 4'S
ALL LUMBER CEDAR PRE-STAINED BEFORE ASSEMBLY
STILES 1 x 4'S

Privacy enclosure creates ideal space beside house for outdoor parties. Wiring for lanterns is concealed within frame that's applied to both faces of FRP. Concrete slab has grass carpeting.

Truck-bed Canopy
VIRGIL RAYMOND, Eagan, Minn.

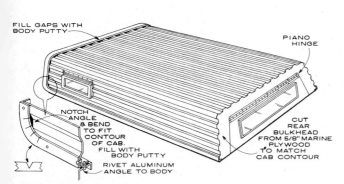

FILL GAPS WITH BODY PUTTY

PIANO HINGE

NOTCH ANGLE & BEND TO FIT CONTOUR OF CAB. FILL WITH BODY PUTTY

CUT REAR BULKHEAD FROM 5/8" MARINE PLYWOOD TO MATCH CAB CONTOUR

RIVET ALUMINUM ANGLE TO BODY

Truck-bed canopy, made from four Type 150 CoolRib panels, needs no inner frame, and can be tailored to any compact pickup as a cargo cover or sleep shelter. Angle frame is easy to shape.

Pool Enclosure
RICHARD L. CATT, Mogadore, Ohio

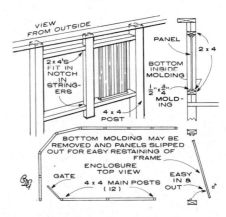

VIEW FROM OUTSIDE

PANEL

2 x 4

2 x 4'S FIT IN NOTCH IN STRINGERS

BOTTOM INSIDE MOLDING

1/2" x 3/4" MOLDING

4 x 4 POST

BOTTOM MOLDING MAY BE REMOVED AND PANELS SLIPPED OUT FOR EASY RESTAINING OF FRAME

ENCLOSURE TOP VIEW

GATE

4 x 4 MAIN POSTS (12)

EASY IN & OUT

Pool enclosure satisfies designer's local safety code, and gives privacy deck for sunbathing. Wood frame is easily restrained.

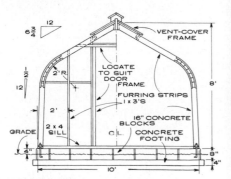

Greenhouse
W. E. BUNTING, California, Md.

VENT-COVER FRAME

12
6 3/4

2' R.

1 1/2 12

2'

LOCATE TO SUIT DOOR FRAME

FURRING STRIPS 1 x 3'S

16" CONCRETE BLOCKS

8'

GRADE

2 x 4 SILL

C.L.

CONCRETE FOOTING

4"

8"
4"

10'

Greenhouse is erected in 4-foot-wide modules, so it can be any length. Unit shown is three modules (12 ft.) long; it took two FRP rolls.

Pool Dome

ROBERT J. KERINS, Niagara Falls, N.Y.

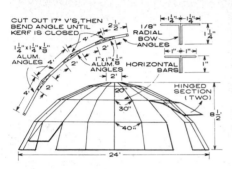

Pool dome, supported by shrewd assembly of aluminum angles, has two hinged sections for access and ventilation. Solar gain extends swim season.

Roof Collector

TOM SALISBURY, Telluride, Colo.

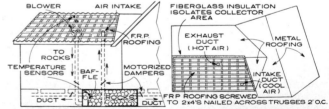

Roof collector is south face of one wing of this mountain home, covered with corrugated FRP. Hot air in space beneath is pumped into rock storage bin and distributed to living areas.

Photo credits: Listed in the order the projects are shown: Kerr — Pete Stevenson; Spencer — Boulger & Kanuit; Honor — Writers Photographers & Artists (Denver); Berglund — Johansen Studios; Raymond — Heritage Photos; Catt — Carpenter's Studio; Bunting — Cosmopolitan Photo; Kerins — Longin Photo; Salisbury — Bill Elizey.

rustic planter

To the wood enthusiast who likes to garden, the container is as important as what it holds. It takes time to construct the project shown here, but unlike a purely practical box, the result is attractive and shows its contents to best advantage.

Quite often, pieces like this can be made from leftover odds and ends of wood. But buying wood for the planter is justified, since the project should show thought and craftsmanship. We chose kiln-dried, heart-grade redwood. Oak or ash would do, but if you choose either, it would be wise to paint the inside surfaces with a liquid asphaltum before filling with soil.

Start the project by cutting the two bottom boards, holding them together with corrugated nails. Drill the drainage holes. Cut the two side pieces, beveling the bottom edges 30 degrees and shaping the top edges in curves similar to those shown in the drawing. Nail these to the bottom and then add the ends. Note that the ends are

cut at an angle to conform to the slope of the sides. Add the two bottom risers with nails long enough to penetrate the end pieces.

We distressed the top edges of ends and sides by working them over with a rasp and then smoothing them with sandpaper. Also, we banged the outside surfaces a bit with a short length of chain. You don't have to do this, but a little rough treatment seems to

make the project more compatible with its function.

We used a tile as the center piece. You can find substitutes such as a length of rectangular or square flue tile. Whatever you use, just set it in place; it does not have to be secured.

Our container holds sedum and Monterey pine. The soil is a fifty-fifty mix of potting soil and clean sand— *R. J. De Cristoforo.*

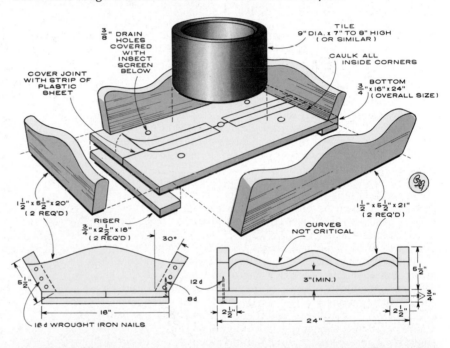

Clear heart redwood was used for this planter, and the edges were rough cut and distressed. Round or square building tile can serve as centerpiece.

cold-frame hot bed

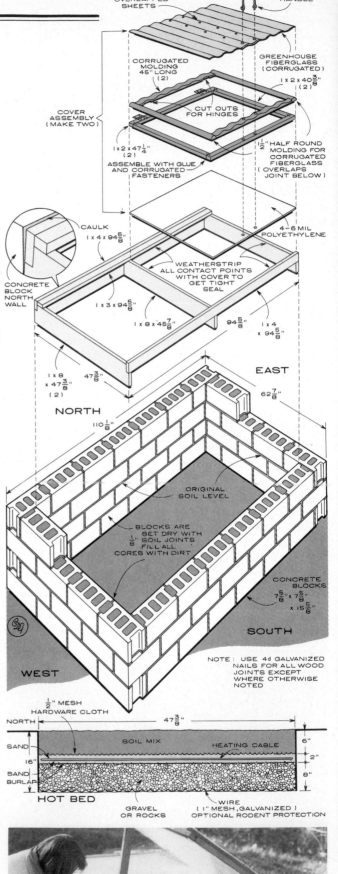

Some call it a poor man's greenhouse. In fact, the modest cold-frame hot bed shown here serves almost as a greenhouse—and for far less effort and money.

Cold frames alone can be very simple. My neighbor lashes old storm windows together and uses the box so created to "harden off" annuals grown indoors. If that's the only use you have in mind, a simple, portable frame, with a polyethylene cover, will do. But a well-built cold-frame hot-bed combination can extend your gardening season at both ends. With a heating cable in half of mine, I get four-season use of it. Here's a sampling:

Spring: Harden annuals started indoors; start early crops of hardy annuals (radishes, lettuce, pansies, etc.); start tender annuals (tomatoes, peppers, etc.) weeks before they can be planted in the garden.

Summer: Start biennial and perennial flowers (covers can be put on in heavy rain); give house plants a "summer vacation" (lathing or cheese cloth can be used to cut intense summer sun).

Fall: Plant hardy crops (carrots, radishes, lettuce, etc.) for harvesting long after frost kills garden; "heel in" garden surplus, such as onions and carrots, before ground freezes; shelter young perennials and biennials from the worst winter weather.

Winter: Sink in pots of hardy bulbs for root development, then bring inside for earliest spring bloom; give hardy bonsai plants necessary winter rest period.

The frame shown takes a couple of weekends to build. It's meant to be a permanent, rugged addition to the garden. Locate it where its sloping roof faces south, and where it gets full exposure to winter sun. (If it can also be sheltered from cold north winds, that's a bonus.) An excellent choice is the south wall of a house. Size is easily adjusted to needs. However, if a frame is too big, the "garden" is awkward to tend; if it's too small, it heats and cools too quickly.

The foundation is the most critical part of construction. First, dig a rough, 5⅓ × 9⅓-foot hole to a 16-inch depth. Set the sod and top soil aside. Use the rest of the soil to build a protective hill along the north wall and cover this with sod. Top soil, lightened with compost or peat moss, will go back into the frame.

I used 15⅝ × 7⅝-inch concrete blocks, setting them in dry and filling in holes with dirt. I left about ⅛-inch between blocks. If your blocks are a different size, build the foundation as shown; check inside measurements; and adjust frame dimensions accordingly. Extra care in leveling and squaring the first row of blocks helps ensure true construction throughout.

I treated my wood with a brush-on preservative. (Even more protection is achieved with pressure-treated wood.) The preservative should be of the water-borne salt type; oil-borne preservatives, such as creosote, give off fumes that are toxic to plants and humans.

If blocks in first row are level and straight, the rest is easy.

As each row is set, fill block holes with dirt.

Wet sand makes it easier to get heating cable to stay put.

Assemble the wood frame outside the foundation.

Fill in foundation with rocks or gravel, burlap, sand, hardware cloth (to keep an errant trowel from hitting heating cable), and soil as diagrammed. Construct the frame and secure in place with masonry nails (one every 1½ feet is plenty).

I chose corrugated fiberglass for the outside cover. It's strong—takes a heavier snow load than flat fiberglass. And it's safe—glass covers make me nervous; I'm afraid a child might fall through. The material must be designed for greenhouse use; others deteriorate with exposure to sunlight. I put polyethylene inside the cover to create a dead air space. This is inexpensive, but it has to be replaced every few years.

The special half-round and ripple "filler strips" for attaching the fiberglass should be available from your fiberglass dealer. You should also be able to get clear sealant and appropriate nails. I used aluminum nails with a deformed shank to help grip the fiberglass better and a neoprene washer at the head.

While the frame is designed to provide warmth and protection, it can do its job too well and overheat. All that's necessary, then, is to prop the top open with a stick. (I use clamps on the top, the kind sold for hanging tools. One end of the stick is secured in a clamp, and the other is poked into the dirt in the frame. The top then remains lifted to the desired height.)

However, automatic ventilation is the answer for frame tenders who can't be home to catch a sudden sunny spell that sends temperatures soaring and threatens to bake a crop of young plants. I prefer the simple vents that use a temperature-sensitive chemical in a cylinder over electricity. "SolarVent" is one such device. It's available from Dalen Products, Inc., 201 Sherlake Drive, Knoxville, TN 37922, and sells for about $32. It's easy to install and can be disengaged for manual operation. I put one on the hotbed side of my frame—*Greg Stone*.

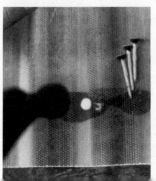

The frame should fit tightly inside the prepared foundation. Caulk any gaps to prevent cold air from getting in.

Drive in nails where they line up with big hole in block.

Lay sealant; overlap panels; use "POP" rivets with washers.

Attach cover with aluminum nails, washers every 4 inches.

Handle is ½-inch rope, with a figure-eight knot on inside.

Fold polyethylene at edges, pull tight, and staple.

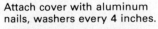

Materials

Wood: One 14-foot 1×8; two 8-foot 1×4s; one 8-foot 1×3; four 8-foot 1×2s; two 8-foot half-round filler strips; two 8-foot ripple filler strips.

Hardware: ¼ lb. 2-inch masonry nails; ¼ lb. 1½-inch aluminum nails (for fiberglass); ½ lb. 4d common nails (galvanized); two 2-inch loose pin hinges; corrugated or Skotch fasteners (small box).

Other: Two 26-inch×8-foot corrugated fiberglass panels (4–5 ounce); one 4×8-foot sheet polyethylene; 20 inches ¼-inch rope; 30 feet weather stripping; 69 concrete blocks; waterproof glue; ¼-inch staples; 4×8-foot sheet burlap; 5 cubic feet builders' sand; 15 "POP" rivets with washers.

easy-to-build outdoor furniture

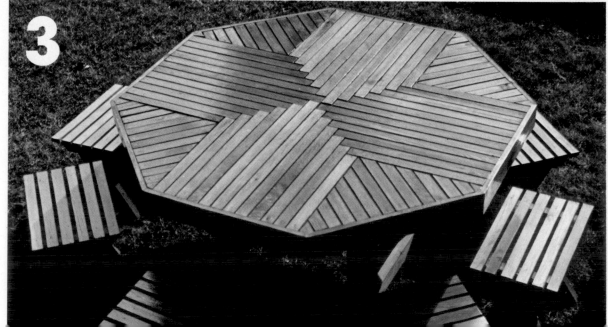

1. Deck Chair

This easy-to-make chair has a reclining canvas seat; the frame is Simpson clear-grade redwood. The chair is one of twenty-three how-to-build-it projects featured in the *Redwood Book of Could/Book of Wood,* available for $2.50 from Simpson Timber Company, 900 Fourth Avenue, Seattle, WA 98164.

For the frame, you need 2×2 wood as follows: Front legs—four 24-inch lengths. Back legs—four 22½-inch. Arms—four 24-inch. Back—three 23-inch. Front crosspieces—two 23-inch. Leg blocks—two 6-inch.

Materials for the seat: 1½ yards of heavy-duty, 36-inch canvas; #10×2½-inch galvanized wood screws (flathead).

The basic construction method:

• Cut all wood to length.

• Assemble front two legs and crosspieces. Join with waterproof glue, reinforced with countersunk screws. For best appearance, fill all screw holes with wood putty.

• Attach arm pieces to inside of front legs using glue and screw. Make sure all angles are square.

• Glue and screw back pieces to arms, keeping angles square. Attach back legs in same manner. Level legs with front adjuster blocks.

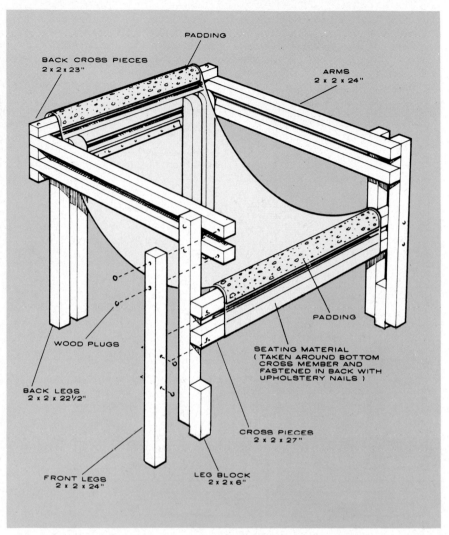

2. Patio Lantern

This unique candleholder can be made of scrap redwood. Upright members are 1⅛ inches square and about 14 inches high. Blocks at the base are 2¾×4 inches and are nailed to a 4-inch-square base, to which a brass candleholder base is bolted. Upper blocks are also nailed to a 4-inch-square block—it has a circular hole that fits the circumference of the chimney. The upper portion, including the glass chimney, lifts out of the uprights for ease in lighting the candle. To make the holder a hanging lantern, attach small chains to the uprights with screweyes—*Designed by William L. Russell, San Diego, Calif.*

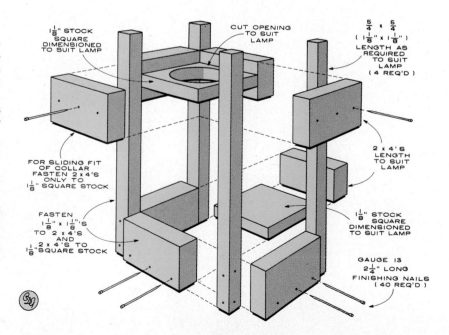

(Continued)

3. Picnic Table

This handsome family-size picnic table, with the unusual, decorative top, was designed by a person who "wanted something different." He was glad to share this design with other readers "because it's easier than it looks."

The table and benches are made of cedar and finished with polyurethane. To prevent rust marks, use only hot-dipped galvanized, stainless steel or aluminum alloy nails.

The top frame, which fits snugly into the lap joints of the leg supports, is secured to them with four hooks and eyes for easy removal for storage—*Designed by Norman Johnston, Ypsilanti, Mich.*

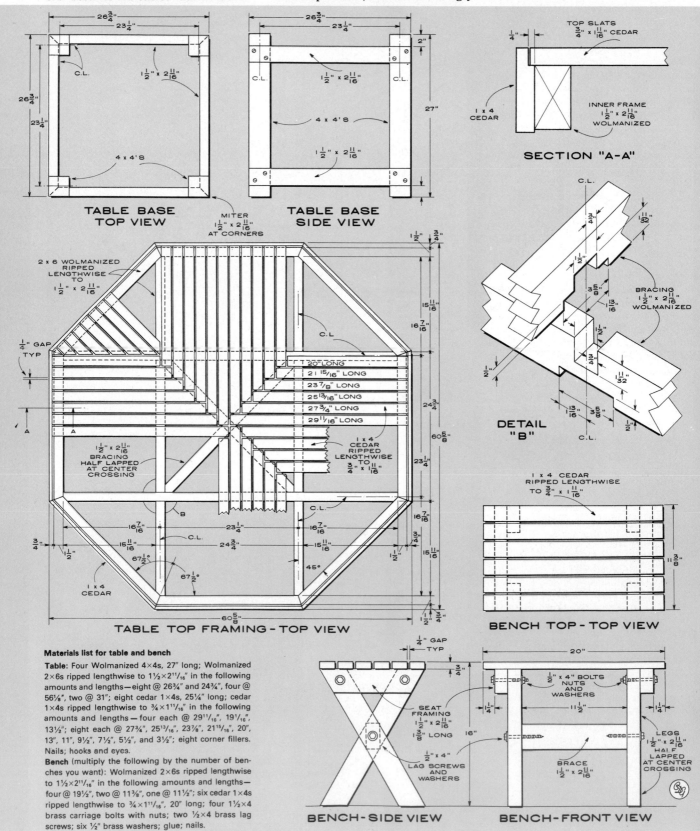

Materials list for table and bench

Table: Four Wolmanized 4×4s, 27" long; Wolmanized 2×6s ripped lengthwise to 1½×2¹¹/₁₆" in the following amounts and lengths—eight @ 26¾" and 24¾", four @ 56⅛", two @ 31"; eight cedar 1×4s, 25¼" long; cedar 1×4s ripped lengthwise to ¾×1¹¹/₁₆" in the following amounts and lengths—four each @ 29¹¹/₁₆", 19¹¹/₁₆", 13½"; eight each @ 27¾", 25¹³/₁₆", 23⅞", 21¹⁵/₁₆", 20", 13", 11", 9½", 7½", 5½", and 3½"; eight corner fillers. Nails; hooks and eyes.

Bench (multiply the following by the number of benches you want): Wolmanized 2×6s ripped lengthwise to 1½×2¹¹/₁₆" in the following amounts and lengths—four @ 19½", two @ 11⅜", one @ 11½"; six cedar 1×4s ripped lengthwise to ¾×1¹¹/₁₆", 20" long; four 1½×4 brass carriage bolts with nuts; two ½×4 brass lag screws; six ½" brass washers; glue; nails.

drop-leaf swim deck

Out on a lake, swimming from a runabout results in a lot of rocking and sloshing as bathers climb back aboard—even with a ladder slung over the side. My solution is a wooden swim deck hinged to the transom. The deck swings up and out of the way when the boat is moving. Materials for the deck (see drawing) cost about $60.

The deck makes swimming more enjoyable and, I think, a little safer. And faced with ever-higher fuel prices, boat owners will be indulging in a lot more "at-anchor" activities such as swimming—*J. R. Holt.*

Position the swim deck at or just above the waterline on the boat's transom. The size of the cutout for the motor depends on whether you have an outboard or stern-drive unit—in any case you'll have to adapt this basic design to your own rig. One-inch hardwood boards can be substituted for the 2-inch pine deck lumber shown here. The deck's depth should be less than the distance from the hinge to the top of the transom. Offset or hatch-style hinges allow ample clearance between the deck and transom.

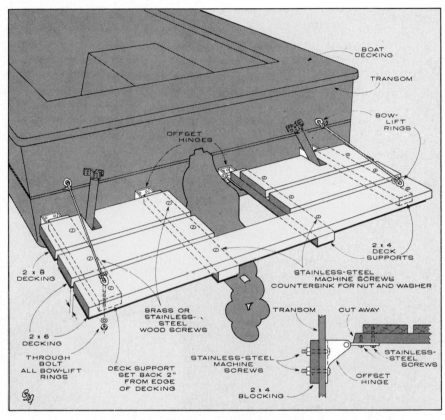

weekender sloop

To create a traditional craft at untraditional cost—that was the challenge we faced when designing this cuddy-cabin camper. The result is an easy-to-build, lightweight version of the classic fishing sloop that first sailed out of Friendship, Maine, a century ago.

Our Little Friendship is as handsome and nice-handling as its namesake. This swift-sailing little sloop paces conventional craft. Yet even beginners can manage its 120 square feet of sail, thanks to self-tending lines on jib and mainsail. And its roomy cuddy lets two people camp overnight on the water—or even on the road. The craft is light enough to be trailered behind today's smaller cars.

You can build the weekender sloop with common tools, using standard lumberyard stocks. The mainsail boom and gaff, for example, are bannister railings. The mast and removable bowsprit are stock full-round moldings. The mast hoops that fasten to the sails are slices of PVC pipe. Mast stays and shrouds are tensioned, not with costly turnbuckles but with traditional deadeyes—handshaped wood blocks. Even the salty-looking wheel is handcrafted from lumberyard spindles, plywood, and 2×4s. The whole boat, including paint, sails—even carpeting—should cost you under $1000—*Susanne and Peter Stevenson.*

BOWSPRIT

HULL SIDES AND CABIN —¼″ PLYWOOD

DECK—⅜″ PLYWOOD

FULL-LENGTH KEEL WITH STEM —3 LAYERS OF 1″ STOCK

HULL BOTTOM —½″ PLYWOOD

1x12 CENTERBOARD —PIVOTS INTO KEEL SLOT

HULL LENGTH	16 FT.
LOA	19½ FT.
BEAM	6 FT.
SAIL AREA	120 SQ. FT.
WEIGHT	APPROX. 500 LBS.

ALL PLYWOOD STANDARD 4x8 PANELS

Don't be fooled by the snug size and easy construction—this is a versatile boat for active people, as the photos on the facing page demonstrate. Clockwise from top: For beaching, its keel-mounted centerboard kicks up and out of the way. When under sail, the clubfoot jib makes tacking a simple matter of spinning the wheel, and the gaff-rigged main keeps heeling to a minimum. Yet the sloop can also be rowed more easily than a dinghy, thanks to its full-length keel. The craft needs no auxiliary motor, even when maneuvering in crowded anchorages. The carpeted cuddy has plenty of sprawling room, because of the sloop's flat bottom. The cabin has sleeping room for two. There's extra stowage and room for a portable head extending back under the cockpit seats. The cockpit also has storage space under aft sections of the seats and in the lazaret. The craft is not only seaworthy and comfortable, it's simple to build. The sails, for example, need no sewing. They're cut from the heavy-duty, woven polyethylene that's sold for tarpaulins. These sun-resistant plastic sails take rugged use. The hull's flat bottom makes it easy to assemble (above). In cross section, the hull is a tapered plywood box that's self-aligning as you build. The laminated keel has a slot for the pivoting centerboard. Underway, both keel and kick-up rudder can be locked in position from the cockpit. The cable-control steering system links the wheel directly to a hidden tiller. For detailed plans, with step-by-step drawings, and materials list, send $10 to Stevenson Projects, Dept. YB, Box 584, Del Mar, CA 92014.

Photos by the authors
Drawing by Adolph Brotman

berming your yard

The flaws in our circa 1950 home included minimal prefab construction, a crushed rock driveway that ended in nothing at one end of the house, sandy soil devoid of vegetation, and a topography as flat as the new, uncarpeted floors.

Some of these conditions gradually yielded to our efforts at improvement, but not the lay of the land. After years of labor, top soil, grass seed, shrubs, flowers, and trees, the terrain—however lush—was still flat and uninteresting.

The good earth

When we excavated for a small addition, that flatness inspired us to have the earth from the hole set aside in our own yard. Our intention was to use it to break up the topographic monotony.

Such an excavation is a direct source of mounding or fill earth. If you're not digging up your own yard, you might be lucky enough to spot a neighbor who is and offer your place as a convenient dumping site for his diggings. But, if you don't plan to ex-

A mound of earth left from the excavation for a new addition to your home can be the makings of a berm. Later, top soil, sod, and other plantings will cover it.

Approximate costs

Ties: 15, at $7.50 each, $112.50
Wood preservative: one quart, $2.50.
Dry mix concrete: one bag, $2.50.
Mound or fill earth: Can vary from nothing to around $60 for a 12-yard load if large truck can reach dump point, more if smaller trucks are needed. It took about 50 cubic yards for this hill, covering about 600 square feet of ground.
Top soil: Check local recommendations for finishing over your subsoil. I used a 6-yard load of pulverized, screened black dirt, $45.
Sod: $1.20 a roll, plus delivery charge. I used 130 rolls, which came to $156.
My total cost: $378.39.

Method for marking contour posts

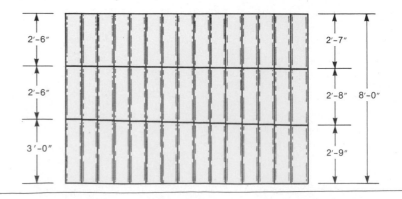

cavate and aren't lucky, turn to your local supplier of topsoil. Most can either provide, or help you find a source of less expensive mound or fill earth.

In the case of our excavation, the operator of the scoop inadvertently imposed a lot of extra earth-moving on us. He failed to see the mind's-eye vision we had of our proposed berm, so he spread the earth too far and in the wrong place. It's a much better idea to have the earth dumped as close as possible to where you will be using it.

Retaining wall

Researching materials for a retaining wall led me to give up on those that required mortar, for which I felt I did not have the required expertise. Of the treated timbers readily available in my locality, I chose from a pile of old creosoted railroad ties that I located through the Yellow Pages. The ties are strong and rustic looking, and they were cheaper than anything else I could find.

Old ties, slabbed on two sides, are about 6 inches thick, from 9 to 11

Railroad ties cut to follow contour of mound, make an effective retaining wall for a berm, as shown at top, left. Berm is shaped with a high crown and an easy grade for mowing, as shown in bottom photo. It can be planted with shrubs and trees as a sound deadener between your home and the street. In any case, a berm is sure to enhance the appearance—and value—of a flat piece of property.

Cut ties with care. Get help if possible. Keep toes clear.

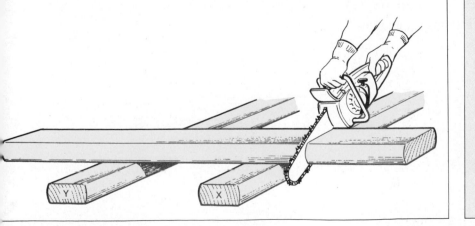

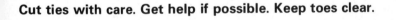

Tools

Shovel: long-handled.
Tamping rod or bar: You can use shovel handle, a 2×4, or any other device that will pack the earth around the posts.
Log saw: large bucksaw, bow saw, or one-man log saw will do, if it's sharp and you want exercise, or a two-man log saw, if you can get help. Easiest of all is a chain saw. If you don't own, and can't borrow one, try a tool rental company.
Rake: for smoothing hill.

inches wide to the rounded sides, and 8 feet long. They may be less than straight in the rounded silhouette. The ties are heavy—you know you've been working after wrestling with a few. So calculate each lift and wear gloves.

Here is the procedure for building your berm:

1. An average of five tie widths, flat surface out, makes 4 lineal feet of wall. I got three segments from each of fifteen ties; creating forty-five widths to achieve about 36 feet of low, curved wall. The ties were laid out, marked, and cut as shown in the drawing. Before sawing, inspect ties for metal and remove any you find.

2. Do the layout—in a curve, angle, or straight pattern, depending on your circumstances. Trench to a depth at least half the exposed wall height and wide enough for post insertion, filling, and tamping.

3. Insert tallest posts at highest point of your wall and work toward lower ends. Control diminishing post-top contour by digging or filling under each post. Use plumb or level to check wall and post vertical. Set each post as true as possible; once you move on, it's impractical to adjust those that came before. Tamp each post with loose soil, using shovel handle end, a rod, or pole. Unless ties are slabbed on all sides, they may not make smooth contacts; if you wish, join rounded sides as I did. Bottom of post to ground line should be one-third to one-half of post length.

4. After posts are set, some contour trimming may be needed. Use concrete to fill any exposed hollow centers and cracks in fresh-cut post tops before painting with preservative.

5. Shovel mounded earth against hill side of posts. Move high crown down into retaining wall and, with long-handled shovel, shape rest into a pleasing contour. Keep slope under 30 degrees for ease in lawn trimming.

6. Condition soil for seeding or sodding and other plantings.

Results

When it's over, you'll be glad you're through and happy with the results. Your property value will increase, and that new slope, a joy to see—*Fergus Retrum.*

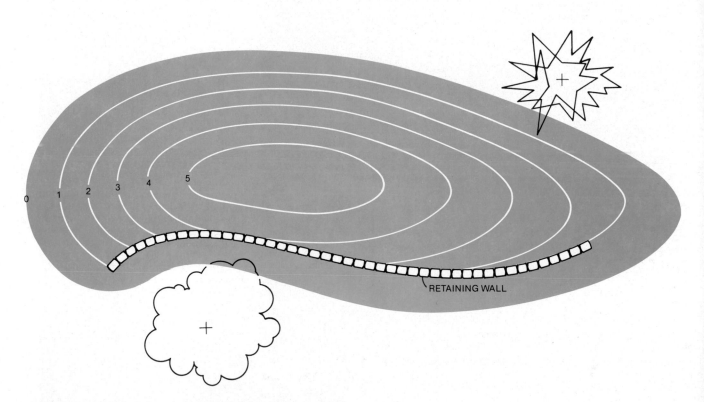

RETAINING WALL

Elevation: Wall side, showing post-setting depths

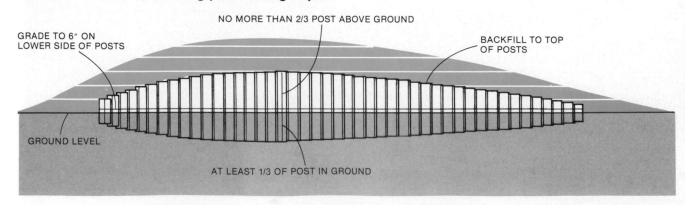

NO MORE THAN 2/3 POST ABOVE GROUND

GRADE TO 6" ON LOWER SIDE OF POSTS

BACKFILL TO TOP OF POSTS

GROUND LEVEL

AT LEAST 1/3 OF POST IN GROUND

wall accents with wood moldings

Look around the room you're sitting in. What hides the seams where walls meet ceiling and floors? If your house was built before World War II, chances are these areas are covered by handsome wood moldings. But this richly carved decoration could be invisible for all the attention we generally give it.

There are other uses, too, for molding strips. They can revive a dull wall, give a custom-designed look to an ordinary room, and even create unique built-ins such as room dividers and canopy beds.

If you live in a modern, post-war house, moldings can create the bold graphics or classic carved paneling that will distinguish your unadorned walls from all the look-alikes in the area. And if you have been wanting an elegant carved wall or wainscoting, you'll find that the look you're af-

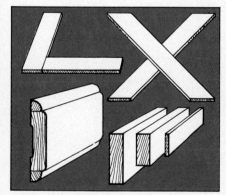

Airy-looking lattice (right) creates a custom bed canopy for this striking room. Painted lattice strips also form the dramatic wall graphics and window frame. Diagram above shows (top row) how to assemble strips for wall frames and canopy lattice. Quarter rounds flank edge casing to form the chair rail (bottom, left). Two sizes of s4s (sanded four sides) molding strips, plus lattice (right), are used.

Paneled room divider (right) echoes this room's elegant wainscoting. Four cove moldings sandwich lattice (above, top) to form divider posts. Cove moldings also frame the plywood panels. Center rosettes are made by mounting base caps atop base moldings (bottom, left) and mitering into four wedges. Crowns and coves nailed to square make divider top; coves and bases nailed to s4s, bottom.

Mirror-backed lattice on one side of corner produces intriguing light-and-shadow pattern. Each grid is best laid out on floor—half the lattice strips trimmed and laid parallel to form the rear diagonal, the other half laid atop, at right angles. Cove strips form frame. Glue and brads hold assembly together as it's raised in front of wall mirrored with mounted sheets or peel-and-stick squares.

The rich look of carved paneling is achieved by nailing s4s molding and base caps to plywood paneling. No solid lumber sold today is wide enough to carve out paneling in one piece as craftsmen once did, so molding is today's means to get this effect. Actual molding type used depends on the effect wanted. Quarter rounds or coves could substitute for the base caps shown here.

FOR FURTHER READING

The Wood Moulding and Millwork Producers (Box 25278, Portland, OR 97225) offer a wide selection of publications that detail the basic profiles available, and give project ideas and tips on how to do them. A partial listing includes: "Design and Decorate with Wood Mouldings" (75¢); "How to Work with Wood Mouldings" (40¢); "How to Finish Wood Mouldings" (40¢); and "From Tree to Trim" ($2).

"Imagine Them Anywhere," a free brochure about prefinished vinyl moldings by the Gossen Co. (2030 W. Bender Road, Milwaukee, WI 53209), is available at hardware stores and home centers.

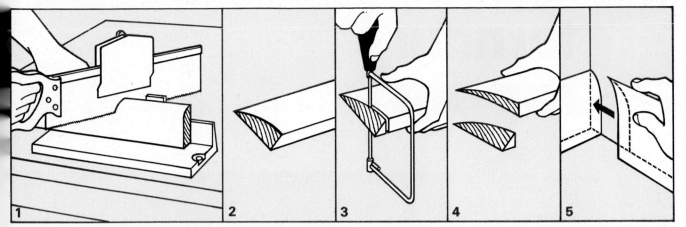

To cope a molding, first set it into a miter box with the wall side of the molding up against the back of the box (1). Trim the piece at a 45-degree angle to expose the exact profile of the molding face (2). Use this as a guide line for the coping saw (3), slicing away excess molding while keeping blade at a 90-degree angle to the molding face. This cut duplicates the curve of the molding (4) so it butts snugly against the face of an adjoining piece (5) to turn a corner.

ter may be possible only by using moldings.

"In the old days, they handcrafted the molding on the spot," Neal Heflin of the Wood Moulding and Millwork Producers told me. "They used wider lumber, and a lot more of it. If you did a room that way today, it would cost thousands of dollars."

Today's wood molding is factory-milled and finished—and a lot cheaper. A major woodworker's catalog (Woodworkers' Store) lists a 1-inch astragal (scalloped shape) molding at 54¢ a foot in pine, and a half-round rope-twist molding (½-inch-wide poplar) at $1.50 for 4 feet. Lumberyard prices vary widely, of course, but most should be in the 50¢-to $2.50-a-foot range, depending on the molding's width and intricacy. That's well under the cost of wall coverings such as fabric, custom wallpapers, and prefinished paneling.

And though most molding projects require careful planning and installation, they are not as tricky as you might expect. Most wall designs can be glued instead of nailed in place, for example. "If you're making a supergraphic, or a wall frame, you can use adhesive," Heflin said. "It's fine in any application that doesn't get stress. For a door casing or a heavy ceiling cornice, you'd want nails," he added.

Designing with moldings

The first step is to become familiar with the varied molding shapes and sizes. A good way to start is by browsing through brochures from manufacturers' associations (see list previous page). There are three basic types of wood moldings. The first, and cheapest, are unfinished strips of milled wood. These give you the greatest design latitude, but you do have the extra work involved in finishing the wood.

Next there are "toned" wood moldings, prefinished with a stain. Finally, there are wood moldings covered with a wood-grain-printed vinyl. These prefinished types are more expensive, but if their colors match your planned decor they can save you time. (The smaller molding designs also come in unfinished or vinyl-clad plastic. These are lighter than wood equivalents, less subject to warp, and can be cut without splintering. Vinyl moldings are often color-matched to a particular line of prefinished paneling.)

Your local home center or lumberyard should have some examples of each of these types. But it's unlikely you'll find a full selection of all possible shapes (or profiles, as the industry calls them). So it's best to plan carefully. Know the effect you want to get and what different molding profiles will give you that effect.

Precise measurements are another timesaver. Moldings come in 2- to 11-foot lengths. The shorter lengths are much easier to work with—and most projects will use lengths under 8 feet. When planning your purchase, list the specific lengths you'll need, then round each measurement to the next largest foot to allow for cutting and trimming. If your project requires mitering, allow for the width of the cut by adding in the width of the mitered pieces. (For an inside dimension of 30 inches, a 3-inch-wide piece mitered on both ends will require 36 inches, for example.)

There's one timesaver you shouldn't use: Don't just hand your list of molding profiles to the lumberyard clerk. Insist on picking out the lengths yourself.

Finish first

It sounds obvious, but in the excitement of creation, you may forget: Staining or painting moldings once they're wall-mounted is a mean job. It's usually best to apply your finish *before* putting it up. Where possible, it's also smart to assemble your molding project on the floor before fixing it in place. For supergraphics, paneling squares, and even some room dividers, you might consider making a jig to ease assembly. Nail a scrap-lumber frame on a panel of plywood so that its inside dimensions equal the outside ones of your graphic.

Not for walls only

Think about ceilings. Moldings can make a modern rosette to highlight a handsome chandelier. They can also turn a plain fireplace wall into a classic showpiece. Dull doors and cabinets can be pepped up with a few well-chosen pieces of molding. They can even give plain unfinished furniture a custom-made look. And moldings can be used structurally to create grilles and railings. Once you get hooked on the possibilities, you'll never lack for home-improvement projects—*Susan Renner-Smith.*

furniture repairs

The accompanying photos illustrate a typical furniture repair—one that includes all the structural elements you're likely to encounter in working on your own furniture. Except for very expensive pieces, where you might find difficult-to-repair mortise and tenon or dovetail joints, furniture today is almost always put together with dowels, screws, and glues. With the glues that are now available, you can forget about sending your broken pieces to a specialist for expensive repair. With a little care (put down newspapers to catch the drips), you can rebuild most joints right in your living room.

Not too long ago, the only way to repair the living room chair shown here would have been to make a new cross member (the piece that split). Today, with epoxy, split pieces can be made as good as new. Used correctly, epoxy makes virtually foolproof repairs. And, for joints, the new wood glues are far superior to anything the old cabinetmaker used to mix up.

Breaks occur gradually—in time, dowels and screws work out of a piece of furniture until they are too weak to hold. If you're alert, you can catch such potential breaks and repair them before they give way. Repair procedure is simple, but allow two or three days for a job, as the glue should set thoroughly between each step.

To repair an actual break: Mix a generous batch of epoxy. Spread it carefully on both sides of the break, then clamp the pieces together, using wood blocks on either side to protect the furniture from clamp marks. Near the edges of the break, apply the epoxy very thinly, or it will ooze out and permanently fasten the clamp blocks in place. (A piece of aluminum foil or waxed paper between the blocks and the break will prevent this.)

Next, thoroughly clean out—but don't enlarge—any dowel holes. Broken dowels may have to be carefully scraped, whittled, or even drilled out.

Remove any screws. Refill screw

holes either with glue and splinters, driving them in, or some other hard-setting material that will create a holding surface for screw threads.

If you plan to countersink a screw and cover the head with a hardwood plug, as in the photos, remove the plug prior to backing out the screw. This is likely to require both a small drill and a sturdy knife blade, as the plugs are well glued when inserted, and sanded, stained, and varnished with the rest of the piece. Plug holes, too, must be carefully cleaned out without enlarging them.

If necessary, get suitable replacement dowels (or make them from doweling) and plugs. Make sure plugs fit the openings tightly; if they're too large, sand them down a little.

Using a good wood glue (don't forget the dowels and holes), reassemble the pieces and clamp if necessary. Replace screws and tighten well to hold the pieces together until the glue sets. Plugs may be glued in after other glue has set.

Unless scars are massive and the piece requires refinishing, just go over the finish with brown shoe polish. Well rubbed in, this works about as well as anything for covering scars in dark-stained wood, especially when scars are in the lower part of a piece where they will not be inspected too closely.

The technique described above will enable you to repair 90 percent or more of the furniture breaks that occur in a home—*John Robinson.*

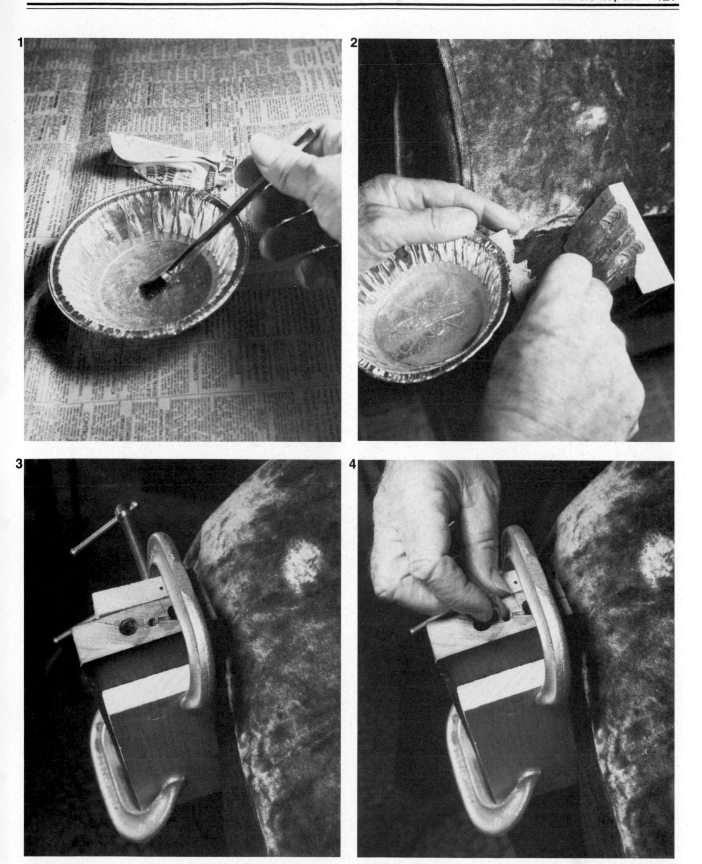

Steps in repair of typical furniture break—split hardwood, broken dowels, loose screw: **(1)** Use epoxy to fuse break in crosspiece. (Avoid the fast-acting kind; it sets up too quickly for this use.) Small brushes, such as the one shown, are inexpensive and disposable. Spread paper to catch drips. **(2)** Spread break apart and apply epoxy generously to both surfaces. **(3)** Tightly clamp split pieces, using wood blocks on both sides to protect furniture. Aluminum foil or waxed paper prevents blocks from sticking. **(4)** To provide new purchase for screw threads, work mixture of powdered wood, sawdust, and glue or some other hard filler into the screw hole.

5

6

9

10

13

14

7

8

11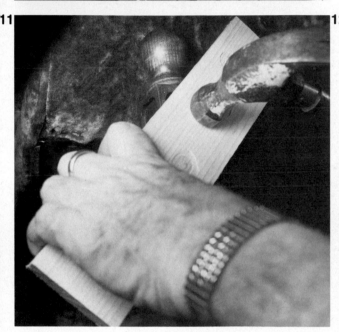

12

For the kind of joint in the chair being repaired, a screw and two dowels are usual elements. **(5)** Note that one dowel is broken. Most well-made furniture has countersunk screwheads **(6)**, covered with hardwood plugs. If possible, remove plug with a knife, or drill carefully. A support makes the job easier. **(7)** Back out the screw and **(8)** remove broken dowel stub remaining in the hole, using either a sharp knife or a drill. **(9)** If you can't find the right size dowel, very carefully sandpaper around a slightly too large one to take off a little. **(10)** Here, a snug-fitting, homemade dowel has been glued in place. Note that the tip has been slightly rounded with sandpaper. **(11)** Use wood glue on dowels and faces of joint, carefully tapping in for tight joint. **(12)** Immediately after joining, put screw in place and tighten thoroughly. For some repairs, you may need a cord tourniquet to keep parts tightly in position, but here the screw is adequate. **(13)** Hardwood plugs are available in hardware stores in various sizes; they're usually displayed near ready-made dowels. **(14)** Very carefully check the plug in the hole and, if necessary, sand it down a little, all the way around. The fit should be slightly snug. Tap the plug into position carefully. **(15)** Here, repairs are completed, but no attempt has been made to refinish the parts. Rubbing brown shoe polish into the scars will make them invisible to all but the most careful inspection. And that's all there is to repairing breaks in most furniture around your home.

15

care and refinishing of wood floors

It's true that professional floor finishers know what they're doing; they also make short work of emptying your pocketbook for their services. Do you need to hire a pro to do the job? Not if you're able-bodied, have plenty of spare time, and are bent on saving money. But prepare yourself—refinishing a floor is a tough number.

To sand and refinish a floor, you need a drum sander, disc-edge sander, and hand scraper; sandpaper (grades 3½, 1½, and 2/0); stain (optional); filler (paste or liquid); varnish, shellac, or penetrating finish; paint brushes; and clean cloths.

You can rent drum and disc-edge sanders at rental service stores or large hardware stores. Be sure to ask how to attach sandpaper to both before you leave the shop. The drum sander does the basic sanding job; the disc-edge sander is used along baseboards and other less accessible areas. For little nooks and crannies, you need a hand scraper, available at hardware stores.

First, put on old clothes, empty the room, and open the windows. (If you use flammable solvents, don't smoke or light a fire during application and drying.) Remove shoe moldings, registers, and electric plates. Try to loosen radiators so you can at least move them out of the way enough to sand under them. Nail down any loose, protruding, or creaking floorboards.

Sanding

A major sanding job is done in three steps, with three grades of sandpaper. The first sanding removes the old finish down to bare wood, takes out deep scratches, and removes high spots. For this, use coarse, open-coat No. 3½ (20 grit) sandpaper.

Move the drum sander lengthwise over the floor, along the grain of the wood. Don't push it—it may take you right into a wall! Just guide it as it moves slowly, under its own power. Start at one wall and move straight to the opposite wall, then walk backwards, pulling the sander back along the same path. Overlap each previous pass by about 3 inches, but be careful—if the sander rubs one place for long, it'll cut through the wood. The cost of repairing that mistake will cancel out anything you saved by doing the job yourself.

To sand close to walls, use the disc-edge sander with No. 3½ paper. Move the sander constantly, and don't tilt it or you'll carve deep circles in the floor.

Use the hand scraper, with the same grade sandpaper, for corners. Keep the blade sharp by turning it upside down and running a fine-tooth

file over it lengthwise. Bear down on the scraper; pull it toward you with one hand, while pushing down on the head with the other. Always scrape with the grain. Vacuum the floor thoroughly after the first sanding.

Now change to a medium-grade, No. 1½ (40-grit) sandpaper to remove the rough surface left by the coarse paper. Sand the floor, using the same technique as before. Use the same paper to edge and scrape, then vacuum the floor well.

Change to fine-grade, No. 2/0 (100 grit) sandpaper and sand as before. Work in socks so you don't leave shoeprints after this final sanding, which produces a smooth surface suitable for the finish. Touch up any rough spots by hand-sanding with medium-grade sandpaper.

Metal key turns mechanism that opens and closes drum on sander (below). Sandpaper is wrapped around drum, and ends inserted in the open slot (bottom). Hold paper in place as you close drum with key. You need a three-prong plug adapter for the drum sander. In using the machine (facing page), get a firm grip on it and, moving slowly (guide it, don't push it), follow the grain of the wood.

Follow the final sanding with a good vacuuming for the entire room (floor, walls, windows, doors, woodwork) and a bath for yourself. You'll need it.

Fillers

The pros mix stain and the fine dust stirred up during sanding to fill imperfections in the wood as they stain. However, that requires a special machine and you're using your own two hands. So make do with paste or liquid fillers.

Disc-edge sander uses a circular sanding disc. Use a wrench to remove the center nut; place sandpaper over the opening, and replace the nut.

Wrap sandpaper around the blade of the hand scraper to sand corners. As you work, use your hand to maintain a constant, even pressure on the scraper.

Filler should be thinned with paint thinner and applied with a good-quality brush. You can color filler by mixing in enough oil stain to get desired tone.

If your floor is open-grain wood (walnut, ash, mahogany, oak), close the cells and tiny crevices with a paste filler, thinned with turpentine. You can color the filler by mixing in a little oil stain. Let the filler set twenty to thirty minutes, then rub it into the pores of the wood. Wipe away any surplus (shows up as blotches or smears) when the filler dries. Remove any smears that persist by wiping carefully with a cloth moistened with thinner or pure turpentine. Be thorough. Any filler you leave on the sur-

Apply equal pressure with both arms to keep the disc sander level. Any tilting of the machine may carve deep, impossible-to-repair circles in your floor.

You will need to use a metal file to keep the blade of the hand scraper sharp. Rub the file evenly over the blade of the scraper to sharpen it.

Sanding sealer is used on unstained floor after sanding. Brush sealer on and let it dry two or three hours. Then sand lightly, vacuum, and apply a finish.

face will cloud after you apply the finish. And there's no way to fix that.

Open-grain wood floors need filler. Without it, the finish sinks into the wood, giving the surface a rippled look.

Staining

Staining your floor gives it color and enhances the grain of the wood. It's an extra step, but it's probably worth the trouble. If you want to stain your floor, this is the time to do it.

Before you start, vacuum or sweep all dust from the floor. If you don't, you'll end up with a sealed layer of dust hiding the grain you've worked so hard to show off. And be sure to check the label of the finish you plan to use to be sure it's made for use over the stain you've chosen.

Floor-care experts recommend three types of stain:

1. *Nongrain-raising stain* (also called "fast-to-light" or "nonsand" stain). This type of stain is made to be dissolved in a solvent that does not raise the grain of the wood. As a result, it does not require sanding before finish is applied. It can be used under any type of finish coat and can be mixed in a wide range of colors. But it's expensive, and you're trying to economize. So read on.

2. *Penetrating oil stain*. This is used by most professionals. It, too, is nongrain-raising, but it tends to bleed or dissolve and mix with later filler coats, varnish, and/or lacquer. To prevent bleeding, seal the stain with a wash coat of shellac.

3. *Pigment oil stain* (also called "wood stain," "pigment wiping stain," or "uniforming stain"). Actually a thin paint, this does not fade or bleed and is easy to apply, but it tends to cover the grain pattern more than other stains. If your floor has an open grain, use a filler before staining with pigment oil stain, or the stain will clog the pores of the wood and make it look muddy.

It's wise to test the color of an oil stain by brushing a little on the floor of a well-lighted closet. Let it stand five minutes, then wipe off the excess. If it's too light, brush on another coat for two minutes. Continue until you know how long the stain should stand for the right color, and follow that timing for the floor. Apply the stain with a wide brush in an even coat, with straight edges to minimize overlap. After it penetrates the wood, wipe up the excess with clean, dry rags. Let the floor dry for 24 hours before applying a finish.

Some floor maintenance procedures and suggestions are shown below. Top row: steel wool is best applicator for paste wax (left), since it rubs away marks as you work. The brush of an electric floor polisher fits over notches on rotor assembly (right). Center row: Some people buff with the polisher brush in direct contact with floor; others prefer using a buffer pad (left). Both do the job well. The main advantage of a buffer pad is that it collects dirt loosened by wax (right). Bottom row: Liquid cleaning wax is easier than paste to spread (left). Like paste, it should be applied in thin coat. Wipe dirt off with soft cloth, then buff. In repairing an old floor, drill holes before driving in finishing nails (upper right)—otherwise, you can split the wood. Countersink nail heads with a punch. Commercial wood cleaning product makes stripping easy (lower right); apply compound with soft cloths. Change the cloth when it gets soiled.

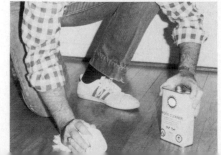

Finishing

The final step in refinishing your floor is applying a finishing coat. Floor finishes protect the work you've already done by putting a protective seal on it. There are three main classes of finishes:

1. *Shellac.* Shellac is economical, flexible, quick-drying, and durable. And you can add toner to it to change the color.

The main varieties are orange, white, and dewaxed. Orange darkens wood; white (clear) does not; and dewaxed is transparent. White shellac is best for most floors. Avoid shellac substitutes; they scratch and mark easily and do not withstand heavy traffic.

Shellac is brushed on the floor and sanded between coats. Never apply it on a warm, muggy day or over a damp surface or it will cloud.

2. *Varnish.* An excellent, transparent finish, varnish outdoes the others in depth and build. Good varnish is extremely hard and durable. Don't economize here; cheap grades become brittle and show scars.

Make sure the surface is completely dry, sanded, and dust-free when you apply varnish. Do the dusting (tacking) with a rag moistened with varnish; the tack rag picks up small particles that no amount of dry dusting could remove.

Abrasion-resistance is high in varnishes, especially those containing urethane. Varnish is more water-resistant than shellac, but it is susceptible to scratching and becomes darker with age.

"Quick-dry" varnishes are usually less durable than the slow-drying ones. Many professionals use *spar varnish,* a dark, slow-drying, moderate-gloss type that is tough, elastic, and durable. (Don't use filler under spar varnish; temperature extremes and the sun decompose it.) *Floor varnish* is harder and faster drying. It is quite elastic and tough enough to withstand grinding heels and scraping furniture.

All varnishes are difficult to patch. No matter how careful you are about it, the patches will always show.

3. *Penetrating sealer.* This type of finish puts tough resins *in,* rather than on the wood. It seals the wood against dirt and stains and makes it very wear resistant. Some sealers (like Wood Finish by Minwax) are colored, so staining, sealing, and finishing can be done in one operation. You also can add some color to any commercial sealing product you use.

Penetrating finishes are the easiest of all to apply. Just brush or wipe the finish on, let it sink in five to fifteen minutes, then wipe away the excess. Your floor probably will need two or three coats, applied at twelve-hour intervals. Wait twenty-four hours after the last application before waxing. Later, you can repair worn spots by applying some of the sealer to the area; unlike varnish patches, sealer patches never show.

Caring for your floor

Once you've refinished your floor you'll want to keep it looking new. The first step toward that end—and to help get an old floor back in shape—is proper basic care.

Cleaning your kitchen linoleum is probably part of your weekly routine and you most likely use a good, harsh cleaning agent like Janitor in a Drum or Mr. Clean. Don't use those products on a wood floor; they'll damage the finish.

Instead, use a liquid cleaning wax (like Truwax) made especially for use on wood floors. Pour a small amount of wax on the floor, then rub it with extra-fine (00 grade) steel wool or a soft cloth along the grain of the wood. The steel wool takes up heel marks and solidified dirt.

Wipe up excess wax with soft cloths to remove the dirt, changing cloths as they become soiled. Then buff the floor with an electric floor polisher. Let the floor polisher move on its own power, with your arm serving only as a guide. Use a buffer pad under the polisher brush and change the pad when both sides are dirty.

Application of wax

Most paste waxes are rubbed onto a clean floor with a soft cloth or extra-fine (00 grade) steel wool. Be sparing; you can't get the wax too thin. Let the coat dry for about five minutes, then polish it with a weighted brush or an electric floor polisher. If the floor is slippery, it needs more buffing.

Self-polishing waxes are less desirable, but if that's what you choose, apply a thin coat with a dry wax applicator. The wax dries to a shine in thirty to forty minutes. Porous floors may need a second coat.

Apply buffable liquid wax in the same way. Then, before it dries completely, buff the coated floor by hand or with a dry wax applicator. If you're using an electric floor polisher, wait twenty to thirty minutes before buffing the dried wax.

Maintenance

If you wax and buff your floor properly to begin with, it won't take a lot of time or effort to keep it in good shape. Unless your floor is exposed to hard wear or excessive moisture, it should need only routine dusting, occasional buffing, and a wax job a couple of times each year.

Use a dust mop or a vacuum cleaner to remove grit and dust from the floor. A little Endust or a similar product will help make dusting go more quickly. For most homes, a once-a-week vacuuming or dusting will do the trick. Use a brush attachment on your vacuum cleaner and be sure to lock it in place, so the brush, rather than the metal, hits the floor.

Since wax doesn't penetrate wood, rebuffing the floor rids it of surface scuffs and will restore the sheen of the wood. Wax two or three times a year with a cleaning wax, a buffable liquid wax, or a paste wax. All must be buffed.

If the floor is old, watch for loose and creaking boards. Keep them nailed down tight. If the old nails

---

Choosing a wax

● Most floor-care experts recommend paste wax, applied in the thinnest coat possible and buffed with an electric floor polisher. Because water-base products will penetrate and damage the wood, use only solvent-base wax. These waxes can be classed in three groups, all of which clean to some extent as they polish.

● Semibuffable paste wax (Trewax, etc.) gives the toughest, longest-lasting finish. Its luster can be maintained for many months, if you buff it occasionally with an electric floor polisher. One problem: The wax must be applied by hand—a tiring and time-consuming job.

● Self-polishing liquid waxes (Gold Label by Trewax, etc.) go on easily and quickly, but they're the least durable. Because they are nonbuffable, their luster can be restored only by reapplying the wax. That leads to a buildup of wax, which must eventually be stripped. And stripping a wood floor is no fun.

● Buffable liquid waxes (Johnson's Beautiflor, etc.) are more easily applied than pastes, but they're not as durable.

Whatever wax you choose must not only rub out into a smooth layer on the floor, but also must resist the abuse of traffic without marking or smearing. No wax can meet both requirements completely; however, very hard waxes—for example, carnauba and montan waxes—come closest.

don't hold well, drill a very small hole at an angle through the loose board and drive in 4-inch, cement-coated finishing nails. Countersink nail heads and cover the holes with plastic wood.

Or, if your floor is well-sealed, try applying a bit of lubricating oil along the cracks between planks. Be sure to wipe off surplus oil. If there are wide cracks between boards, fill them with wood putty.

If wood pegs in a pegged, wide-board floor come loose, reset them with white wood glue.

Glue splinters down with white glue as soon as you notice them.

Stripping

If your floors are not overwaxed, there never should be a buildup that requires complete removal (unless you use self-polishing liquid wax). However, when scuffs become hard to buff out, it's a sign that your floor should be stripped of old wax.

Don't use water or water-base stripping compounds like those used on resilient floors. (The water damages wood.) Instead, use a waterless floor cleaner. Be careful if you use naphtha; it is highly flammable.

Bad spots

Deep scratches require a thorough sanding of the surrounding area to level the surface of the wood. Some scratches on a floor with a shellac finish can be filled with a melted shellac stick of the proper color. And deep scratches in a stained floor can be stained to match surrounding wood.

Surface scuffs often can be rubbed out with paste wax and steel wool. Or, on floors with a shellac finish, use alcohol. Scratches in painted floors can be sanded, spackled, resanded, and repainted.

Or try Varsol, a petroleum product that takes up heel marks, cleans tar off your car, kills weeds, and maybe even cures sinus trouble. (It's sold at Exxon stations in 2-gallon containers. Or you can bring your own container and buy smaller portions.) Use a rag moistened with Varsol to rub the mark away. A warning though: Varsol also takes the wax off your floor; the spot must be rewaxed.

To remove dents, try this: Turn a bottle cap upside down over the dent and heat the cap for brief periods with a warm iron to raise wood.

For treating special problems—burns, paint spills, and the like—see "Special problems" above—*Denise Allen Zwicker.*

Special problems

Wood floors are just as susceptible as any others to spilled drinks, cigarette burns, water damage, and other such catastrophes. Repairing the damage is just a matter of learning the proper strategy:

● Fresh paint: Use the appropriate paint solvent.

●Dry paint: Rub with a rag that has been dipped in a mix of rottenstone (a cleaning powder you can buy at hardware stores) and salad oil.

●Rust: Mix one part sodium citrate with six parts water and seven parts glycerine. Add whiting and stir to a thick paste. Spread on stains and let it dry two or three days, then scrape it off. If stains remain, repeat the process.

●Cigarette burns: Scrape blackened area *carefully* along wood grain, until you reach brown wood. Wipe out color with benzine, paint thinner, or bleach; smooth with sandpaper or steel wool; apply stain; finish to match surrounding wood.

Filling in with plastic wood sounds easier, but it's hard to find any to match the floor color. You can, however, mix ordinary plastic wood with an alcohol stain that matches the floor.

●Crayon and lipstick: Use liquid cleaning wax.

●Oil and grease: Try wiping with paint thinner or benzine, but don't rub the oil further into the wood. Or place cotton saturated with hydrogen peroxide over the stains; then soak another piece of cotton in ammonia and spread it on top until the cotton dries. Repeat the process until the stain disappears.

●Alcohol: If you break a bottle of wine on the floor, use a dampened cloth or mop, but be sure to dry the floor thoroughly; if you don't, the water will penetrate the wax and turn it white. The only solution, then, is to rewax.

Wipe alcohol stains with a rag dipped in salad oil and rottenstone, rinse with benzine, and apply wax. Really old stains will require a little extra work with the same treatment, unless the floor has a shellac finish. In that case, rub out the stain with 00-grade steel wool; brush on new shellac, diluted fifty-fifty with denatured alcohol; rub well with steel wool; reapply shellac, and rub down again.

●Chewing gum: Chill the gum with an ice cube until it's brittle. Then scrape it off with a dull knife. Remove any residue with trichloroethylene.

●White water marks: Rub with cigarette ashes and salad oil. Or daub spots with spirits of camphor. Let the camphor dry for half an hour; then rub with a rag dipped in oil and rottenstone, clean off residue with benzine, and apply wax.

Water allowed to stand for long periods (e.g., under planters) eventually will stain wood almost black. There are three things you can try on these marks: (1) Rub with coarse steel wool and a good floor cleaner or paint thinner. (2) Sand, first with medium, then with fine sandpaper. (3) Bleach with three applications of oxalic acid. If one of these suggestions works, even out the finish around the marks with fine sandpaper, apply new finish, and wax. The only other alternative is deep sanding and refinishing.

●Candle wax: Scrape as much as you can away with a dull knife, then use naptha or trichloroethylene to clean the rest.

●Mildew: For this, you must use water. First, scrub with a rag dipped in a strong solution of chlorine bleach and wrung out. Then rinse with a rag dipped in water and wrung out. Dry thoroughly.

●Food: Most foods are neutral and will not affect the floor finish. Use water to remove any food residue, then dry thoroughly.

Rottenstone and salad oil can be used to atone for a number of sins (left); the mixture even will remove dried paint and old alcohol stains. Be careful when scraping a burned spot (top, right). A sharp knife blade or too much pressure can seriously damage the floor. Scrape carefully along the wood grain. With dark water stains, sanding is imperative (bottom, right). Use medium sandpaper to remove the damaged wood; switch to fine paper to smooth the finish.

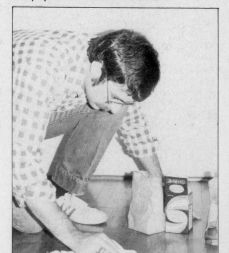

silence squeaky floors and stairs

Squeaking floors and stairs don't have to be tolerated along with your mortgage as part of home ownership.

Squeaks result when wood changes shape. For example, if a floor had been laid to close tolerance, moisture could have caused wood to swell, resulting in a slight buckle that has created a gap between floorboards and subflooring. When someone walks over the area, pressure on the floorboards results in their rubbing together, and a squeak is produced.

Squeaking floors also result when joists and bridging weaken. Joists are wood beams running from wall to wall that support the floor. When one warps or sags longitudinally, that portion of flooring it is supposed to support is left unsupported. This creates a dip in the floor, and a squeak.

Bridging, which consists of wood strips nailed diagonally between joists to give joists rigidity, can loosen when pressure from above is exerted. This produces a squeak.

Furthermore, if there is insufficient bridging, the rigidity joists need to provide firmness will be lacking. This can result in the floor sagging as well as squeaking. Sagging may also result when very heavy furniture, such as a grand piano, is placed in the home.

In the case of squeaking stairs, noise is generally created when a tread and riser loosen and rub against each other.

The remainder of this article treats squeaking floors and squeaking stairs separately. Methods which are successful in eliminating squeaking floors are outlined in the accompanying chart. In addition to the chart you'll find a step-by-step procedure that will prove successful in eliminating squeaking stairs.

In the chart, you'll notice that repairs are made either from below (in basement or crawl space) or from above to the finish flooring itself. If you are tackling the situation from below, first pinpoint the trouble area by having someone walk back and forth over the noisy portion of the

Typical flooring

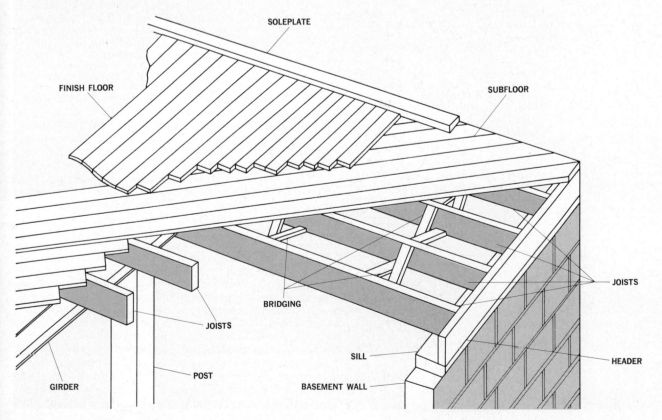

Methods of eliminating squeaking floors

Material and use	Procedure	Material and use	Procedure
Wood shims (wedges) for taking up a gap between joist and subfloor. Wood shingles or scrap lumber that is beveled thin enough so it can be driven between the joist and subfloor can be used.	This repair is made from below. After pinpointing the squeaking area, drive the shim between the joist and subfloor. The shim takes up the slack created by the subfloor and joist parting company.	8d (pennyweight) annular flooring nails. Use standard nails for softwood (fir, pine) floors and hardwood nails for hardwood (maple, oak) floors.	This repair is made from above. Walk back and forth over the floor, testing for loose floorboards. Where one is found, drill pilot holes ½ inch from where the board butts against the adjoining board. Drill two holes — one on each side. Drive nails at an angle into the board. Countersink nailheads, and cover them with wood filler. Nails should also be used in this manner where a floorboard has warped and is pushing up against the floorboard next to it.
Plastic wood or plastic resin glue to seal wide cracks between floorboards.	This repair is made from above before a floor is to be sanded and refinished. Filling wide cracks between floorboards with wood filler or plastic resin glue (force the compound into the crack with a putty knife) can take up the slack and relieve a squeaking condition as well as enhance the floor's appearance.	Dry graphite to "lubricate" cracks between squeaking floorboards when dry air has caused boards to shrink.	This repair is made from above. Insert the tip of a pencil-type graphite applicator between floorboards and press graphite into the crack. This is a temporary repair.
No. 10 1¼-inch wood screws for pulling together subfloor and finish floor. This gap results when moisture causes surface flooring to swell and buckle slightly.	This repair is made from below. Locate the squeaking area. Drill a 1-inch-deep pilot hole through the subfloor. If it is difficult to estimate 1 inch, place a thin piece of wood 1 inch up on the drill to serve as a depth stop. When the depth stop comes in contact with the subfloor, stop drilling. With someone standing on the floor so pressure is exerted on the weak area, screw a No. 10 1¼-inch wood screw into the subfloor to pull together the finish floor and the subfloor. If the squeak remains, insert several more screws, spacing them 4 inches apart, but if a maximum of five screws fails to help, forget it. This method won't do the job.	Adjustable floor jack and 4×8-inch beams to relieve a sagging condition which is so bad that the methods suggested above won't work.	This repair is made from below. Place a support beam on the floor and rest the jack on the beam to prevent concrete damage resulting from pressure. If the sag is concentrated in one relatively small area, the jack may be forced against the joist in that area. If the sag is extensive, place a beam across joists and extend the jack. In either case, raise the jack until resistance is felt on the jack handle. Now, keep the jack in this position for no *less* than 24 hours. Then, if you can, turn the jack handle to raise the jack only ¼ turn more. Let the jack remain in this position for 24 hours. In other words, never exceed ¼ turn of the jack handle for each 24 hours until the sag has been removed. Putting excessive pressure on the floor with the jack at any one time can cause extensive damage.
Hammer, block of wood, and piece of scrap carpet (or other suitable material) to use as padding.	This repair is made from above. If your floor is covered by carpeting or tile, and it is not possible to tackle repair from below, try this: Place padding on the floor over the squeaky floorboard, place a block of wood on top of that, and hammer down on the wood sharply. You may just reset some loose nails. If this doesn't work, repair cannot be made until the floor covering is removed.		
Hammer and nails to secure bridging that has loosened; handsaw for bridging pieces that are rubbing together.	This repair is made from below. Grasp each crosspiece and try to twist. If the piece is loose, nail it to the joist. Try to insert a piece of thin cardboard (the kind used as backing for a laundered shirt is suitable) between crosspieces. If this demonstrates that pieces are touching, shave them apart with a saw.		
A piece of 2×8-inch lumber cut exactly to the width of the space between joists for use as bridging where a squeak exists and there is no bridging. This may also be used to reinforce a floor that is sagging.	This repair is made from below. Drive the 2×8-inch piece of lumber up at right angles to the joists until it is firmly wedged against the subfloor. Toenail the support to the joists.		

floor as you, below, pick up the sound. Mark the troublesome area with chalk for easy identification.

To temporarily relieve a squeaking step condition, force dry graphite into the crack made where the noisy tread and riser join. If a permanent solution is desired, try one of the following:

1. If the squeak occurs when you step on the front of the tread, drive several brads opposing each other at an angle through the tread into the riser. An alternate solution, if the underside of the stairway is open, is to cut two blocks, and glue and screw them to the riser from below so blocks provide the tread with additional support.

2. If the squeak occurs when the riser presses down on the tread because a space exists between the tread and riser, equip yourself with thin wood shims. Apply wood glue and insert shims at equal intervals between the riser and tread using a hammer and driving block. Cut off exposed ends with a sharp knife or chisel so shims are flush with the tread. Nail a strip of molding over the crack between riser and tread to hide the repair.

3. If the entire stair seems to creak no matter where pressure is applied and the underside of the stairway is open, install two equally spaced long-arm shelf brackets. This will sufficiently reinforce the step and stop the noise—*Art Hughes.*

Added support in the form of wood shingles between joists and subfloor provides strength and will relieve squeaks.

A support piece driven between and nailed to joists will reinforce a floor that is sagging and squeaking.

Drill a pilot hole 1-inch deep into the subfloor (left). If necessary, use a depth stop. A few wood screws in an area is an effective method in pulling parted subfloor and finish floor together (above right).

Treating wide floor cracks before sanding may relieve a squeak and will lead to a neater finish.

A squeak may be caused if bridging is loose. Strengthen support pieces with nails (left). Pressure from above may cause two pieces of bridging that are in contact to rub.

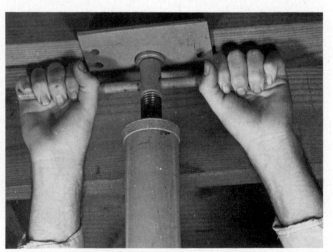

Use a floor jack cautiously to avoid damage. Raise only one-quarter turn per twenty-four hours.

How to eliminate squeaks from your stairs

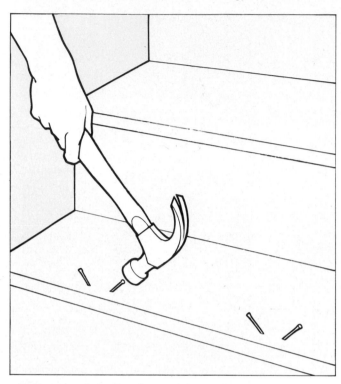

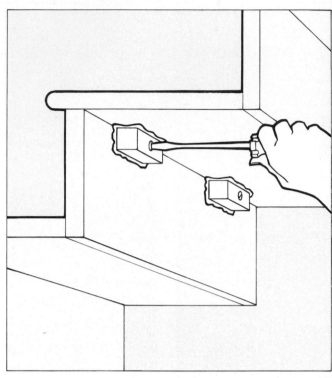

Often a squeak can be taken out of a tread by simply reinforcing the tread with brads. Notice how brads are arranged.

A squeak in a step may be eliminated from the blind side with wood blocks, glue, and screws.

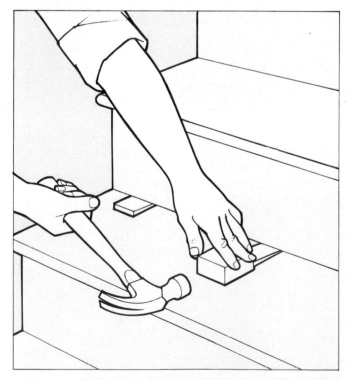

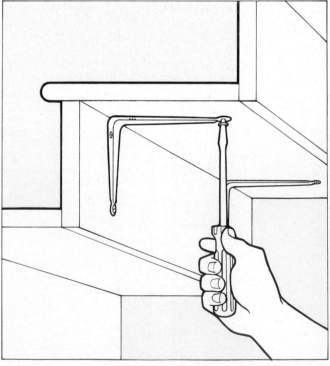

Shims are effective in closing a gap between riser and tread that may be responsible for a squeak.

Shelf brackets provide overall support for a weak tread and riser. Install them as shown.

fast furniture finishes

Y ou may have spent hours sanding, scraping, staining, and sealing a piece of unfinished furniture. But it's the final finish that makes your work look either professional or amateurish.

For years, I was convinced that varnish was the only good finish—dust, bubbles, brush marks, sags, and all. Over the years I've experimented with brush application of lacquer, shellac, and linseed oil—the other basic finishes. All took considerable time and effort to apply, but each produced a handsome top coat.

Now, store shelves are crowded with tung oil, polyurethane, and other synthetic-resin varnishes. The labels claim these products will solve everyone's finishing problems: No sanding between coats. Satin and antique finishes right out of the can that look hand rubbed. Fast, foolproof.

But do these new products produce fine finishes? To answer this question, I did extensive testing.

There are three basic types of clear top coats: *penetrating finishes* that sink into wood pores and leave a relatively thin surface coating; *padding finishes* (applied with a pad) that

leave a micro-thin surface coating; and *surface finishes,* either satin or glossy, that simply deposit a protective film on the wood. I tested a selection of all of these on several different woods. I followed the manufacturer's directions for each product, except in the last test of glossy surface finishes. Here, I also tried old application methods.

My primary criterion in judging the results was appearance of the final sample. The second—but important—consideration was how well the finish protected the wood from water and alcohol. I noted ease of application, but did not consider it in judging the finish, since I was primarily concerned with results.

The result of each test is detailed in the tables. Here are my conclusions: Some new finishes are clearly superior to the traditional ones. With these you will get the same good looks, with less effort. Other finishes, while easier to apply than traditional ones, will give inferior results if you simply follow the manufacturer's instructions. But if you use more traditional finishing procedures, the newer finishes can look as good as the old.

Penetrating-oil finishes

As a group, penetrating-oil finishes are the easiest to apply. There are no worries about brush marks, dust, bubbles, or sags. Although the procedures vary slightly from product to product, you basically slop the finish on, wait, then wipe off the excess.

Linseed oil is the original penetrating finish. Some craftsmen swear by it; others condemn it as a finish that is all work for little result. Some say you must apply it monthly for a year, then yearly forever after. That may be exaggerating a bit. But four months after using linseed oil on my test sample, I could still smell the finish, which meant it hadn't yet dried.

The new penetrating finishes are mixtures of oils, synthetic and natural resins, and petroleum solvents. All are easier and quicker to apply than linseed oil (see table for details).

Like linseed oil, the new finishes produced a natural-wood look and texture with a slight sheen; but linseed oil resisted alcohol and water somewhat better. For this test, half of each sample was waxed; then separate puddles of Gordon's gin and water were left to stand overnight.

Penetrating finishes

	Product	Main ingredients	Application	Teak	Final appearance (non-waxed sheen) Pine	Mahogany	Water and alcohol resistance
Old finish	Linseed oil	Polymerized vegetable oil	Cut linseed oil 1:2 with turpentine (use only "boiled" oil; raw won't dry), apply, let soak, then wipe: once daily for a week, once weekly for a month	Slight	Slight	Moderate	Good
New finishes	DPS (deep-penetrating sealer)	Tung oil	Apply, let drain off, wait 24 hours, repeat	Slight	Flat	Slight	Bare finishes had good resistance. With optional "protective" wax coating, all showed slight clouding
New finishes	Tungseal	Tung oil	Apply, let penetrate, wipe dry, repeat (two coats on mahogany and teak, four coats on pine)	Slight	Flat	Slight	
New finishes	Watco Danish Oil	Linseed oil	Apply, wet-sand with 600A wet or dry paper, wipe dry. Apply second coat when dry, let penetrate, wipe dry	Flat	Flat	Slight	

Padding finishes

	Product	Main ingredients	Application	Myrtle Burl	Final appearance Walnut	Mahogany	Water and alcohol resistance
Old finish	French polish	Orange shellac	Dribble some shellac onto a wad of surgical cotton, enfold in a cloth pad, moisten with alcohol, lubricate sparingly with linseed oil. Rub thin coat onto surface with circular motion. Let dry 24 hours. Repeat for three more coats. Apply two final coats with the grain to eliminate swirl marks. Waxing is optional.	Rich, mirror-smooth, transparent shine, highlighting color and figure of grain	Rich, mirror-smooth, transparent	Rich, mirror-smooth, transparent	None
New finishes	Pad Lac	Shellac pre-mixed with moisteners and lubricants	Apply about ¼ oz. onto pad, tap pad to disperse liquid throughout, rub thin coat on surface with circular motion. Wait 24 hours. Repeat for three more coats. Apply two final coats with the grain	Same as above	Same as above	Same as above	None
New finishes	Rapid Pad	Same as above	Same as above	Glossy and transparent, but soft	Glossy, transparent, soft	Glossy, transparent, soft	None

On balance, I judge the packaged penetrating-oil finishes to be as good, or better than, linseed oil.

Padding finishes

French polish is a top coat of shellac rubbed on in very thin coats by a pad moistened with alcohol and lubricated with linseed oil.

Surface preparation for padding a top coat is very important. The padded film is so thin that it will not correct surface defects. So the wood must be thoroughly sanded, and a sealer coat of diluted shellac applied by brush before padding the finish on.

French polish application is time-consuming (see table) and very difficult to master, but if you do it right, you get a finish that's unsurpassed in bringing out the rich color and grain of the wood. Unfortunately, the finish is not water or alcohol-resistant. Nor is it as durable as varnish under normal wear.

The modern versions of French polish are prepared substitutes that don't need alcohol or oil for successful application. They are easier to apply successfully than the traditional French polish, but the wood surface must be prepared the same way.

In my test the Pad Lac sample looked as fine as the finish obtained by traditional French polishing.

Rapid Pad also looked good, but the finish was so soft I could scratch it with my fingernail.

Surface finishes

If you want a more durable high-gloss finish, you can apply several coats of varnish, lacquer, or shellac. Some of the coating sinks into open wood pores but most stays on the surface, forming a thin, protective skin.

For a satin or antique (flat) finish that doesn't penetrate the wood, you can use lacquer or varnish products clouded with silica. These give the dull finish that you formerly got only

Satin and flat surface top coats

	Product	Main ingredients	Application	Leveling on pine	Sample appearance Pore filling on mahogany	Pore filling on cherry	Initial sheen
Old finishes	Varnish (gloss ZAR)	Polyurethane (today's most widely available equivalent of rubbing varnish)	3 coats: first and second thinned, light sanding between coats	Good	Fair	Fair	Gloss
	Shellac	Natural resin in alcohol	8 coats: thorough sanding after fourth and seventh coats	Poor	Good	Good	Gloss
New finishes	Antique ZAR	Polyurethane with silica	3 coats: first and second thinned, light sanding between coats	Good	Fair	Fair	Flat
	Deft Clear Wood Finish	Nitrocellulose, coconut oil, alkyd lacquer	3 coats: light sanding between coats	Good	Poor	Poor	Flat
	Satin brushing lacquer	Nitrocellulose lacquer	4 coats: light sanding between coats	Very poor	Fair	Good	Flat
	Satin Minwax	Polyurethane with silica	3 coats: light sanding between coats	Good	Fair	Fair	Satin
	Satin Varathane	Polyurethane with silica	3 coats: light sanding between coats	Good	Fair	Fair	Satin
	Wood Glo	Polyurethane with silica	2 coats: light sanding between coats	Good	Poor	Poor	Flat

Gloss surface top coats

	Product	Main ingredients	Application	Appearance after application of finish Walnut	Cherry
Old finishes	Gloss brushing lacquer	Nitrocellulose lacquer	6 coats: first coat thinned as sealer, other coats full strength; thorough sanding and steel-wool rubdown between all coats	High gloss, brush marks, surface pores filled	High gloss, brush marks
	Shellac	Natural resin in alcohol	8 coats: first coat diluted, other coats full strength (3-pound cut); thorough sanding after fourth and seventh coats	High gloss, brush marks, surface pores filled	High gloss
	Varnish: All varnishes are listed below because today's available varnishes have such altered resin content (synthetic instead of organic) that they can't be classified as old finishes				
New finishes (applied according to manufacturers' directions)	Deft Wood Armor Gloss	Acrylic-latex finish	3 coats, full strength: light sanding between coats	Moderately glossy surface, pores not filled, but not as prominent as above	Moderately glossy surface, pores filled equal to Gloss Varathane, surface wavy with grain
	DPS/PF	Tung-oil varnish	2 coats DPS sealer: let dry; rub with 0000 steel wool and DPS, wipe clean, immediately apply DPS/PF; let dry, repeat rubdown and second coat DPS/PF	Glossy surface, pores not filled, surface wavy with grain	Glossy surface, pores not completely filled
	Gloss Varathane	Polyurethane varnish	3 coats, full strength: thorough sanding after first coat, light sanding after second	Surface glossy, pores not filled, surface wavy with grain	Surface less glossy than Gloss ZAR (below), pores better filled, surface wavy with grain
	Gloss ZAR	Polyurethane varnish	3 coats: first and second thinned, third coat full strength; thorough sanding after first coat, light sanding after second	Surface glossy, pores not filled, surface wavy with grain	Glossy surface, pores not filled, surface wavy with grain
New finishes (using old methods)	Barrett Coachman	Alkyd varnish	6 coats: first coat thinned as sealer, other coats full strength; thorough sanding and steel-wool rubdown between all coats	High gloss, mirror-flat surface, pores filled	High gloss
	Hour Varnish	Tung-oil varnish	6 coats: same procedures as above	High gloss, mirror-flat surface, pores filled	High gloss, brush marks
	Gloss ZAR	Polyurethane varnish	6 coats: same procedures as above	High gloss, mirror-flat surface, pores filled	High gloss, mirror-flat surface

by rubbing down gloss varnish with pumice and rottenstone (see table).

Thirty years ago, most varnishes were solutions of natural gum resins in linseed or tung oil. Today's varnishes are made from oils, resins, and chemicals dissolved in petroleum solvents. But there is no universal varnish. Each product is formulated for a particular job. Bar-top varnish, for example, must resist water, alcohol, and detergents, and must have a good, long-lasting gloss. Floor varnish must be more flexible and have good abrasion resistance; high gloss is less important. Neither of these is satisfactory for fine furniture.

Like varnishes, the components of lacquer have changed over the years. The original lacquers were basically shellac. Today's lacquers are made from nitrocellulose (and other bases), resins, plasticizers, and solvents. Though trickier to work with than most varnishes, lacquer has an advantage: It really is colorless. Varnishes described as "water white" are actually pale yellow.

Shellac is an organic resin dissolved in alcohol. Once widely used as a top coat, shellac is most often used today only as a sealer, because of its poor alcohol and water resistance. But in my tests, shellac was highly effective when applied properly.

Film-finish tests

The traditional way to produce a satin or antique finish is to rub down shellac or gloss varnish with pumice and rottenstone. Since many new finishes don't require this final step (see table), my objective was to see if they were as good overall.

I tested old and new products on unstained, unfilled wood samples. All—except for the brushing lacquer and shellac—brushed on easily and leveled well. As in previous tests, I let puddles of gin and water sit overnight on waxed and unwaxed samples of the finish. The shellac sample surprised me. It came through unscathed. Since all other samples (both satin and gloss) were undamaged, as well, I didn't include the tests in the tables.

Although satin and antique finishes can hide many surface defects, none of the finishes used match paste filler in filling wood pores.

In appearance, the new products produced results almost as good as the old rubbing with pumice and rottenstone. On close examination, the surfaces were not quite as smooth.

For the final gloss-finish test, I added an extra step. Besides applying new finishes according to manufacturers' directions, I also used old methods on some samples. One new finish, gloss ZAR, served as control.

The sanding made a difference. While the fast-finish samples displayed the pored surfaces noted in the previous test, the samples that were heavily sanded between coats were glassy smooth. Final rubbings with pumice and rottenstone gave them a high-gloss, glare-free mirror finish.

My conclusions? There is no way you can produce a good varnish, shellac, or lacquer surface-film top coat without sanding between coats—sanding with great care before the final coat. Container instructions that say no sanding is required mean that succeeding coats adhere without sanding. But for a smooth finish, sand between coats—*Thomas Jones.*

Photo by Greg Sharko

Rubbing and waxing	Final surface	Finish evaluation		
		Pine	Mahogany	Cherry
Sanding 400A and oil, pumice and oil, rottenstone and oil, wax on half of surface	Satin	Excellent	Fair (pores not filled)	Not tested
Same as above	Satin	Excellent	Excellent	Excellent
None	Flat	Excellent	Fair (pores not filled)	Excellent
Waxed	Satin	Excellent	Fair (pores not filled)	Good (pores not filled)
Pumice and oil, rottenstone and oil, wax	Satin	Poor (brush marks still show)	Poor (brush marks, and pores not filled)	Poor (brush marks, and pores not filled)
None	Satin	Excellent	Fair (pores not filled)	Not tested
None	Satin	Excellent	Fair (pores not filled)	Not tested
None	Flat	Excellent	Fair (pores not filled)	Good

Final-coat rubdown	Final appearance (not waxed except where noted)
Rub with pumice and oil, rottenstone and oil, compound; buff with lamb's-wool pad on hand drill (no wax)	Mirror finish
Same as above	Mirror finish
Not done	Satin
Rub down with pumice and oil, rottenstone and oil (mfr.'s procedure), paste wax, and buff	Glossy when waxed
Not done	Glossy
Not done	Glossy
Rub with pumice and oil, rottenstone and oil, compound; buff with lamb's-wool pad on hand drill (no wax)	Mirror finish
Rub down as above (no wax)	Mirror finish
Same procedure as above	Mirror finish

Tables show importance of sanding between coats. Another secret to a smooth finish: Use disposable polyfoam brushes. They apply a thin coat of varnish without brush marks or dropped bristles. Although most poly brushes are marked "not for shellac or lacquer," they can be used for both. They may last for only one coat—but if you buy in box lots, the brushes will be cheap enough to be discarded after one use.

When sanding before the first two coats, use 280-grit garnet or aluminum oxide paper. Or use 320 or 400A wet or dry silicon carbide paper. A felt-backed block will keep the paper flat on the work. Sand until the surface is dull except for pores and depressions. Then rub with 0000 steel wool to dull these spots. For the last sanding, use the 320 or 400A silicon carbide paper lubricated with water (oil for shellac). Rub with 0000 steel wool, clean thoroughly, and let dry.

SOME MAIL-ORDER SOURCES

Constantine, 2050 Eastchester Rd., Bronx, NY 10461 (Wood-Glo, Pad Lac, Watco, lacquer); **Craftsman Wood Service**, 1735 West Corland Ct., Addison, IL 60101 (brushing lacquer, Watco, Barrett, Deft); **John Harra Wood & Supply Co.**, 511 W. 25th St., New York, NY 10001 (DPS, DPS/PF); **Mohawk Finishing Products**, Amsterdam, NY 12010 (lacquer, Rapid Pad); **Woodworkers Store**, 21801 Industrial Blvd., Rogers, MN 55374 (Barrett, ZAR, Deft, Minwax, Watco).

how to wire a home workshop

If your workshop is a maze of extension cords and you're always blowing fuses or tripping breakers, you're flirting with disaster. Don't chance it. Wire that workshop to handle the load you're likely to impose on it, and enjoy the safety, convenience, and peace of mind it will bring.

Table saws, radial-arm saws, large drill presses, and other power tools with a ½-hp rating or more should have an individual circuit. The surge of power in the line the moment the motor is started up requires it. So does under-load power consumption—a table saw, for example, may draw two or three times as much power when a board is being cut than when idling.

Many of these motors can be operated on either 120 or 240 volts. Given the option, utilize the 240-volt operation—it's better for the motor in the long run. To convert a motor from one voltage to the other, remove the small end plate and arrange the wires on the terminal board inside to correspond with the wiring diagram or manufacturer's instructions for the voltage desired. A 240-volt motor must have a 240-volt receptacle and plug. This prevents plugging a 120-volt tool into a high-voltage outlet.

If you have more than one heavy-duty power tool, one circuit can handle all of them, *if* they all operate on the same voltage and *if* you never run more than one tool at a time. The instruction manual that came with the power tool will give you the electrical data needed to wire for it adequately.

Other circuits

A separate 120-volt circuit will be needed to operate any other small tools you use. Install receptacles in strategic locations to operate tools like grinders, hand drills, sanders, or extra drop lights for close work. This circuit should be run with #12 copper wire and fused with a 20-amp fuse or circuit breaker. (For brevity, any fuse assembly or circuit breaker will hereafter be referred to as an "overcurrent device.")

A 15-amp lighting circuit may be needed if you plan to install a lot of lights, or if you plan to use many high-wattage bulbs. In the average workshop, however, the lighting needs can be supplied by an existing circuit that supplies some other part of the house. Remember, the 20-amp circuit mentioned above can also be used for extra lighting. A reflector flood lamp with a clamp-on assembly works well for lighting up specific work areas.

The type of general illumination used is a matter of preference. Fluorescent fixtures produce an even, diffused

Drawing below shows the wiring for a typical home workshop. Note special provision for tools operating on 240 volts.

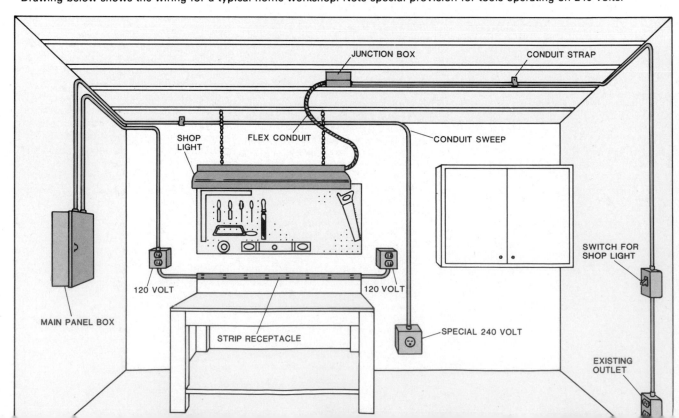

light that generally works out well. But if you're one of those who finds the stroboscopic effect irritating or that it tends to make moving tools appear stopped, incandescent lighting is your choice. Incandescent light glares more than fluorescent, making certain kinds of work hard to focus on, and it's slightly more expensive to operate, requiring more fixtures to get ample light.

Materials

The workshop circuits will be run in type NM (nonmetallic) sheathed cable, commonly called Romex. In the event that any cable needs to be buried in the earth, type UF or a type suitable for direct burial will need to be used. When purchasing cable for a specific power tool, be sure to buy the correct wire gauge (see chart, next page). Thin-wall aluminum conduit (½ inch) will be needed to encase wires running on the surface of a wall or flat finished ceiling.

Also needed: metal outlet boxes with covers; conduit connectors and conduit straps for holding conduit snugly in place; couplings for connecting two lengths of conduit; and receptacles and overcurrent devices rated at the proper voltage and amperage for the wire used (see chart).

Running circuits

Running the circuits for a workshop is nothing more than running the cable from the circuit or panel box to the location of the power tools. Ca-

Below is a neat mini-panel. If a panel has a main circuit breaker like this one, the two hot leads connect to the breaker. If there's no breaker, the hot leads connect directly to the buss bar lugs.

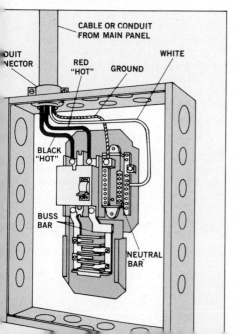

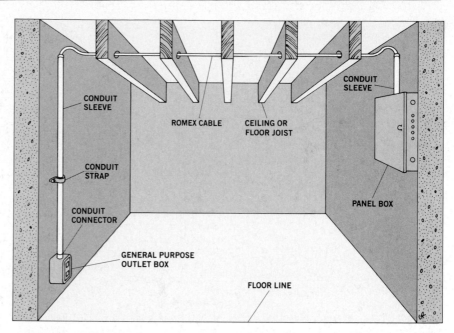

If your plans are to finish off the ceiling on which you're doing your wiring work, be careful not to drill holes too close to the edge of the beam. That way, you'll avoid having the cable penetrated by a nail when the ceiling work is done.

This main circuit panel, below, shows a 240-volt connection for large motors and a 120-volt connection for small motors.

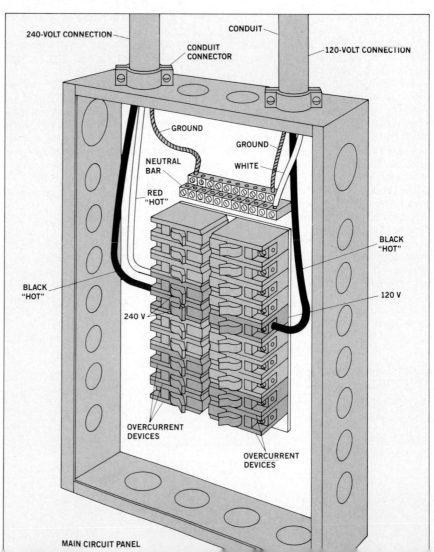

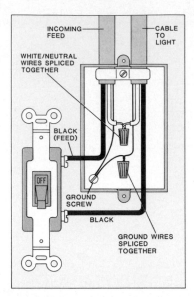

A typical single-pole switch connection. Note: All metal boxes must be grounded.

ble consisting of two insulated conductors and one ground conductor is suitable for both the 240-volt circuits and the 120-volt circuits.

In basement installations where there are overhead wood beams, holes should be drilled through the beams. The cable can then be drawn through the holes to the receptacle location. Sleeve the cable running down the wall in conduit. Connect the conduit to an outlet box, and install the receptacle and cover. (Use bushing on conduit sleeve to protect cable.)

Garage installations may be similar, or if an attic is available, the cables can be run up the wall from the panel, through the attic, and then down the wall to the location of the receptacles. Again, sleeve any cable running on the surface of the walls.

If your workshop is located in a place that has no attic access, and does have a finished ceiling, the circuit can be run entirely in thin-wall conduit. Run it up the wall from the panel box, across the ceiling, and down the wall to the location of the receptacle. Use a conduit bender to get around corners, or purchase ready-made Sweep Ell's. Strap the conduit to the ceiling and wall surfaces as necessary to provide for a firm installation.

In the latter case, the use of Romex

isn't necessary. The completed conduit run serves as the ground connection, and two individual conductors (Type TW) can be drawn through the conduit to provide the necessary voltage.

After the cable or conduit assembly has been run, the receptacles can be connected by attaching the white wire to the white terminals, the black wire to the dark terminal, and the ground wire to the green terminal.

Panel box

The connection for the 120-volt circuit requires a single pole (S/P) overcurrent device; the connection for the 240-volt circuit, a double pole (D/P) overcurrent device. Before making the connection, shut down the main switch that controls the entire house. All lights will go out, so have a flashlight ready. Work cautiously, because the main lead-in wires may still be energized.

Secure the overcurrent devices in place. On the 120-volt circuit, the ground wire connects to the multiple terminal where the other ground wires are; the white wire connects to the multiple terminal where the other white wires are and the black wire, to the new overcurrent device. On the 240-volt circuit, the ground wire connects to the ground bar; the red and black wires connect to the two terminals on the new (D/P) overcurrent device.

Turn the power back on and you should be in business. Before plugging in any power tools, check the receptacles with a voltage tester.

If an extra 15-amp circuit is needed for lighting, use the same method of connection as above for 120-volt operation. The only difference is the HOT cable, coming from the panel, should feed a switch first and then run to the light.

When taking a feed off of another source in the house, the connection is white to white, black to black, and ground to ground; just be sure you have a continuous HOT, and not something that is controlled by another switch.

Adding a subpanel

If your workshop is a great distance from the main panel box, it might be best to install a subpanel, or mini-panel box directly in the workshop. This is a small circuit box of perhaps 30- to 50-amp capacity, and is wired from the main panel box by a single cable with four conductors (three insulated and one ground) large enough to handle the entire workshop load (see chart). The workshop circuits could then be wired from the subpanel, saving on wire, conduit, and voltage drop.

In the main panel box, the ground wire and the white wire connect to the ground terminal and the white terminal respectively. The black wire and the red wire connect to the overcurrent device, supplying the subpanel with 240 volts. If there are no spaces left in the main panel box to install another circuit breaker, the subpanel may have to be fed from the main lugs supplying the entire house. That is a job for an electrician. The subpanel connection is white to white, ground to ground, black wire to buss bar, and red to opposite buss bar.

Once the subpanel is wired, the individual workshop circuits can be wired from it. If there is any doubt about working inside the main panel box, wire everything up to the point of the main connection, and leave the final connection to a pro. You will have already saved a great deal of money—*Lloyd Lemons, Jr.*

Right wire for the tool

240 volt		120 volt	
Motor size	Wire size	Motor size	Wire size
½ hp—370 watt	#14 cu.*	¼ hp—180 watt	#14 cu.
¾ hp—550 watt	#14 cu.	⅓ hp—240 watt	#14 cu.
1 hp—746 watt	#14 cu.	½ hp—370 watt	#12 cu.
		¾ hp—550 watt	#12 cu.
		1 hp—746 watt	#12 cu.**

* cu. is the abbreviation for copper
** A 1 hp—120 volt motor with a wire run over 75 feet should utilize #10 cu. wire.

Right wire for the circuit

Romex cable size copper conductor	Current capacity
#14 AWG*	15 amps
#12 AWG	20 amps
#10 AWG	30 amps
#8 AWG	40 amps
#6 AWG	55 amps

*American Wire Gauge

how to solvent-weld plastic pipe

Plastic pipe has become the universal problem solver for the do-it-yourself plumber. With most code restrictions toppling, you can plumb water-supply, drain-waste-vent, sewer-septic, or irrigation systems with easily cut, lightweight thermoplastic pipes and fittings. Best of all, most plastic components can be speedily joined with solvent cement.

Solvent welding is just about foolproof. There's no flame to start a fire while the water pressure is off. A saw, knife, and brush are the only tools needed.

Plastic pipe used for cold-water supply or drainage, including PVC, ABS, and polystyrene (often just called styrene) can be solvent welded. So can CPVC (chlorinated PVC), used in hot-water systems. A few plastic-pipe materials—notably polyethylene, polybutylene, and polypropylene, used for chemical-resistant fixture traps—are so resistant to solvent attack that they must be joined mechanically.

Solvent-welding cement consists of plastic filler (of the same material as the pipe to be joined) dissolved in a mixture of active solvents. The mix can be clear or pigmented. The handiest cements come with daubers or brushes for easy application.

To make a solvent-welded joint, cement is applied to the pipe end and fitting socket, which are immediately pushed together. The resulting joint can be handled gently within a minute, take water flow within a half hour, and handle full water pressure in two hours. A full cure takes about twenty-four hours. These time periods vary somewhat, depending on temperature, humidity, and solvent used.

During a complete cure, the solvents evaporate, leaving only pure plastic resin, which becomes one with pipe and fitting. The joint is actually

Solvent welding plastic pipes is easier and safer than sweat soldering copper pipes—especially when plumbing is overhead. Eye protection guards against solvent drip. Good ventilation is essential when working with strong solvent chemicals.

welded with plastic, hence the term solvent welding. A solvent-welded plastic piping system is joined into one continuous fitting from beginning to end. No weak spots are left for corrosive attack.

Solvent-welding tips

For advice on good do-it-yourself solvent welding, I talked to Ken Pepper of Genova, Inc. (Davison, Mich.), maker of vinyl (thermoplastic) plumbing products. Pepper, an authority on solvent cements, outlined three basic steps that will ensure success for the home plumber. "First, make sure the parts to be joined fit properly; next, clean the mating surfaces thoroughly; and finally, use ample amounts of a quality cement," he advised.

Plastic plumbing parts are designed with an interference fit. This provides space for the solvent cement, yet leaves no voids when the solvents evaporate. Unfortunately, a poor fit may be the rule rather than the exception. Pipe and fitting dimensions are specified by the American Society for Testing Materials. Often, the pipe-only manufacturer reduces the outside diameter and wall thickness of his pipe to the smallest prescribed ASTM tolerance to ensure that his pipe will fit into every manufacturer's fittings. The fitting-only maker expands his fitting sockets to the larger ASTM tolerance so they'll fit over every pipemaker's pipe. The result is a sloppy fit between the two. And if the additional ASTM out-of-round tolerances in pipe and fitting don't happen to coincide during as-

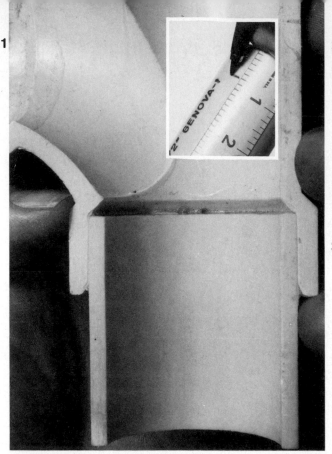

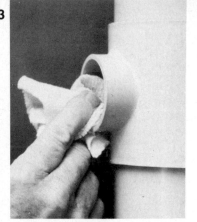

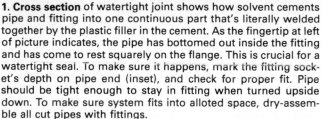

1. Cross section of watertight joint shows how solvent cements pipe and fitting into one continuous part that's literally welded together by the plastic filler in the cement. As the fingertip at left of picture indicates, the pipe has bottomed out inside the fitting and has come to rest squarely on the flange. This is crucial for a watertight seal. To make sure it happens, mark the fitting socket's depth on pipe end (inset), and check for proper fit. Pipe should be tight enough to stay in fitting when turned upside down. To make sure system fits into alloted space, dry-assemble all cut pipes with fittings.

2. Cutting pipe perfectly straight and scraping off plastic curls stuck to pipe end are essential steps for a good solvent-welded joint. For the best bond, the entire inner surface of the socket must contact the pipe. An off-square pipe end can reduce this vital contact by as much as 20 percent. Using a special plastic-cutting wheel attached to a good pipe cutter as shown will ensure straight cuts without a miter box. A hacksaw is easier—but only if you have a good eye and a light touch. Be sure to inspect pipe closely for gouges and cracks; cut pipe end if necessary.

3. Apply an etching primer-cleaner to both fitting socket and pipe ends to remove joint-spoiling dirt and grease. Etching also readies mating surfaces for full solvent attack. When cleaning, be sure to avoid rubbing off the socket-depth mark on pipe end. Piping must be kept dry: Water would mix with solvent cements, displacing plastic-attacking solvents and creating leak-prone unwelded spots in the joint. Once a joint is welded, water and dirt can't hurt it.

4. Telltale bead of solvent circling assembled joint shows that enough solvent cement has been applied for a secure joint. For best results, apply cement liberally to pipe end, to fitting socket, and *again* to pipe end. This sequence ensures that excess cement is squeezed out of the joint, where it can be wiped off, and not forced down into the pipe bore or fitting, where it would impede water flow. After applying solvent, join pipe and fitting as quickly as possible. Push them together with a slight twist to bring the fitting to correct alignment and break up any areas where cement is thin. Make sure that pipe bottoms out. Hold for 20 to 30 seconds.

sembly, the joint may be far too loose for successful solvent welding.

The only cure for too loose a joint is to find another pipe and fitting with an acceptable fit. The best way to do that is to buy pipes and fittings of the same brand. A sloppy fit is almost unheard of between parts of the same brand. Even so, it's good solvent-welding practice to test-fit each joint.

The second essential step is to clean the mating parts of the joint. Some instructions call for the use of sandpaper or steel wool for this. Ken Pepper frowns on this advice.

"That's what you do in sweat soldering," he says. "Solvent welding is very different." Pepper fears that sanding might remove too much material from the parts, leaving the joint loose or with flat spots. Instead, he

recommends a two-step welding process using a cleaner-primer before solvent cement.

Pepper also notes that the biggest single cause of joint failure is inadequate coating of the joining surfaces with cement. That's why he advises coating the pipe end *twice* with cement. "It's tough to use too much cement," says Pepper. "Only when solvent cement runs down the inside of the pipe have you used too much."

What about mistakes?

Warnings to the contrary, you may get away with pulling apart a pipe-fitting assembly after the joint has been doped and assembled. But you'd better be quick. In just seconds it will be held so tightly that a weight lifter

couldn't get it out. (You should only try a separation on piping used in nonpressurized systems.) If you're successful, both the pulled-out pipe and its fitting may be used again. But if you fail to pull the joint apart, you'll have ruined it in the process. You must then cut out the fitting and replace it with another one. Two pipe couplings will enable you to install the new fitting.

Suppose you put solvent cement on a pipe and fitting, but discover an error before joining them? You needn't throw them away. They're still fully usable. Just keep them clean until the next use.

In all cases, be sure to give the used pipe a double application of cement to get full softening through the aborted doping.

Choosing and using cement

A solvent-cemented pipe joint is tested at conditions that are more severe than any of those that will be encountered in normal use. The basic ASTM test for a solvent-welded CPVC joint, for example, calls for the twenty-four-hour-cured joint to be immersed in 180°F water for thirty minutes, then pressurized to 521 psi with the same hot water. The heat and pressure are held for at least six minutes to simulate 11.2 years of usage at 100 psi and 180°F.

A properly welded joint is grossly overdesigned. It will stand up to hot-water pressures that can burst the fittings. The joint works continuously and indefinitely. Even so, you should use a quality solvent cement as insurance against problems. Trouble is, you can't tell a good cement from a poor one by looking, smelling, or shaking.

A quality cement contains plenty of highly active plastic-attacking solvents that soften piping walls. These work with sufficient depth and speed for good welding. A good cement is not oversaturated with plastic filler. It needs unattached solvents to work. But it contains enough plastic filler to bridge any reasonable gap. A quality cement also sets quickly enough to be efficient to use.

Finally, a quality solvent cement contains enough spare dissolving power to permit its continued use after some of the solvents have evaporated.

The most active attack solvent in a good cement is tetrahydrofuran (THF). THF is quite costly, so cheaper solvents contain less of it and more of such lower-cost solvents as methyl ethyl ketone and cyclohexanone.

Most solvent cements contain all three of these solvents in varying degrees.

Because cost can be so affected by the generous use of THF, quality can sometimes be judged by price. But you can be assured of quality if you buy the whole system—pipes, fittings, and solvent cements—from the same firm. Besides using materials designed to work together, you'll have one responsible organization to deal with should you have complaints. Otherwise, one manufacturer may blame another's product.

Another caution: Keep the cement can capped as much as practical. Screw the cap down snugly or at least enough to mesh the threads. The solvents in all cements evaporate quickly when exposed to air. That's one of the criteria for a good cement. But if too much solvent evaporates, there may not be enough left to soften a joint's mating surfaces properly.

Evaporation also makes a cement thicken in the can. If a solvent cement thickens so it will not pour, get a fresh can. Don't try to thin it, even with a cleaner-primer; these have different formulations. And never mix an old, thickened cement with a fresh, properly constituted one. Ordinarily, a solvent cement will keep for a number of years if evaporation is prevented.

Yellowing of solvent cement in the can indicates aging. CPVC cements are especially affected. There's no problem as long as the solvent will pour readily. But if a solvent cement turns rusty or dark brown, it's useless.

Temperature also affects solvent cements. Most are formulated to work best at, or near, room temperature. In really hot weather, they tend to dry too quickly; in icy temperatures they may set too slowly. There are special hot- and cold-weather cements, with high-temperature limits of about 90° F and low-temperature limits of 40. Even a normal solvent cement may be used beyond these limits if conditions are allowed for. In hot weather, work more quickly. In cold weather, allow for more holding and curing times.

When you've finished the last joint on a solvent-welded pressurized-water-supply system, wait a half hour or longer if possible. Then flush water through the system without pressurizing it. To do this, make sure that all outlets, such as faucets, are fully open. Open the main valve slightly to let water flow slowly into the new system. As water reaches the lowest outlet, it will begin flowing out there. Adjust this faucet to a steady trickle. Move through the house, adjusting each flowing outlet in turn. The trickles of water will dissolve and carry away any solvent vapors left within the piping system. This trick also expedites curing of the cement and helps purge the system of tastes and odors.

Aften ten minutes of trickling, shut the main valve completely for a half hour. Reopen it a crack for another ten minutes of trickling, then repeat once again.

Finally, pressurize the system by fully turning on the main valve. Flush out any debris from each faucet by opening it fully, then closing it. Don't forget to flush toilets, too.

If you've followed Ken Pepper's simple solvent-welding tips, you need never worry about leaks—even if you've been less than perfect at it. As Pepper says, "A good solvent cement is very forgiving"—*Richard Day.*

Matching plastic plumbing with cement

Material	ABS cement	Styrene cement	PVC cement	CPVC cement	All-purpose cement
ABS	■		■		■
Styrene		■	■		■
PVC			■		■
CPVC				■	■

How much cement you'll need

Pipe size (in.)	Approx.* no. of joints per pint of cement
½	255
¾	170
1½	68
2	38
3	30
4	21

*Varies with user and cement type

There's a cement for almost every kind of plastic pipe, and some are versatile enough to work with most plastics (see chart, above left). But these are often more expensive. Consider two factors when picking a solvent: attacking power and duty (temperature resistance). A cement designed to work with ABS—a plastic with low resistance to solvent attack—won't be able to handle PVC pipe. Nor will that cement be able to withstand the high temperatures and pressures that a CVPC pipe may be subjected to. But a CVPC cement could certainly weld ABS. If your project uses two kinds of piping, you might find it simpler to use a higher-rated cement, despite the added expense. Use the table above (right) to estimate how much cement to buy. Remember that applicators can't be used interchangeably with different-size pipes.

air tools

Pro mechanics and trades people long have flexed pneumatic muscles. Why shouldn't you too enjoy the benefits of air tools? They're lighter and generally more maneuverable than electrics of the same power. Air-vane motor power is more controllable. An air tool is unharmed by overloading, even by a dead stall. And it seldom overheats. Besides all this, you'll find air tools that you can't duplicate as electrics. And to make the switch still more attractive, prices of do-it-yourself air tools have been dropping. Here's a complete rundown on air tools: what's available, what they do, and what they cost.

If you have a suitable air compressor—piston type of ½ hp or preferably more, with air tank and pressure regulator—you're on the way to assembling an air-tool shop. That's the big cookie. (If you're starting from scratch, we'll give you tips on compressor selection later on.)

Two kinds of air tools

As you shop, you'll find two types of tools: air power and pressure. One type of air-power tool uses an air-vane motor: Air expanding between two vanes turns a rotor. Gearing and other mechanical action provide rotary or reciprocating action. Air-power tools can also be piston powered, with a piston, cylinder, and valve—much like a steam engine. An air-pressure tool does its work like a spray gun, blowing something out along with the air.

Air drill. This is perhaps the number-one ambassador of air tools. Super lightweight and with an infinitely variable trigger throttle, it does any job handled by an electric drill—but better. The drill's trigger instantly varies drill speed and power from a creep to full bore. Maximum torque is always available even at stall.

To experience the control of an air tool, start a drill bit without center-punching first. With an electric the expected happens: The bit wanders away from your mark. But with an air drill you start so slowly and smoothly that the drill makes its own start-up hole, right on target.

Paint spray gun. If you already

have a compressor outfit, it's likely a paint spray gun came with it. The $35 convertible bleeder/nonbleeder, internal-mix/external-mix, siphon-feed/pressure-feed spray gun that comes with many compressors is great for around-the-house painting in enamels and latexes.

A bleeder spray gun, used only with a tankless air compressor, emits air continuously from the air supply. Nonbleeders emit air only when you pull the trigger. They are used with an air line and air-storage tank. An internal-mix spray gun blends air and paint inside the gun's nozzle, while an external-mix blends outside the nozzle. The internal-mix gun is best for slow-drying paints; the external-mix is best for fast-drying ones. Siphon feeding is used to break up hard-to-atomize paints like lacquers. Pressure feeding lets the gun lay on more material quickly, as you'd want for house painting.

A convertible gun, while it can be changed to suit a variety of paints and projects, lacks the finesse to put down a really smooth finish. For fine finishes on cars or furniture, use a top-of-the-line, $100-plus, external-mix spray gun. Such guns are built

with the quality, controls, and size for professional work.

Hammer-chisel. An air hammer-chisel is just the ticket for muffler and body/fender work. Long, arm-tiring hammering sessions are compressed into a few seconds by the hammer-chisel's piston-delivered blows—some 2,000 a minute. A small packet of bits will handle a large packet of projects. These include nut busting, dent pulling, riveting, metal forming, slitting, and pipe splitting. Get the longest-bodied air hammer-chisel you can afford. Unhappily, the economy-priced $39.95 unit we purchased had such a short stroke as to be practically useless. The farther the piston moves, the harder the bit will strike.

Safe use of an air hammer-chisel calls for adequate eye protection. And when installing or removing a bit, always disconnect the tool from its air source. Accidental triggering would send the bit flying. Likewise, always firmly install the bit retainer before connecting the gun back to its air.

Die grinder. If you do much precise grinding or polishing on such things as auto-engine cylinder-head ports and valve reliefs, cleaning tight welds, or pipe deburring, the ultra-

Automobile-engine cylinder-head port is polished with an air-powered die grinder.

high-rpm die grinder is for you. Wailing happily at 23,000 rpm, the die grinder spins ¼-inch-shank cutting bits and burrs as well as polishing cones. Just be sure that the bits you use can withstand the high rpm. A shattering stone scatters its pieces with high velocity.

Needle scaler. Another metal-working tool is the needle scaler. It does much the same job as a sand-blaster, but doesn't scatter abrasives. A needle scaler will scour the rust out of extremely irregular surfaces. It works with an internal piston, as on an air hammer-chisel. But with the scaler, a set of hard metal needles is shot onto the work at up to 5,500 times a minute. The needles conform to whatever shape is there, chipping the surface away to something solid. Needle scalers are great for removing graffiti from masonry buildings or for autoshop and welding work. They do leave the surface rough, however.

Air wrenches. These are the most basic of air-powered tools. Handiest of all is the compact ⅜-inch-drive impacter. You'll love it. Small enough to fit the palm of your hand, it packs up to 75 foot-pounds of torque, enough for most jobs around the house and garage. A two-way butterfly throttle lets you tighten or loosen, depending on which way you press it. A wide assortment of sockets and screwdrivers and other accessories is available. All should be of tough impact design.

The ⅜-inch impact wrench will not handle big jobs such as car-engine cylinder-head bolts or wheel lugs. For these you need a ½-inch impacter that will twist 200 foot-pounds and more.

The air ratchet is another handy air wrench. Since it does not impact, it transfers torque to the user. This is actually a help in judging how tight the fastener is getting. An air ratchet can also be used to hand-tighten a fastener that has been run down under air power. Impact hardware need not

Air tools displayed at right were purchased for less than $50 apiece. (If you're planning heavy use, it's best to pay a little more.) The tools are: (1) dual-action random orbital-disc sander; (2) ratchet socket wrench; (3) die grinder; (4) grease gun; (5) ⅜-inch drill; (6) tire-inflater chuck; (7) blowgun; (8) ⅜-inch palm-sized impact wrench; (9) hammer-chisel with bit; (10) engine-cleaning tool; (11) sandblasting gun; (12) ½-inch impact wrench; (13) caulking gun; (14) hammer-chisel bits; (15) orbital-pad sander; (16) air compressor.

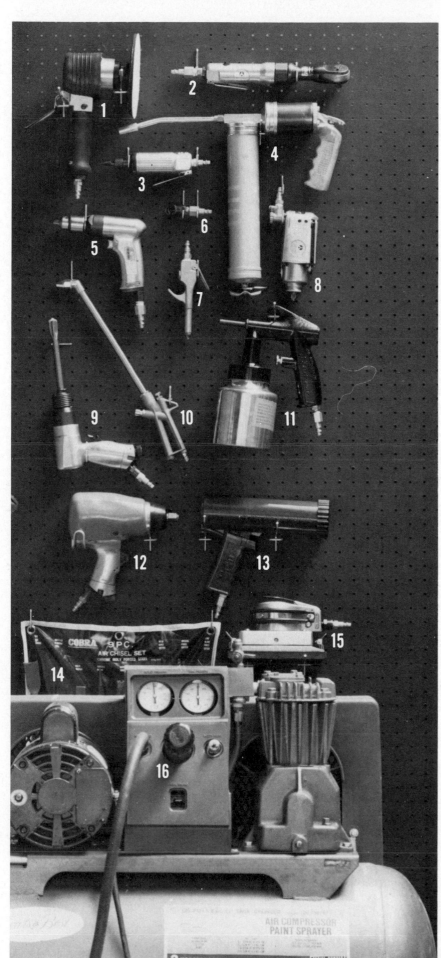

Swimming-pool repair in water—hazardous with electric drill—is safe with air-powered tool. Hose reaches from compressor, wheeled to pool-side for use.

Sandblasting gun has innumerable uses around the house and garage. Here it's used to clean oil-fouled spark plugs. Protect your face, hands, and lungs.

Needle scaler has hardened-steel captive needles at business end. Needles vibrate against the work to remove heavily encrusted paint and rust in corners.

Artist's airbrush is handy tool for spraying small amounts of paint. Stenciling rig shown was fed from CO_2 bottle with regulator and gauges for on-off use.

Sandpaper polishing cone is one of many useful die-grinder options. Cone threads onto its arbor and stays until removed. Layers of paper extend cone life.

be purchased; use the air ratchet with standard sockets.

Grease gun. An air-powered grease gun is made for those who do their own auto-lube work. It will take only a few lube jobs to save the tool's under-$35 cost. An air greaser takes the standard 14½-ounce cartridges of various types of grease. It also accepts bulk grease loads, though you'll get greasy loading it. The gun pumps out grease at up to 9,000 psi.

Air sanders. If you're involved in auto-body/fender work or furniture finishing, look at the nifty air sanders you can use. Most basic is the orbital-pad sander, sometimes called a finishing sander but also great for rough sanding and feather-edging. The air model easily tops electrics. It's so small you can do single-handedly what you'd want both hands for with an electric model.

Another air sander that some in auto-body repair prefer is the ran-

dom-orbital-disc sander, also called a dual-action (DA) sander. Fitted with a 7- or 9-inch sanding pad and disc, it not only spins as a normal sander does, but moves the pad laterally to create a random-orbital finish. The uses for it are the same as for the orbital-pad sander, though it's heavier and harder to control. You probably wouldn't need both sanders.

The air disc sander is great for grinding down old paint, removing rust, and preparing metal for painting. It thrives on tough going. And if you make a set of progressively smaller pads, you can use sanding discs right down to the nubbins.

Caulking gun. The homeowner who has suffered forearm fatigue from working with cold, balky caulk will appreciate the air-powered caulking gun. It's a low-ticket air tool costing about $15. Air power takes the strain out of applying caulks, sealants, and adhesives from the fa-

miliar 11-ounce drop-in cartridges.

Trades tools. In addition to the most popular air tools, you'll find a number of more specialized ones, such as air nailers and staplers, used in the building trades. Most often these are supplied with pressurized gas from a high-pressure portable tank with gauge and regulator. The tank, with a short hose, is carried near the work site. Tank-filling, once you have the tank, costs little, considering how far a tank goes. These tools may also be supplied by an air compressor.

Air-pressure tools

Some air tools do not develop torque or impact power; they spray. For use with an air-storage tank, all of these should be of the nonbleeder type—that is, air flows only when you trigger the tool.

Sandblaster. This is one of the foremost air-pressure tools. Once you have it you'll wonder how you got

In-line oiler fitted to inlet of air tool meters small amounts of lubricating oil as tool is used. Cost is about $12. Oil from the device may contaminate some finishes.

Air-supply hose with swivel head is called a whip; it lets tool work in tight spots. This $12 model is fitted with quick-coupling male adapter and control valve.

along without it for scouring off rust, removing paint, etching glass, cleaning concrete (great for graffiti), and texturing wood, among other things. You can also use a sandblasting gun to spray liquids, though a paint spray gun works better for this. The sandblast gun throws a stream of silica sand or other abrasive at whatever you aim it. The sand is held in a quart cup or a larger accessory hopper. (Air use is increased slightly with the hopper.) The gun sells for $30 to $40.

Depending on grit used—No. 30 is average—the texture of the parts being sandblasted can be varied from cat-tongue rough to silverware smooth. Mandatory equipment for sandblasting is face mask, gloves, and dust respirator.

Bleeder-type sandblast guns can usually be converted to nonbleeder operation in a few minutes; the same is true for conversion between pressure- and siphon-feed tools. With

pressure feeding you get more sand; with siphon feeding, less. As with sandpaper, high grit numbers become progressively finer. You can buy aluminum oxide grit for heavy sandblasting jobs; glass beads give metal, wood, and glass a fine polish.

Cleaning gun. A different sort of spray gun is the cleaning gun, or engine cleaner. Cost is under $30. While air flows through, a siphon tube brings up solvent, such as degreaser, from a container on the floor. The solvent may be nothing more than diesel fuel or soapy water. One of the mix-with-paint-thinner degreasers is ideal for degreasing car engines, lawnmowers, and such. These are low enough in cost to spray with some abandon. You rinse with water from a garden hose.

Pressure washer. Another kind of spray cleaner works directly with a garden hose. Air pressure speeds hose water from the tool, as though you

were using a ten-cent-a-minute jet-spray, carwash tool. The pressurized water encourages dirt and grime to let go, and some units have a built-in detergent dispenser. Pressure washers cost $80 and more, but they have many uses around the house and garage, so one might pay off faster than you'd think.

Blowgun. This is a superuseful tool. It cannot be topped for shop dusting. You can use a blowgun for drying parts, blowing out pipes, getting leaves out of a boat, overhauling a typewriter, and much more. For all its simplicity, a blowgun is among the most dangerous of air tools.

The problem is that high air-line pressure, when fed through the tiny blowgun nozzle, builds physically damaging pressures, especially if held in contact with the body.

Modern blowguns are safer. Some have side relief holes that let air escape without harm when the outlets are blocked. The newest ones prevent air outlet contact with the body. Some, such as the Safe-T-Blow, employ the COANDA effect for safer, more efficient operation.

You can increase the safety of the old-style blowgun by regulating its air pressure to 30 psi. But this will reduce the effectiveness of the air stream.

Tire inflater. The tire-inflater chuck is the cheapest of all air tools. If you have a compressor, you probably already have one. You can put air into anything that has a Schrader valve and some things that do not. With a basketball needle and pressure gauge, it enables you to pressurize tires, balls, and air mattresses (use care to avoid rupture). Air chucks are available in plastic or brass, long or short.

The list of air tools on these pages will give you ideas of what other air tools are available.

Air-tool accessories

A host of accessories is available to make your air tools more useful. Some, you'll find, are more necessities than accessories.

Quick connectors. A set of quick couplers is a must for air-tool efficiency. It consists of one female master coupler with built-in air cutoff and male couplers. The master coupler installs at the end of your air hose. The ¼-inch pipe threads (or ⅜-inch in a large-air-draw installation) make a direct fit. A male coupler—with either male or female pipe threads—screws to the air inlet of each air tool.

Table A: Air tools for the home shop

Tool	Air requirement (scfm)	Pressure requirement (psi)
Artist's airbrush	1	5–50
Blowgun	1–6	30–90
Caulking gun	1–2	40–70
Circular saw	8–18	90–125
Cleaning gun	4–6	90
Die grinder	4–18	90–125
Drill (⅜-in. chuck)	4–6	90–125
Grease gun	3–4	30–150
Hammer-chisel	4–7	90–150
Impact wrench (⅜-in. drive)	2½–3	90–120
Impact wrench (½-in. drive)	3½–5	90–120
Inflater chuck (tire)	1½	60
Nailer	5–10	90
Needle scaler	3–4	90
Paint spray gun	½–11½	10–70
Polisher	20	100–125
Pressure washer	8½	40–90
Ratchet socket wrench	8½	90–125
Riveter (hydraulic)	1–2	85–110
Router	8–10	90
Sandblasting gun	2½–6	30–90
Sander (belt)	8–10	90–125
Sander (disc)	4–8	90–120
Sander (orbital pad)	4–7	90–120
Sander (random orbital disc)	2–9	40–100
Sander-filer (straight line)	6–8	90–125
Saw-file	4½–6	80–120
Screwdriver	2–6	90–120
Shears-nibbler	3½–8	90–100
Stapler	1½–6	90
Vacuum cleaner	8–10	90–125

Table B: Capacities of home-quality air compressors

Compressor size (hp)	Power	Typical voltage requirement	Typical air delivery (scfm @ 90 psi)
½	Electric	115	1.2
¾	Electric	115	1.7
1	Electric	115/230	3.7
2	Electric	230	6.0
3	Electric	230	6.2
3	Gasoline		3.5
4	Gasoline		7.5
5	Gasoline		9.5

Plugging a tool into the hose then takes only a second. It's off just as quickly.

Filter. If you do much critical paint spraying, you'll want an air-line filter. Some are made to hook to your belt as you spray. A filter prevents water and oil droplets from spoiling a paint job. Main-line tool oilers are also available, but they are not recommended.

Extra air hose. To extend the reach of your air tools, it's handiest just to wheel the compressor. But additional air hose may be desirable. It should be at least 5/16 inch to prevent excessive pressure drop between compressor and tool, especially on high-draw air tools. Even the 3/8-inch-I.D. air hose is not too big for good air flow. You should try to hold air-line pressure drop to 5 psi or, at most, 10 psi. Handiest hose of all is the self-coiling type, available in 1/4 and 3/8 inch. Flexible whip hoses, sometimes used at each tool, are 1/4 inch, but only a couple of feet long. If you need a longer reach, it's better to use extra air hoses.

Portable air tank. This is another handy accessory. Usually with about 9-gallon capacity, it fills and holds air via a Schrader valve. The tank often comes with a pressure gauge and short hose with tire chuck. An air tank may be filled by your compressor or by the local service station's air hose. (Unless you're a good customer, better ask first.) Unfortunately, a portable tank does not contain enough air to change a flat tire with an impact wrench. This proves a strain even for a 20-gallon compressor tank full of air. A 9-gallon portable tank sells for under $40.

Compressor basics

The basic air compressor for use with air tools comes with motor, 12- or 20-gallon lightweight or heavy-duty ASME storage tank, tank-pressure gauge, adjustable pressure regulator with gauge, safety blowoff valve, and pressure switch with automatic unloader. It should be capable of producing at least 90 psi or, better yet, 120 psi and up.

Other compressor considerations are horsepower and air delivery in standard cubic feet per minute (scfm). Typical horsepower figures for a homeowner-style air compressor range from 1/2 to 5. Most likely, the one you need falls between those extremes, say 1 or 2 hp. As for scfm, compressor output should match the air use of the heaviest-drawing, con-

tinuous-use air tool you expect to use. Sprayers, sanders, drills, and hammer-chisels are considered continuous-use air tools. Others, such as impact wrenches, rest between uses and should not be scfm determiners.

As you might guess, a compressor's air delivery depends on its horsepower. Delivery also depends on compressor efficiency. And because air delivery drops as pressure increases, scfm for compressors are given at two pressures, typically 40 and 90 psi.

To tell what size compressor you need, look up the scfm figures for your largest-drawing, continuous-use air tool in Table A and go to Table B to see what compressor is needed. Also double-check the scfm and horsepower figures on the actual compressor you plan to purchase. The figures given may not apply specifically to a compressor. In Table A the scfm ranges allow for various makes and sizes of air tools.

You may find that a 1-hp (3-hp gasoline) compressor will handle your needs. Expect to pay $250 to $400. However, a larger 2-hp (4-hp gasoline) unit will do a better job. It costs $350 to $550. There are few air tools the higher-hp models will not handle. When in doubt, go for the larger compressor. Playing catch-up with a too small air compressor is maddening. A larger tank is no help, either. It merely forestalls the wait.

Air-tool maintenance

Install your compressor where it will not draw in dust produced by air-tool use. That will help lengthen its life. Follow the manufacturer's instructions on electrical wiring, lubrication, and maintenance.

Air-powered tools need one drop of fine oil every day they're used. It's amazing how many mechanics like Marvel Mystery Oil for this. Special air-tool oil, light machine oil, or automatic-transmission fluid also may be used. Put the drop into the tool's air inlet after each daily use, then store it so the oil will run down into the air-vane motor. Wipe off the outside of the tool regularly, too. Air-pressure tools, such as sandblasters, need no oiling.

Here's a Catch-22 of tools. Air sanders used on surfaces to be painted should not be oiled if you wish to avoid heavy degreasing. Yet if you don't oil them, they'll eventually freeze up and have to be junked or repaired. The answer is either very light oiling so that no excess oil bleeds from the tool's exhaust ports—

a neat trick if you can do it—or using a National orbital-pad sander, which seems to run indefinitely without oiling.

When you shop for air tools, you'll find three qualities available: industrial, professional, and do-it-yourself. Forget industrial quality unless you really need air tools so well built that they cost more than $300 each. These tools are built to standards beyond what you'd need for use at home. They're made to run continuously while supplied with proper line-oiling and designed to be fully serviceable. Furthermore, many are significantly heavier than home and shop tools, since they are intended for counterweighted support from above when in use. Instead, select air tools from either professional or do-it-yourself quality.

Lots of pro-quality air-power tools sell for $75 to $100. If you want good service and can afford to spend the money, go for these. They are lightweight and are designed for auto-mechanic and trades use under tough but not continuous service. They feature serviceable design, quality materials, and careful workmanship, provide plenty of power for fast working, and may be repaired when necessary.

But if you're on a budget, the do-it-yourself-quality air-powered tools at $50 and even less will get you into air most easily. These tools are practically all imported, built to sell at low price. While they, too, may be repaired, the best bet is to discard and replace them when they give up. In occasional use, if you're lucky, some of the better ones may last you a lifetime—*Tom Wilson* and *Richard Day.*

FOR FURTHER INFORMATION

Black and Decker Mfg. Co., Towson, MD 21204; Campbell-Hausfeld, Harrison, OH 45030 (paperback book recently published at $5 postpaid covers compressors and air tools in depth); Chicago Pneumatic Tool Co., 2200 Bleecker St., Utica, NY 13501; Executive Trading Co., P.O. Box 35558, Los Angeles, CA 90035; Ingersoll-Rand Co., Tool and Hoist Div., 28 Kennedy Blvd., East Brunswick, NJ 08816 (industrial-quality tools, but huge selection); Jet Engineering Co., Inc. (blowguns), 5406 Coal Ave., S.E., Albuquerque, NM 87108. **Montgomery Ward and Co.**, 619 West Chicago Ave., Chicago, IL 60607; **National-Detroit Inc.**, P.O. Box 2285, Rockford, IL 61111; **J.C. Penney Co., Inc.**, 1301 Avenue of the Americas, New York, NY 10019; **Rockwell International**, Power Tools Div., Suite 600, Popular Towers, 6263 Popular Ave., Memphis, TN 38138; **Rodac Corp.**, 1005 East Artesia Blvd., Carson, CA 90746; **Sears Roebuck and Co.**, Sears Tower, Chicago, IL 60684; **Silvo Hardware Co.**, 2205 Richmond St. Philadelphia, PA 19125; **Skil Corp.**, 5033 Elston Ave., Chicago, IL 60630; **Snap-On Tools Co.**, 8028-28th Ave., Kenosha, WI 53140; **U.S. General Supply Corp.**, 100 Commercial St., Plainview, NY 11803; **J.C. Whitney and Co.**, P.O. Box 8410, Chicago, IL 60680.

computerized drill press

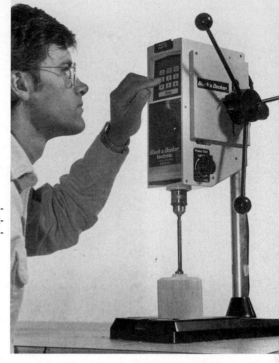

Control panel includes the push-button plate barely visible LED display.

What do you get when you combine a tiny computer chip with a 3.3-amp variable-speed motor, then add a chuck, housing, and base? The Black & Decker Electronic Drill Press—the first computerized tool for the home shop and priced at $180 to $200. Here's what I found out when I tested the tool: You and the computer communicate through a touch-sensitive control panel and an LED readout screen. At the touch of a finger you select drilling speed, set drilling depth, or ask the tool to give you rpm or depth readouts *as you drill*.

Let's go through a typical shop operation and see how all this works. Say you want to drill a ¾-inch-diameter hole in a wooden chair seat for the leg. The seat is 1 inch thick, and you want the hole ¾ inch deep.

First you position the work on the drill-press base and clamp it in place. Then lower the bit until it touches the work. Press the SET DEPTH key. You have now set the computer to the zero point for this particular job. The LED display will read 0.000.

Now check the speed-selection chart on the side of the drill press. For a ¾-inch hole in wood, it tells you to put the tool's power shift knob in the HEAVY DUTY position and press speed selector key 5. Turn the power shift knob counterclockwise until the arrow points down. Press 5.

The drill press will start running, accelerating smoothly up to speed to avoid jolting your work out of position. Slowly feed the bit into the work. The computer feeds power to the motor according to load, helping to keep rpm constant. At the same time, it displays the depth of the hole continuously in 0.02-inch increments. When the readout reaches 0.74 inches (there is no 0.75 because it's an odd hundredths number), stop drilling.

If, for any reason, you want to check drill speed as you bore, simply press the DISPLAY RPM key. Then the rpm will appear on the display. Touch the DISPLAY DEPTH key and the depth readout will reappear. When you want to stop the press, touch the STOP key.

While the controls may sound complicated, they're really simple. The control panel, for example—keys and all—is made of a single sheet of plastic, perfectly sealed against dust and dirt. The speed selection and display command keys are fairly stiff; there's little chance of starting the press accidentally. The STOP key, on the other hand, is sensitive, so you can shut things down quickly.

You'll rarely need to, however. The computer has some logic circuits that protect both you and the tool itself. Say you overfeed the bit while drilling metal, and the bit breaks through and binds. The computer will automatically shut the motor off and display error code "D" (instantaneous stall) on the LED panel. The motor will not start again until you depress the desired speed selector key.

If you try to start the press without removing the key from the chuck and placing it in its special holding pocket on the drill-press head, the motor will not start and the LEDs will display error code L.

SPECIFICATIONS

Max. diameter of workpiece	10⅞"
Quill travel	2.90"
Rpm range	400–2,700
Max. depth (chuck to base)	8¾"
Drilling capacity (wood)	¾" dia.
Drilling capacity (metal)	⅜" dia.
Chuck type	⅜" geared
Motor	3.3 amps, double insulated
Depth control	Visual according to readouts, or automatic by stop collar

Should you overload the tool until the motor overheats, the LEDs will begin flashing the code LOAD. At this point, you should press speed selector key 6 and allow the motor to run unhindered at full speed until it cools off and the LOAD display stops flashing.

To test this feature, I put a squeeze-type wooden brake on the chuck and tightened it until the motor overheated. The LOAD display appeared and stayed on for exactly 30 seconds while the motor cooled.

The computer can also help you avoid mistakes. If you release the quill feed handle after drilling a hole and let the quill snap sharply back to the raised position, you may jolt the depth sensor off its zero point. If so, the readout will display error code "p," warning you to reset to zero.

All this electronic wizardry is more than flash. The tool works, and it works well. The chuck runs smooth and true, with none of the wobble I've seen in some other small drill presses. The depth readouts are easy to read and dead accurate. To check them, I drilled a piece of wood with a brad-point bit until the tip barely broke through. I noted the depth readout, then drilled several more holes to the same reading. Each matched the depth of the first hole.

To check the motor's ability to maintain a constant speed under load, I chucked an oversize Powerbore bit in the press and fed it quickly into various types of wood, watching the rpm readout as I bored. A fast feed rate could cut motor speed about 200 rpm, but that's not bad. Only when I used a 1¼-inch spade bit in oak could I seriously bog down the motor. Remember, however, that a spade bit of that size is well over the maximum capacity of a tool this size (see table above).

Complaints? I have a few. The head is difficult to raise on the column. The handle on the chuck key hits the drill-press head, so you can't turn it a full 360 degrees. You have to be very careful to turn the power shift knob firmly into the LIGHT DUTY position or you will be greeted by a loud grinding of gears—A. J. Hand.

power screwdriving

W hy use a screw when a nail will do? That used to be my basic rule for choosing fasteners. Today that rule has changed 180 degrees.

The reason? Power screwdrivers. Once you start using them, you just don't want to drive nails anymore. Picture this:

You want to fasten two boards. You grab your power driver and slip a screw onto its bit. Holding the work with your left hand, you press the screw into position with your right hand and squeeze a trigger. In the time it takes to swing a hammer three times, the screw is driven into place, countersunk neatly below surface. No banged fingers, no hammer dents in your work.

"Wait a minute," you say. "That sounds too easy. You forgot to predrill and countersink for that screw."

The fact is, with a power screwdriver and the right screw, you often don't have to predrill or countersink. And a screw has much more holding power than a nail, looks better than a nail, and can be removed just as easily as it is driven.

But don't dash out—yet—to get a power driver. There's more than one way to drive a screw with power. The true power screwdriver is the fastest and most convenient tool. But you can also do very well with a good ⅜- or ¼-inch, variable-speed, reversing drill. And today's cordless electric drills are surprisingly effective, too. Which is best for you? Let's take a look at each.

True power drivers

These are commercial-grade tools made for professionals. But if you drive a lot of screws, you might like one. What sets them apart from the other tools is a combination of speed, power, and convenience features. The Milwaukee Screw-Shooter (photo right) is a good example. It has a top

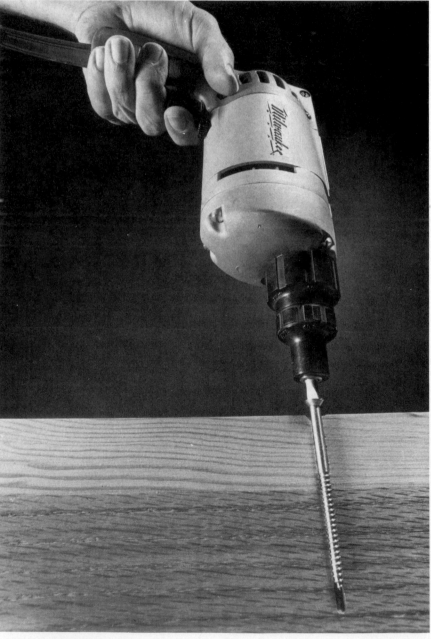

Power drivers like the Milwaukee shown here are designed for heavy-duty work. They can easily drive a No. 16 screw into softwood without a pilot hole.

speed of 1,000 rpm and a 4.5-amp motor with enough power to sink a No. 16 screw into softwood without the need for a predrilled hole.

Unlike a drill, it has no chuck. Driver bits snap into a simple holder for quick changes without the need for a key. The tool also has a positive-drive clutch. Press the driver against the screw and the clutch engages, turning the bit. Release the pressure and the bit stops turning.

Combine this clutch with an adjustable depth-sensing nosepiece, and you can drive screws automatically to a preset depth. Once that depth is reached the clutch disengages. This is convenient if you want to drive a lot of screws to uniform depth in a hurry.

The positive-drive clutch is best for general home and shop work, but for driving a lot of sheet-metal screws, a tool with a torque-release clutch is more convenient. You set it to release at a given level of torque. This lets you make sure the screw is driven up tight, but not so tight that the head twists off.

Prices for a basic power driver with positive-drive clutch start at around $120. An adjustable, depth-sensing nosepiece might bring the price up to $140 or so. For home use, there's no sense in going much higher than that.

Variable-speed drills

Most of these have enough power to drive screws without predrilling. Overall, they are almost as good at driving screws as true power drivers. They lack some of the conveniences, but make up for the lack in other ways.

Example: Drills have chucks instead of snap-in bit holders. That makes bit-changing a little slower. But it also gives the drill more uses than just driving screws.

Chucks have another advantage, I have discovered. Now and then, while driving a screw, you will twist its head off. With a variable-speed drill, you can simply tighten the chuck over the shaft of the broken screw and back it out. You can't do that with a power screwdriver.

True, variable-speed drills don't have clutches. But in my experience you can get by without them. A clutch is convenient when teamed with a depth-sensing nosepiece, but otherwise it is of no real advantage. A good

Cordless drills are the most convenient way to drive with power, but they are not designed for heavy, continuous work. Clockwise from left: Skil 2016, Black & Decker 9082, Skil 2003, JC Penney 0032.

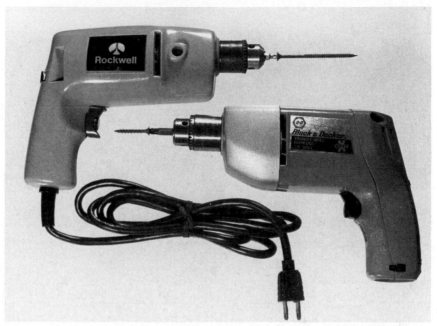

Variable-speed, reversible ⅜-inch drills such as the Rockwell 4150 and Black & Decker 7156 (above) will drive screws nearly as well as power drivers.

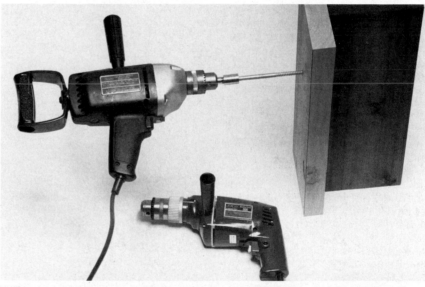

Half-inch, variable-speed drills such as the Sears and Skil Xtra-tool (above) have enough power to drive lag screws if you first drill a pilot hole in the work.

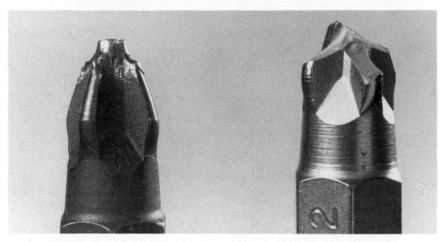

Extra drivers to keep on hand: Common, soft-tempered type (left) wears quickly if abused. Hardened, snap-in type (right) won't wear easily but can often break.

variable-speed trigger gives all the control you need without a clutch.

My advice: If you want to drive a lot of screws fast, get a power driver with a depth-sensing nosepiece. It will speed your work and hold up longer than a variable-speed drill. Otherwise, a ⅜-inch variable-speed, reversing drill will do the job well for about one-third the cost.

Cordless drills

I have to admit I was skeptical about the ability of these tools to drive screws when I first got them. But they soon won me over. Cordless drills are not as fast or as powerful as the tools mentioned so far, but they're awfully convenient. I now keep one fitted out with a driver bit at all times and rarely use an ordinary, manual screwdriver anymore.

All four of the cordless drills I tested have the power and capacity to tackle typical household tasks. Using the Skil 2003, for example, I drove a 2-inch screw into pine seventy-five times—without predrilling—and removed it seventy-five times, as well. The tool was still going strong. If the batteries run out, two of the drills (JC Penney 0032 and Skil 2016 Boar Gun) recharge in an hour. The Boar Gun also has snap-in power packs. With a pair of these you should never be without power. The Skil 2003 recharges in three hours and the Black & Decker in sixteen.

All four tools are reversible, but not all are variable-speed. The Skil 2003 and JC Penney drills each have a two-speed trigger. Pull the trigger partway back and it gives you 100 rpm. Pull it all the way back and it gives 300. In practice, this system works as well as true variable speeds.

The low speed is slow enough to give you the control you need to start a screw or snug it up. And 300 rpm is fast enough to drive a screw home in two or three seconds.

Most interesting of the cordless drills is the Skil Boar Gun. It has a variable-speed trigger plus a two-speed "gear shift." In the low range you get 0 to 250 rpm and the highest torque of any of the cordless drills. In the high range you get 0 to 750 rpm and the highest speed.

I wouldn't use any of these cordless tools for heavy-duty, all-day driving, but for casual around-the-house work they're my favorites.

Choosing screws

If you're going to drive screws with power, it pays to use the right screws. Ordinary screws just don't make it. For efficient power driving you need screws with Phillips or Robertson (square drive) heads—screws that will slip into a screwdriver bit and stay there. They won't fall off as long as you keep the tool horizontal or pointed upward.

Magnetic bit holders are also available. These transfer their magnetism to the bit, and will hold a screw in place in any position. The socketlike nature of the heads also helps to keep the screw in line with the bit, pointed wherever you point the driver.

All this makes it very easy to start a screw, even with one hand and no pilot hole. That's something you just can't do with slot-head screws, even if you use a bit designed with a collarlike "finder."

Phillips bits are also unlikely to slip off a screw and damage your work. I have power-driven hundreds of Phillips screws and never had the

driver dig up my work. That frequently happens when I'm working with slotted screws.

Screws for power driving must also be tougher than the average screw. The best types are case-hardened: Their heads won't twist off or strip. Both of these problems are fairly common especially if you don't usually predrill the holes in your work.

Hardened Phillips or Robertson screws are most easily available as so-called "drywall screws." A good builder's-supply outlet should have them in lengths from 1 to 3 inches. Some of the more specialized screws can often be located by looking under "screws" in the Yellow Pages. If you can't find screws locally, write to Nutty Co., 135 Main St., Derby, CT 06418, or Equality Screw Co., Box 1296, El Cajon, CA 92022. These two outfits specialize in mail-order screws. My favorite screw is Equality's 2¼-inch cabinet-assembly screw. It's a good length for use with ¾-inch stock and has a self-drilling tip, which eliminates the need for a pilot hole, and a bugle head, which in most cases draws down flush without need for countersinking. Unlike some screws it is not threaded all the way up to the head. Without the threads, the head is pulled into the top workpiece by the fastening end as you tighten the screw, and your two pieces of work are drawn firmly together.

What about attachments?

In the course of preparing this article, I tested a variety of screwdriver attachments. One was a simple, positive-drive clutch you can chuck in your drill. Verdict: no good. It wobbled excessively, making it difficult to control where the screw was going. And it offered no real advantage. Anyway, you don't really need a clutch unless you want to team it up with a depth-sensing nosepiece. And those nosepieces don't work with accessory clutches.

Another common driver attachment is the speed reducer. Some work well, multiplying the torque of even a lightweight ¼-inch drill and slowing its speed down to a rate conducive to driving screws.

All of them, however, force you to use two hands to drive a screw. The cheap, plastic kind tends to break if used aggressively. The good ones, with heavy metal housings, usually cost almost as much as a ⅜-inch drill. I think you'd be happier with the drill—*A. J. Hand.*

a hotter torch

Until now, the propane torch, familiar to most do-it-yourselfers in home and shop applications, has been limited by its inability to generate and transfer sufficient heat to the work target. Various methods have been tried to improve torch performance—oxygen "pellets"; higher heating value gases, such as MAPP; and oxy-propane mixtures. Still, there were shortcomings.

With the advent of the Spitfire torch, things started looking up. It was developed using the design principles of the Turbo-torch, employed in the plumbing and heating trades since 1968. The key to the performance of the Spitfire torch is what the manufacturer calls *swirl combustion.* Here's how it works.

Propane from the supply tank is pressure controlled (automatically in the 400 models; manually in the 300 models), allowing the gas from the tank to enter the torch through a small, but precisely-sized hole (orifice). Just in front of this orifice, toward the tip, are the air intake holes. The correct amount of air is introduced at these holes by the jet-pump venturi action (a pressure less than the pressure of the surrounding atmospheric air is created by gases moving through the shaped passage—much as in your automobile carburetor). This air mixes with the gas and proceeds toward the tip through a three-bladed built-in rotor, which causes the gas/air mixture to rotate or swirl.

At this point, combustion begins. Then the hot gases expand, causing a high-velocity swirl. This acts like a centrifuge, spinning the heavier, inert gases to the outside edge. The net result: The hot, inner part of the flame is insulated and the greatest quantity of heat is concentrated right where you want it—on the work.

This heat concentration is enhanced by the stainless-steel torch tip, which will not conduct heat from the flame. Furthermore, the flame tends to wrap itself around the workpiece to heat the area more evenly.

When using a 400-model torch, keep the valve open all the way to avoid the heat working back from the tip, causing a reddish glow and eventual damage to the torch. On 300 models, as the gas leaves the supply tank, the pressure and temperature drop, requiring compensating valve adjustments.

Lighting any model is easier if you choke it slightly by partly blocking off the air intakes with your fingers. On the 400 model, the torch tip can be rotated 360 degrees on its fitting—a convenience when you're working in awkward spots. Neither torch should be used with the tank inverted.

Operations using soft 50/50 solder up to silver solder occur within the 400 to 800° F range. The Spitfire torch will handle this quite easily. Ordinary propane torches will also do these tasks—generally, more slowly. But that's where the Spitfire and or-

The Spitfire model 400 All Metal Repair Kit (right) contains all the makings: propane; regulator; small and standard torch; 50/50 solder and flux; aluminum solder and flux; brazing rods; fan spreader; heat shield; igniter. With the Spitfire torch, it doesn't take a lot of muscle to braze repair a metal chair (below).

For bench soldering or brazing, it's best to work on a noncombustible surface—for example, Transite. In photo above, we're soldering ½-inch copper.

Using the Spitfire torch, a good pipe cutter, and snips, it takes hardly any time at all to accomplish even a big task like installing a water heater.

Typical braze-repair of a metal ladder/chair is shown here. First step is to close the joint with bar clamps. Then all you have to do is apply heat and rod.

To avoid the possibility of getting burned while removing paint from surfaces, be sure to keep the torch and fan spreader ahead of your putty knife while you work.

dinary propane torches part company.

This little fellow will generate and target enough heat so that you can braze (brass solder) a fusion that occurs at 1400 to 1600° F! It won't weld; that occurs at 2800° F. But the ability to braze puts you in a different ball park. Now you can repair breaks in bike frames, lawnmower parts, barbecues, lawn furniture, auto parts, metal toys, metal chairs, and more things than we could possibly mention. You'll be able to heat and bend metal, work art metal, do metal sculpture, or heat stubborn nuts and bolts that refuse to yield to normal wrench disassembly. You'll be able to remove paint in a jiffy, using the torch and fan spreader with a putty knife; thaw frozen pipes; start barbecue fires; remove, install, and repair asphalt tiles; and repair gutters.

Perhaps one of the most interesting features of this torch is its ability to sweat-solder copper pipes and fittings without first draining out the water. However, don't forget to open all valves and faucets on the copper branch first. Otherwise, the part of the trapped water that changes to steam can damage the copper.

When brazing, never try to fill a large gap with brass. The best way to effect a good joint or repair is to keep the parts closed against each other, with clamps or other similar devices, if necessary. Make sure that all coatings, such as paint or galvanized surfaces, are scraped clean.

There are a number of accessories for the torch that are handy for jobs around the home. For example, there's a small tip, which can be screwed in to work small pieces more effectively. Also, there's a heat shield that snaps on the tip to allow you to apply sufficient heat to copper pipes and fittings without causing unneces-

When there's plumbing right next to the floor joist, you can use the heat shield, as shown above, to divert the flame. This prevents scorched woodwork and a possible fire.

Another difficult job made quick and easy: shown above is the procedure for brazing metal pipe nipples. Using Spitfire and flux-coated brass rod brazing takes just a couple of minutes.

Heat metal bars before you try to bend them. In the event that too much heat transfers to the vise, insert an asbestos insulator between the vise jaws.

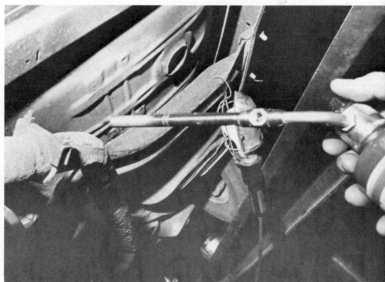

Nails and bolts on the underside of a car are often rusty. In this case, snap off the expendable pipe clamp, or when that's not possible, you can use the torch to swell the nut.

sary damage to nearby joists or studs. To distribute the heat from the tip (as opposed to a concentrated source), get the flame spreader. It's good for paint removal and thawing frozen pipes. Spare flints, sealing rings, solder, flux, and brazing rods are also a necessary part of a complete kit.

When you have a couple of repairs under your belt, you'll wonder how you ever got along without this handy torch. It's available at home and discount centers, hardware stores, and chain stores or write: Wingaersheek Inc., 2 Dearborn Road, Peabody, MA 01960—*Bernard Price*.

A little bending, a little brazing, and, in almost no time, you can create a wall sconce like the one shown here and many other decorative and useful items.

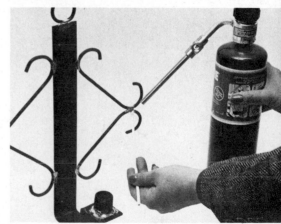

sander/stripper and specialty cutter

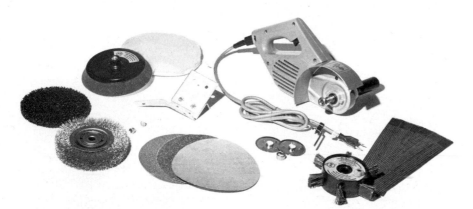

Workwheel and its accessories (left) will sharpen tools, sand flat and contoured surfaces, strip, and polish. *Below, upper row of photos:* Left: Stripping peeling paint is a lot easier with the wheel and its Flap Wheel. Center: Buffing down car wax is speedy with bonnet and cushion pad. Right: To lock or unlock shaft nut for changing accessories, insert lock pin and turn wrench. *Bottom row:* Left: Clean 'n Strip wheel (abrasive impregnated nylon) brings a rotary mower blade down to bare metal in seconds. Right: Bracket allows bolting Workwheel to bench for use as stationary sanding tool.

Black & Decker now has a pair of portable power tools designed to handle many of the tougher and more tedious jobs you're likely to come across in your shop or home maintenance work.

The Workwheel

It's normally a big chore to strip paint or rust from metal—but not if you use the Workwheel. The "wheel" does stripping jobs with a minimum mess and none of the smell and danger that go along with the use of caustic chemicals. With the wheel you can apply as light or heavy a touch as you need.

The model 7470 Workwheel can be purchased separately (about $50) or as a complete kit with accessories (model 7471; about $99). The wheel turns at two speeds, 2700 or 3400 rpm. It has a removable 6-foot power cord for easier storage, draws 6 amps, and weighs 5½ pounds. With accessories, it not only strips, but can buff and polish, sharpen tools, and sand both flat and contoured surfaces.

One accessory is the Clean 'n Strip wheel, a nylon-mesh disc impregnated with abrasive. It's mounted with a small sleeve and a pair of washers to ensure stability, concentricity, and balance. Rust, scale, and paint on metal disappear under it.

A cushion sanding pad combines a mounting nut, a thick foam body, and a slick surface. Contact adhesive-coated sanding discs may readily be attached to the pad, but should be centered by eye to minimize vibration. The semiflexible pad provides an excellent backup for the sanding disc. When bench-mounted, the pad and disc may also be used as a sharpening tool. The pad serves as body for the polishing bonnet as well.

Other accessories are the wire wheel, which needs no explanation, and the Flap Wheel, which does. This wheel is basically a cup and cover in which a supply of six abrasive strips is stored on a hub. Six "arms" of abrasive strip feed out through slits in the radial edge of the cup, where they're backed up by little brushes. As you use the Flap Wheel, the abrasive doing the work deteriorates. You can feed out new strip by rotating a knob, geared to the hub, and then starting the motor. Due to centrifugal force, the strip moves radially outward and, after the motor is stopped, the excess may be trimmed to the length of the brushes with scissors.

Also available for use with the wheel are Flap Wheel brushes; abrasive strips, both 80 grit unslashed and 120 grit slashed; and abrasive sand-ing discs in several grits for use with the cushion sanding pad.

Eye protection and, perhaps, a dust mask are important when you work with the wheel because the abrasives generate a fair amount of powdered paint, dust, wood, rust, and scale. Always unplug the tool when changing accessories, and be sure to remove the locking pin when you're done—before starting up again.

We found the Workwheel easy to use with the rear grip and side post for balance and control. The two-speed trigger was properly positioned and functioned well.

Changing accessories was no problem, with one minor exception—the lock nut in the Flap Wheel bore is a little low and, when all the way down, requires extra muscle on the wrench. Results with all accessories were excellent. And the wheel is light enough to allow extended use without tiring the user.

Rotary cutter

You can operate the Model 7975 Rotary Power Cutter with one hand. The business end consists of hardened steel, self-feeding cutting blades (wheels), so you never have to force the tool forward. You simply depress the variable speed trigger until you reach the rate of speed you desire.

For blind (notch-shaped) cuts, use the reversing switch to back out before starting the remaining cuts. This switch is handy if you should experience a slight jam up (we didn't). Incidentally, the switches are located so the index finger can be on the trigger while the thumb is on the reversing switch, all without moving your hand from its grip on the machine.

Never force the tool through a serious jam up. You know when one occurs—there's a clackety-clack noise from the clutch drive as it does its work to protect the cutter from damage. When you hear the noise, shut off the cutter, back it out, and start again.

The cutter is designed to cut many—but not all—materials. It can be used, for example, on fiberglass cloth and insulation, carpet and padding, vinyl flooring, wire screen, foam rubber, roofing paper, and sandpaper. Among the no-no's: laminated plastic, vinyl asbestos flooring, asphalt flooring, plywood paneling, Lucite, Masonite, and Styrofoam. It's a good idea to keep the provided list handy; the list also gives maximum thickness of material that the cutter can wade through. By observing the limits, you'll get years of service from the tool.

Both the Workwheel and the Rotary Cutter are available in home centers, chains, discount stores, hardware stores, and lumberyards. For more information, write: Black & Decker, Towson, MD 21204—*Bernard Price.*

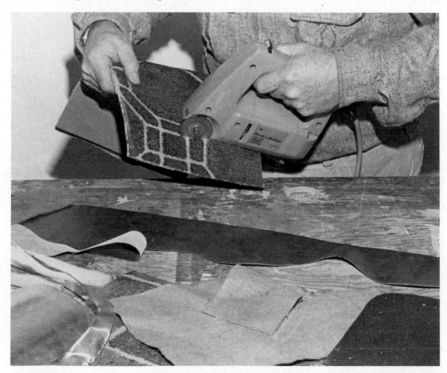

Here's Black & Decker's Rotary Power Cutter (Model 7975) zipping through some indoor-outdoor carpeting. And look at all the materials it will handle as well.

better-grip, different-twist wrenches

There was a time when the "monkey wrench" and "end wrench" were about the only items in the tool box that could be used on nuts and bolts. And they did the job, if you had the time and patience to manipulate them. They're still with us, but in different forms, together with some new wrenches that are both easier to handle and capable of handling more difficult situations.

New tools are the result of continuous evolution. The Crescent wrench (named for the Crescent Tool Company, Jameston, New York, where it was manufactured), for example, replaced the monkey wrench. End wrenches became "open end," to differentiate them from the new idea—the "box wrench." Wrench handles began to take different shapes. And along came the socket wrench, the

ratchet wrench, and dozens of aids and accessories to make all wrenches more versatile.

You can get a lot done with a couple of adjustable wrenches. The 6-inch size opens to a bit more than ¾ inch, and works in fairly close quarters. The 10-inch size, for heavier work, opens to a bit more than an inch.

In use, the adjustables handle just like open-end wrenches. There is, however, a newcomer. The *ratcheting adjustable* (made by Evans) is intended for hexagonal nuts. Set completely over the nut, it functions like a box wrench and must be lifted for each stage of the turning. However, when the wrench is handled like an open-end wrench, it grips the nut in one direction, but slips backward in the other, making a ratchet action possible. The

Below is a new combination wrench by S-K Tools — open on one end and socket on the other. Beneath that is a traditional combination wrench — open on one end, box on the other — long considered the most versatile of the nut-and-bolt tools. Both wrenches come in sets, in sizes that can handle most home jobs.

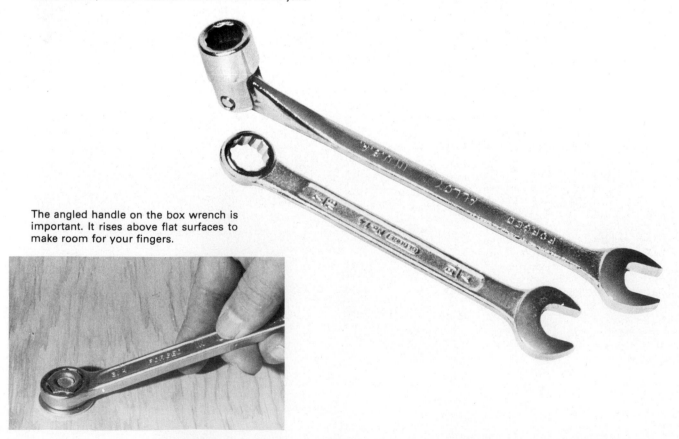

The angled handle on the box wrench is important. It rises above flat surfaces to make room for your fingers.

"swing" is about 60 degrees, which means it is not as convenient as a regular ratchet wrench. However, it is handier than a regular box or a standard open-end wrench, since it doesn't have to be lifted and reset with each turn.

You can set yourself up, also, with open-end wrenches that function exactly as the ratcheting adjustables do. A set of these wrenches costs more than a couple of adjustables, but when your nut-and-bolt activity increases, they are handier.

Combination wrenches are those with an open-end on one end of the handle and a box on the other. Normally, you use the box, but when you can't lift the wrench off the nut for a new bite, you use the open-end. This makes the wrench a little handier than either the open-end or the box.

Box wrenches have the box on both ends—two different sizes per wrench. Thus, they supplant the open-end, double-end wrench—when you can lift the tool off the nut for new bites. Box wrenches come with straight handles, with angled handles, and with offset handles. The purpose of the angled or offset tools is to make room for your fingers when you must apply the wrench on a flat surface, as might be the case lag-screwing one large-area element to another.

Any time your needs call for a lot of wrenching, sockets may be the answer. Their utility arises not only from the tight grip of the wrench on the nut, but also from the many aids and accessories that have been ingeniously invented for use with them. Add to this the range of sizes in socket wrenches (and nut drivers) from $5/64$ inch up.

Basically, the socket system is a set of sockets and a driver or handle, which is usually ratchet-engineered. Smaller socket systems may have a ¼-inch drive, medium-size sets, a ⅜-inch drive; and bigger outfits, a ½-inch drive. Do include a driver converter in your system. A tremendous convenience, it allows you to drive ¼-inch drive sockets with your ⅜-inch handle. Also, there are extensions that let you reach deep into confined areas. These range from 3 inches up to a foot or more in length. Another handy driver is one in the form of a brace (as in bit and brace) that lets you drive nuts or lag screws faster than would be possible with any standard handle.

When you set yourself up with sockets, you can **(1)** buy a tool box and fill it with sockets and drivers as you need them. Or, **(2)** buy complete sets that provide both inch and metric in ⅜-inch and ¼-inch drive. For lighter work, there are socket sets **(3)** ranging from $7/32$ inch to ½ inch. Then, add to the versatility of your tools, with **(4)** square sockets, special swivel converters, etc.

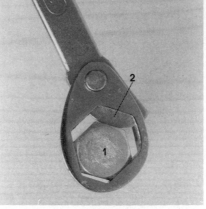
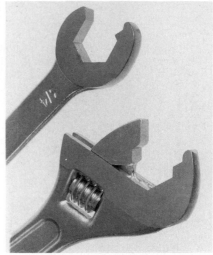

Ratcheting is no longer an operation that can be performed only with ratchet drivers. Shown at left, above, is a box wrench, by S-K Tools, mounted in a ratcheting handle — two ends, two sizes, the same as nonratcheting tools. At right, above, is a ratcheting tool by Weaver that fits several nut sizes. The nut (1) nests into the end of the wrench and the arc (2) holds it. On the backswing, the arc moves back to the next face.

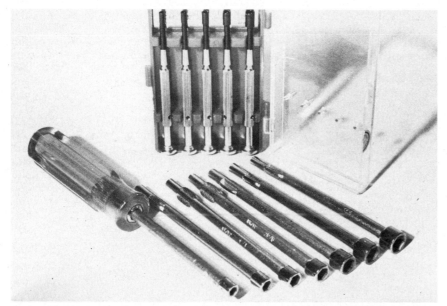
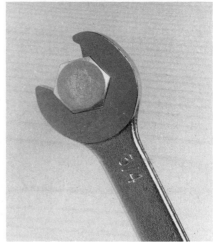

Nut-driver tool kit provides a full range of small-size sockets with a handle the shafts fit into. Handle the tools as you would a screwdriver. Shown also, a set of tiny nut drivers for work on projects that are down to jewelry size.

It's worthwhile to shop around for eccentric converters like this one from Crescent. This converter fits into the socket and is driven by a ratchet drive, but you can also use it at an angle in normal rotation when you want to guide the handle over obstacles.

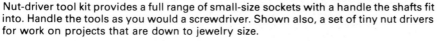
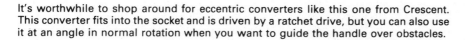
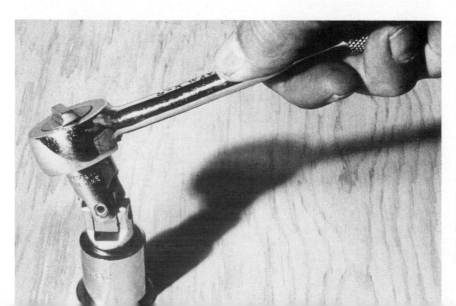

The three photos above show wrenches with unusually-shaped jaws, by Bevco Industries, 1712 S.E. Ankenny, Portland, OR 97214. In the top photo, note the jaw shapes. In the center photo, the tool serves like a box wrench. In the bottom photo, the adjustable open end can be set to permit new bites for slight turns made in tight quartoro, giving you noarly tho oapability of a ratchet wrench.

Knob-drive socket set, from S-K Tools, includes ³/₁₆-, ¼-, ⁵/₁₆-, ⅜-, ⁷/₁₆-, and ½-inch sockets, and ¼-inch drive shaft and ratcheting knob. Handy for work in close quarters. Other ¼-inch drive handles, extenders, etc., can be worked into system.

Recent entry in the wrench field is a ball-end tool that has five hex-wrench "boxes" on each end. Look for it in catalogs featuring specialty tools.

One of the new combinations of ratchet and adjustable comes from Howard Products. It's a tool that can be adjusted to fit the nut, then adjusted to drive in or loosen. The only problem is the difficulty of fitting the tool into tight quarters.

Socket sets are the simplest way to rig yourself up for the socket system of nut driving. Sets come in all three driver sizes, and usually include a special ¹³/₁₆-inch socket, intended for use on standard spark plugs.

However, it is possible—and often sensible—to buy wrench equipment a piece at a time, as the need for each size or function arises.

Two changes in the world of nuts and bolts are now in process, both of which can affect your selection of tools.

• The nut-and-bolt industry has just about completely switched to hexagonal nuts, bolts, and lag screws. This means you should be equipping yourself with hexagonal or 12-point wrenches. The 12-point tool is a little handier than the hex model, since it repeats with a 30-degree swing of the handle, while the hex socket calls for 60 degrees. This lets it work in tighter quarters.

But, while the industry is switching to hex nuts and bolts, the typical household is full of square nuts on items that might need repair work. Although an open-end or adjustable wrench will work as well on square as on hex, if you want to set yourself up with square sockets, you'd better *start shopping* because they're getting scarce.

You can use a 12-point socket or box on a square nut. However, the fit is not always close enough, and you could end up stripping the points out of the wrench or rounding the corners of the nut.

• The other significant change in progress is the seemingly inevitable switch to metric measurements. And most outlets now stock wrenches in metric sizes.

You might be able to use metric wrenches on inch-designated nuts and bolts, but not with guaranteed satisfaction. As an example, take the nut that calls for a ¾-inch socket—a perfect fit. The 19mm socket will fit over the nut, but it's a loose fit. The answer, of course, is the adjustable wrench—where it will work.

If the nut to be driven is not bigger than about ⅜ inch, the quick and easy answer may be the nut driver. It is nothing more than a screwdriverlike tool with a socket on the end, instead of a tip. The best way to set yourself up is with a complete set of nut driver sizes, all driven by a single handle into which each driver fits. The typical set ranges from ³/₁₆ inch to ⅜ inch.

Smaller than that? You can get a set of nut drivers as small as ⁵/₆₄ inch —*Jackson Hand.*

choosing door hinges

Shopping for hinges can be confusing. There seems to be an almost limitless variety of sizes and styles. And the selection of hinges at home centers and larger hardware stores is only a small portion of the types manufactured.

While special-application hinges were once available only in large sizes for industrial and commercial uses, many are now designed for home use. You might even discover some of these earlier hard-to-find hinges now displayed in blister packs; yet for many types, your hardware store will have to order them for you because there are too many types to keep in stock.

But whether you are looking for a new hinge to close a door automatically or swing it open wider, or whether you simply want to rehang a wobbly door, you still must determine the style, size, and number of hinges.

Hinge size must be matched to the width and thickness of the door. The selection of either a standard or heavyweight hinge is determined by the weight of the door; the type of bearing depends on the expected frequency of opening and closing. The required hinge height is derived from the combination of door thickness and width (see chart next page).

Determining the necessary hinge width is more complicated. You have to take into account the door thickness as well as the inset (if any), backset, and the clearance required (see drawing).

The hinge width is calculated from this formula:

Hinge width = 2 (door thickness − backset) + inset + clearance

Clearance is the distance that the door must be away from the plane of the wall in order to open a full 180 degrees and lie flat against the wall. To open fully, the door must clear the jamb casing, any raised molding on the door face, or the chair rail. If there is a perpendicular wall on the hinge side of the door and the door can open only about 90 degrees, then the clearance requirement is zero.

There is no absolute standard for the amount of backset. One-eighth to ¼-inch is usually used on 1⅜-inch-thick, lightweight doors, keeping the hinge screws as nearly centered in the edge of the door as possible. Exterior doors 1¾ inch thick should have a ¼-inch backset, and thicker doors, ⅜ inch.

Though it's common practice to hang lightweight doors with only two hinges, all walk-through doors up to 90 inches tall should have three hinges. Taller doors (up to 120 inches) should have a fourth hinge, with an additional hinge added for each extra 30 inches of door height.

Cheap utility hinges are not an adequate replacement on the doors in your home. Standard-weight hinges of the appropriate size are used for residential doors, unless the doors are unusually heavy. In this case you should substitute a heavyweight hinge of the same size. Doors that are opened and closed constantly should have low-friction or ball bearings. All residential doors, with the possible exception of the front door, are classed as low-frequency-of-operation doors for which plain bearing hinges are specified.

Hinge handedness

Many kinds of loose-pin and specialized hinges are "handed." That means they are made for either left-hand or right-hand door installations and cannot be switched to the other side. Here's how to determine the handedness of a door (and its hinge): With the door opening *away* from you as you face it, the door is left-handed if the hinges are on the left side—and this door takes left-hand hinges. If the hinges are on the right side, the door takes right-hand hinges. (To confuse matters, this method of identifying hinges is the opposite of that used by cabinet manufacturers.)

To determine the handedness of any loose-joint hinge, open the hinge with its face toward you and the pin pointing up. If the knuckle of the right leaf is at the bottom, it is a right-hand hinge. If the knuckle of

Door thickness	Door width	Hinge height (min.)
¾"–1⅛" (cabinets)	24" (max.)	2½"
	36" (max.)	3"
1⅜" (interior doors)	32" (max.)	3½"–4"
	over 32"	4"–4½"
1¾" (exterior doors)	36" (max.)	4½"
	48" (max.)	5"
	over 48"	6"
2"–2½"	42" (max.)	5" (hvywt.)
	over 42"	6" (hvywt.)

Spacing for door hinges

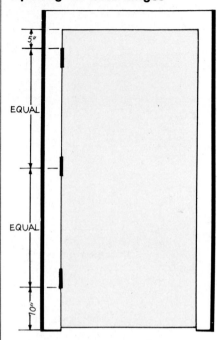

Factors affecting hinge width

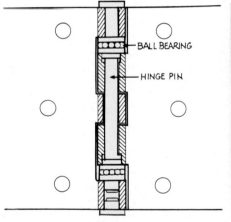

Butt-hinge parts

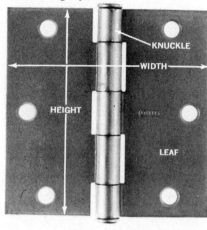

Ball-bearing hinge for heavy-duty use

Rounded-corner hinge

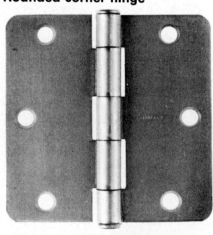

Low-friction bearing hinge from Stanley

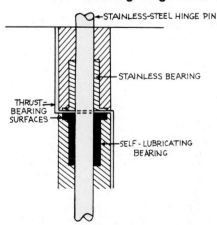

A security hinge has a stud on one leaf that fits into a hole in the opposite leaf. To make your own security stud, drill a 5/16-inch hole through both leaves and then mount the hinge. Drill a pilot hole into the jamb, insert a ¼-inch lag screw, and cut off the head. Mortise for rounded-corner hinge (above) can be cut with a router.

Swing-clear mortise hinge

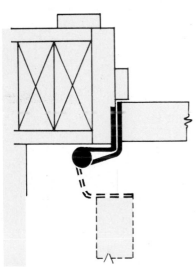

The swing-clear hinge allows a door to clear the doorway when opened only 95 degrees.

Compact spring hinge from Stanley employs a coil spring; it's UL-approved for fire doors.

Full-surface hinge

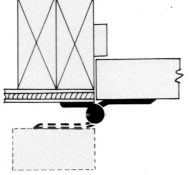

Full-surface hinge requires no mortising; it's usually used on shop or shed doors.

the left leaf is at the bottom, it is a left-hand hinge.

Alternatives to the butt

Most doors today create a barrier to people in wheelchairs—or a squeeze to people on crutches. Doors hung on conventional hinges can extend up to 2 inches into a doorway when open—which can also make it inconvenient to move large objects in and out. The solution to this vexing problem is a swing-clear hinge—long available for commercial applications. Now Stanley is making these much-needed hinges in 3½- and 4-inch sizes to replace old hinges in existing jamb and door mortises. The Stanley F248 hinge will take the door completely clear of the doorway when the door is opened about halfway.

Stanley is also marketing a new spring hinge, model 2060, which can replace standard mortised hinges. These hinges look like any other premium-grade, concealed-bearing hinge. The spring action is provided

Soss concealed hinge

Concealed hinge has no exposed knuckles. The Soss 216 is for medium-weight doors.

by a reliable internal coil that should be adjusted after the door is hung. Only one of these spring hinges is needed to shut a lightweight door; up to three may be needed on heavy doors.

Another way to keep your doors where you want them is to use gravity pivot hinges. Designed only for lightweight doors, these hinges will automatically close a door or hold it open 90 degrees in either direction. For heavier doors, the double-action floor hinge, often used on swinging kitchen doors, will do the same chore.

There may be occasions when you cannot or do not want to mortise the hinges in either the door or jamb, or both. For this purpose butt hinges are also made full surface, half mortise (mortised in the door only), and half surface (mortised in the jamb only). The surface-mounted door leaf is usually attached with through-bolts rather than wood screws, for greater durability.

Security is also a consideration in choosing door hinges. Outward-opening doors can be forced open easily if hung on ordinary butt hinges—you just remove the pins and pop the door out from the hinge side. There are two ways to prevent this: The hinge pin can be locked with a set screw that is accessible only with the door open, or you can use a hinge that has a security stud (see photo preceding page). This stud prevents the hinge leaves from separating when the door is closed, even with the pins out. Most hinges can be specially ordered with security studs, but you should have

Tee and strap hinges

Double-action floor hinge

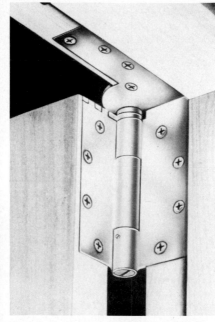

The pivot-reinforced hinge is designed to withstand abuse. It replaces normal top hinge on door.

Sizes available in standard and heavyweight hinge types

Type	Weight	Frequency of use	Mounting	3"	3½"	4"	4½"	5"	6"
Butt	Standard	Low	Full mortise	X	X	X	X	X	X
Spring butt	Standard	Average	Full mortise		X	X	X		
			Half mortise				X		
Butt	Standard	Average	Full mortise		X	X	X	X	
			Full surface				X	X	
			Half mortise				X	X	
			Half surface		X	X	X	X	
Butt	Heavy	High	Full mortise				X	X	X
			Full surface				X	X	X
			Half mortise				X	X	X
			Half surface				X	X	X
Swing-clear butt	Standard	Average	Full mortise		X	X	X		
			Full surface						
			Half mortise			X			
			Half surface			X			
Swing-clear butt	Heavy	High	Full mortise				X	X	
			Full surface					X	
			Half mortise					X	
			Half surface					X	
Pivot-reinforced	Heavy	High	Full mortise					X	
Olive	Standard	Average	Full mortise						X
Paumelle	Standard	Average	Full mortise					X	
Paumelle	Heavy	Average	Full mortise					X	X

little trouble drilling and adding a stud to a butt hinge yourself. Some hinges can carry concealed wiring and switches to activate an alarm if the door is opened by an intruder.

The butt hinge is the most economical for hanging a door, but there is other hardware you can use. If you think conventional hinge knuckles mar the appearance of your doors, you can use Olive or Paumelle hinges to minimize the exposed barrel. (Examples of each are at the center of our lead photo. Olive hinges—so named because the concentrated barrel is shaped like an olive—can be ball-bearing or pin; Paumelles have a chrome ball bearing for vertical load and a nylon bushing over the pin for lateral load. Farther left in the photo is a Victorian shutter hinge to hold

shutters open.) Soss—or other brands of hidden hinges—eliminate all visible trace when the door is closed. Another way to minimize the visibility of hinges is to use pivot hinges instead of butts. These are familiar on cabinets, but they are also made in sizes capable of handling large doors. Ordinary tee or strap hinges are used on some period doors, as well as on outdoor utility doors and gates and doors that can't be hung with conventional butts, such as doors made of narrow planks or plywood.

If you have a problem door that seems to be always pulling off its hinges, Stanley has a drastic solution. It's called a pivot-reinforced hinge, and it's billed as boy-proof. A pivot and butt hinge are joined into one compact, interlocked unit with a sin-

gle hinge pin. The pivot hinge is mounted as the top hinge, one to a door (shown above, left). The intermediate and bottom hinges are normal butts.

I've identified most hinges as Stanley, here, because that company makes, and sells nationally, such a broad range. But other manufacturers often offer equivalent types, if your hardware store or home center stocks another brand.

Before ordering a special hinge, ask its price. Some of them cost quite a bit more than a pair of simple butts. The table above summarizes availability of the most familiar types. Remember: The weight of your door and how often you'll open it determine whether you should choose standard or heavyweight hinges—*Thomas H. Jones.*

how to buy lumber

The buying of lumber and plywood can be a confusing experience. Here's what you should know about the way wood is classified and graded so you can buy the right materials for your projects and get the most for your money.

What's called *rough lumber* has been sawed, edged, and trimmed at a sawmill; it shows marks on all sides. *Surfaced* or *dressed lumber* that you buy in a lumberyard has also been through a planing machine to smooth the sides, but not always all sides.

Softwood lumber grading standards have been set by the government. The actual grading is done by inspectors of such associations as the Western Wood Products Association (WWPA), Northeastern Lumber Manufacturers Association (NELMA), and Redwood Inspection Service (RIS).

For grading purposes, all softwood lumber is divided into two groups: green lumber and dry lumber (moisture content is 19 percent or less). All softwood lumber is further divided into three use classes: (1) yard lumber for ordinary construction and building purposes; (2) structural lumber for use where high stress will be encountered; (3) factory and shop lumber for manufacturing into molding, siding, and furniture.

Lumberyard stock is almost exclusively dry yard lumber, and classified as board, dimension, and timber.

Boards

Board means a thin piece of lumber that, considering its thinness, is both long and wide. Softwood lumber boards are made in eleven standard thicknesses, but most of those sold in lumberyards are ¾ inch thick. Widths are standard, too.

Softwood boards are sorted into select or finish grades (good stuff) and common grades (knotty). They are graded after being surface-planed, and looking at the good side. A board is graded as a whole, not in sections. In the common grades, it is not the number of knots that determines the grade, but their size, and whether they are sound, loose, or missing, plus such things as warp, wane, splits, rot, and other defects. In select grades, both number and size of knots are limited.

What each board grade is called depends on where the tree grew. Western woods are graded mostly under WWPA rules. Lumber from the northeast comes under NELMA grading rules. Idaho white pine, although graded under WWPA rules, carries its own grade designations.

Each board grade describes the type, size, and number of defects permitted in the worst board in that particular grade. Most boards in a grade surpass requirements. However, these gradings are made when the board is just out of the planer; if a board is improperly stored, it may develop a lot more warp than that allowable at inspection.

Dimension lumber

Dimension lumber is 2-by, 3-by, and 4-by softwood used for framing—joists, studs, rafters, planks, light posts, etc. The lumber is divided into several classes, such as Light Framing, Utility, Studs, Joists and Planks, Appearance, Structural Light Fram-

STANDARD

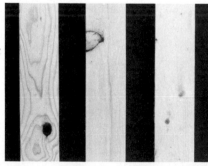

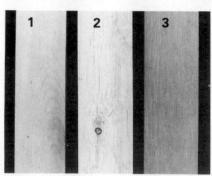

ECONOMY

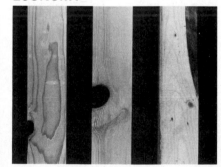

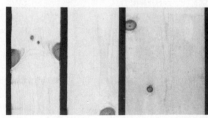

At top: Standard (left) and Economy (right) 2×4 dimension lumber. Center, left: Select boards—1 is B & BTR pine; 2 is C & CTR pine (there's only one knot in this 8-foot 1×6); 3 is Clear All Heart redwood. Center, right: Except for knots, these boards, bought as knotty pine, would meet C & BTR Select. Bottom: Common lumber—1 and 2 are second-best quality (No. 2 Common, Sterling, etc.) normally found in yards; 9-inch pocket puts 3 in No. 3 Common grade (several scattered pockets allowed).

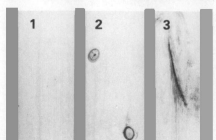

Top: Fir plywood A grade veneer, left, with five boat patches visible in this about 4-square-foot panel, and, right, C grade veneer (knots and knotholes up to 1½-inch diameter allowed). Center: Fir plywood, D grade veneer (knotholes up to 3 inches allowable) at left, and right, Lauan (Philippine mahogany) underlayment surface veneer (good side has few, if any, defects; backside may be another story, with wide splits possible, though much of panel will be usable on both sides). Bottom: Birch veneer plywood. Most "veneer" in yards is not graded, much is imported. You can buy it good-one-side (G1S) or good-two-sides (G2S).

ing, and Machine Stress-Rated. Only dimension lumber in the first three of the classes is usually available in retail lumberyards.

Light Framing. Light framing dimension lumber is sorted into several grades. Construction, the top grade, is for general framing; although it has good appearance, it is graded primarily for strength and serviceability. Standard, also for general framing, is almost as good, but bigger knots, knotholes, and other defects are permitted.

Utility. For noncritical framing, such as studding, blocking, plates, bracing, and rafters. Allowable knots and knotholes are bigger still, and more warp and other defects are permitted. Economy—in this grade almost anything goes except that the ends can't be broken or slabby.

Studs. There is only one stud grade and it's called *Stud.* It is suitable for all stud use including load-bearing walls. In Economy Stud, as in Economy Light Framing, almost any defect is allowed.

Joists and Planks. This class of dimension lumber is intended for use full length to support floors, roofs, etc. Grades are Select Structural, No. 1, No. 2, and No. 3, and Economy, with grade quality requirements similar to those for Light Framing, except for allowable knots.

Appearance Framing. This class has only one grade—Appearance. This dimension lumber is for exposed use in housing and light construction. In strength, it is equivalent to No. 1 Structural Light Framing with no unsound knots allowed. There are also tight limits on defects affecting the appearance of the lumber.

Structural Light Framing. Grades of dimension lumber in this class have strength and stiffness that

are specified percentages of those of clear straight-grained wood. Grades are Select Structural (67 percent), No. 1 (55 percent), No. 2 (45 percent), No. 3 (26 percent), and Economy, for which there is no specified fiber stress in bending value.

Other classes of dimension lumber include Machine Stress-Rated lumber, in which class each piece is non-destructively tested; Foundation lumber (red cedar and incense cedar heartwood only); Decking; and Scaffold Plank.

Timbers

Timbers have a minimum thickness of 5 inches and are produced in several classes and grades.

Beams and stringers are 5 inches or more in thickness, and more than 2 inches wider than they are thick, making the minimum dimensions in this class 5×8. There are four grades.

Select Structural is graded primarily for strength, but most pieces can be used exposed where good appearance is important. Other grades, in descending order of strength and appearance are No. 1, No. 2 (No. 1 Mining), and No. 3 (No. 2 Mining).

Posts and timbers are 5×5 and

TABLE I. Typical grading softwood lumber

USE		Grading based on 1"x8"x12' piece. Defects in other size pieces proportional. Grading based primarily on WWPA rules. Rules for other lumber may vary, particularly on allowable knots.	Northeastern Lumber NELMA	Western Lumber WWPA	Idaho White Pine IWP	West Coast Lumber WCLB	Redwood RLB	Western Red Cedar WCLB & WWPA	Southern Pine SPIB
SELECT & FINISH	Lumber of exceptional quality and appearance. Many pieces absolutely clear.	Two sound, tight pin knots (½" max.) or slight traces of pitch, or a very small pocket, or equivalent combination. Very light torn grain, skip and cup. Wane on reverse side on an occasional piece.	—	B & BTR 1 & 2 Clear Superior Finish	Supreme	—	Clear All Heart Clear	Clear Heart	B & B Finish
	Lumber of fine appearance for high quality interior trim and cabinet work.	Two small, sound tight knots (¾" max.) or light pitch, or a small pitch streak, or two very small pockets, or equivalent combination. Very light torn grain, cup and crook. Light skip. Wane on reverse side on an occasional piece.	C & BTR Select C Select	C Select	Choice	C & BTR Finish	—	A	C Finish
		Four small fixed knots (¾" max.) or four small pockets, or medium pitch, or equivalent combination. Medium stain, scattered light torn grain, light crook, short split on end, wane on reverse side.	D Select	D Select	Quality	D Finish	—	B	D Finish
COMMON	Best quality knotty lumber with all sound tight knots	Sound tight knots and smooth red knots 2¼" max. Very light torn grain and cup. Very short splits, one each end. Light crook and pitch. Two small dry pockets. Wane on reverse side on an occasional piece.	Finish and 1 Common	1 Common	Colonial	Select Merchantable	Select Heart Select	Select Merchantable	No. 2 Board
	Knotty lumber for exposed paneling and shelving and exterior house trim.	Sound and tight red knots 3" max., sound and tight black knots 1⅜" max. Light torn grain, cup, shake. Medium-light crook, short splits (one each end), three small dry pockets, medium wane, some firm hearth pith, 12 scattered pinholes.	Premium and No. 2 Common	2 Common	Sterling	Construction	—	Construction	No. 2 Board
	Knotty lumber for use where appearance and strength are important in shelving, paneling, siding and fencing.	Sound and tight red knots 3½" max., unsound knots, loose knots, knot holes 1½" max. Medium torn grain and crook, cup. Light-to-medium shake. Some unsound wood, heavy pitch, split up to ⅙ of length. Only one knot in a board can be the maximum size.	Standard No. 3 Common	3 Common	Standard	Standard	Construction Heart Construction Common	Standard	No. 3 Board
	Knotty lumber for general construction—subfloors, roof and wall sheathing, concrete forms and crates.	Fixed, firm and tight knots up to ⅔ width 3" loose knots and knotholes. Heavy torn grain, cup, wane. Large pockets. heavy streaks and patches of massed pitch over ½ area. Medium to heavy shake full length, split ⅓ length. Pinholes and small holes unlimited.	No. 4 Common	4 Common	Utility	Utility	Merchantable	Utility	No. 4 Board
	Lowest grade knotty lumber.	Large knots, very large holes, unsound wood, massed pitch, heavy splits, shake, wane in any degree or combination. But some pieces may be only slightly below No. 4.	No. 5 Common	5 Common	Industrial	Economy	Economy	Economy	—

larger, but the width cannot be more than 2 inches greater than the thickness.

These are graded Select Structural (good appearance), No. 1 and No. 2.

Plywood

Plywood is made of an odd number of thin layers of wood (called veneers) that are glued up and sandwiched together, with the grain of the veneers alternating at right angles. Softwood plywood—usually called *fir plywood*—is manufactured in this country under U.S. Product Standard PS 1. Most plywood you find in a lumber yard is marked with a grade-trademark of the American Plywood Association (APA). This mark tells you everything you need to know about the plywood.

Fir plywood is not exactly the right name, because many woods besides fir are used. But fir plywood, to use the common term, is what you get when you go to the lumberyard and ask for plywood. The plywood is made in two types and many grades.

The two types are exterior and interior. One difference is the glue. Exterior is always made with waterproof glue, while water-resistant glue may be used on the interior type, though waterproof glue is sometimes used here, too.

Each type is made in many grades. The grades are based on surface veneer quality and the plywood's intended use. The face veneer grades are N, A, B, C, C-plugged, and D, running from best to worst.

N: Smooth surface, natural finish veneer. No open defects, and not more than six repairs (with wood) allowed per 4×8 panel, made with the grain and well-matched for grain and color.

A: Smooth, paintable. Not more than eighteen neatly made repairs per 4×8 panel.

B: Solid surface veneer. Shims, circular repair plugs, and tight knots up to 1 inch across permitted.

C: Knotholes up to 1 inch across permitted, plus occasional 1½-inch knotholes within specified limits. Splits permitted.

C-plugged: Improved C-grade veneer with splits limited to ⅛ inch in width and knotholes and borer holes limited to ¼×½ inch. Synthetic compound repairs permitted.

D: Knots and knotholes up to 2½ inches across the grain permitted, with some up to 4 inches permitted within specified limits.

These grades spell out veneer quality. Plywood is also divided into Appearance and Engineered grades. The common A/D Interior and A/C Exterior are appearance grades.

Engineered grades are used for sheathing, subflooring, underlayment, and decking, where strength and solid integrity is of more importance than the appearance and the surface finish.

Other plywood

Lauan plywood is imported from Korea, Japan, and elsewhere, mostly as ¼-inch underlayment. Lauan actually can be any of several wood species, all of which look like mahogany. Besides using it as underlayment, it is the best all-around choice for anything needing ¼-inch plywood, such as drawer bottoms and cabinet backs.

All plywood is made of veneer, but *veneer plywood* means plywood of something better than the fir used for the face veneers and, usually, for the inside veneers, too. This is the plywood to use for furniture or anything you plan to put a clear finish on. Choice of veneers includes pine, birch and most other domestic hardwoods, redwood, mahogany, and even exotic imported woods.

Not all plywood has veneer cores like fir plywood. *Lumber-core plywood* contains a thick center core made up of strips of lumber, glued up and faced with cross-banding veneer and face veneer. Lumber-core plywood costs more than veneer-core plywood, but is better for furniture work

Typical grade marks for dimension lumber

Western Wood Products Association (WWPA) Lumber was produced and graded at mill 12 (name of brand could substitute for number). The lumber had moisture content of more than 19 percent (S-GRN) at time of grading. Wood species is Mountain Hemlock (M HEM). Grade: Standard.

Western Wood Products Association (WWPA). Wood had moisture content of 19 percent or less when graded (S-DRY), and Utility grade shipment is a mixture of Mountain Hemlock, Hemlock and Fir (M-H HEM FIR).

STUD ASPEN

Northeastern Lumber Manufacturers Association (NELMA). Wood had a moisture content of 19 percent or less (S-DRY) at grading time. Species: Aspen (ASPEN). Grade: Stud.

Typical grade marks for plywood

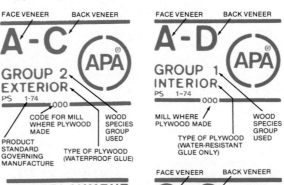
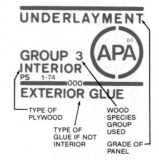
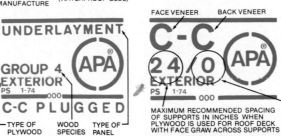

At top: Left, A-C Exterior plywood; center, A-D Interior plywood; right, underlayment—face veneer is Plugged-C; inner plywood construction resists surface indentation. Bottom: Left, A-D Interior plywood. Right, numbers indicate maximum recommended spacing for roof decking and subflooring in inches.

Wood characteristics

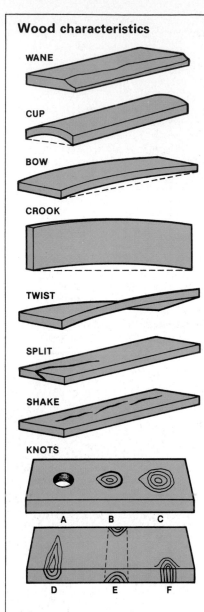

WANE

CUP

BOW

CROOK

TWIST

SPLIT

SHAKE

KNOTS

A   B   C

D   E   F

While manufacturing defects are also a factor, lumber grades are determined primarily by natural characteristics of a log that appear in the lumber. These include. . .

Wane. Presence of bark or lack of wood on edge or corner of board.

Cup. Curvature of wide face of board, edge to edge.

Bow. Curvature of wide face, end to end.

Crook. Curvature of narrow face of board, measured end to end.

Twist. Deviation from flat plane of all four faces.

Split. Separation of wood, usually at end of the lumber, due to tearing apart of wood cells.

Shake. Lengthwise separation of the wood. Shakes usually occur between or through the annual growth rings.

Knots. Varieties include: **A.** Knothole through two wide faces. **B.** Sound, encased, fixed round knot through two wide faces. **C.** Sound, watertight, intergrown through two wide faces. **D.** Sound, watertight, tight intergrown spike through two faces; **E.** Intergrown round knot through four faces; **F.** Edge knot.

---

that calls for doweling, splines, or dovetail joints.

"Plywood" is also made with a *flakeboard* core. Face veneers are applied directly to the flakeboard.

Veneer, lumber-core, and flakeboard plywoods all have advantages and disadvantages. Here's a rundown of what you can expect from each:

Veneer (all inner plies of wood veneers). General thickness: ¼ to ¾ inch. Remarks: Best screwholding power from face or back of panel. Core imperfections and grain may "print" through face veneer. Exposed edge difficult to stain; shows core voids and imperfections. Most susceptible to warpage. Most difficult to work.

TABLE II. Dimension lumber and timber grades (Requirements

DIMENSION

	LIGHT FRAMING 2" TO 4" THICK 2" TO 4" WIDE 6' AND LONGER				STUDS 2" TO 4" THICK 2" TO 6" WIDE 10' AND SHORTER	
	CONSTRUCTION	STANDARD	UTILITY	ECONOMY	STUD	ECONOMY STUD
TYPE OF KNOT PERMITTED	Sound, firm, encased, and pith. Must be tight.	Any kind	Any kind		Any kind, well spaced	Any kind
SOUND KNOTS, SIZE PERMITTED — WIDTH OF PIECE 2"	3/4"	1"	1 1/4"		3/4"	Knots up to 3/4 of cross section permitted
3"	1 1/4"	1 1/2"	2"		1 1/4"	
4"	1 1/2"	2"	2 1/2"		1 3/4"	
5"	—	—	—		2 1/4"–3"	
6"	—	—	—		2 3/4"–3 3/4"	—
8"	—	—	—		—	
10"	—	—	—		—	
12"	—	—	—		—	
14"	—	—	—		—	
SPIKE KNOTS ACROSS WIDE FACE	1/4 of cross section	1/3 of cross section	1/2 of cross section		N.A.	N.A.
LOOSE KNOTS & KNOTHOLES, SIZE PERMITTED — WIDTH OF PIECE 2"	5/8"	3/4"	1"		3/4"	Knotholes up to 3/4 of cross section permitted
3"	3/4"	1"	1 1/4"		1 1/4"	
4"	1"	1 1/4"	1 1/2"		1 1/2"	
5"	—	—	—		1 3/4"	
6"	—	—	—		2"	—
8"	—	—	—		—	
10"	—	—	—		—	
12"	—	—	—		—	
14"	—	—	—		—	
KNOTHOLE SPACING	1 per 3 lin. ft.	1 per 2 lin. ft.	1 per lin. ft.		1 per lin. ft.	
SLOPE OF GRAIN	1 in 6	1 in 4	1 in 4		1 in 4	—
SHAKE	Several heart shakes up to 2' long, none through	1/2 of thickness at ends. elsewhere longer, some through	Surface shakes at ends, same as split through; 1/3 length		At end, same as split if through; elsewhere 1/3 of length	Not limited
SPLITS (MAX.)	Length equal to width of piece	Length equal to 1 1/2 times width of piece	1/6 of length of piece		Length equal to twice width of piece	1/4 of length of piece
WANE Typical, many exceptions	1/4 of thickness 1/4 of width	1/3 of thickness 1/3 of width	1/2 of thickness 1/2 of length		1/3 of thickness 1/2 of width length unlimited	1/4 of thickness 3/4 of face length unlimited
WARP Includes bow, crook, cup, twist or any combination	1/2 of medium	Light	Medium		1/2 of medium	Crook and twist 1" max. in 8' stud
UNSOUND WOOD • Spots and streaks only • Must not destroy nailing edge	Not permitted		1/3 of cross section		1/3 of cross section	

ALL LUMBER CHARACTERISTICS ALLOWED EXCEPT BROKEN OR SLABBY ENDS LARGE KNOTS AND KNOTHOLES, UNSOUND WOOD, HEAVY SHAKE, SPLITS AND WANE OR ANY COMBINATION PERMITTED. PIECES 9' AND SHORTER MUST BE USABLE FULL LENGTH

NOTE: AT EDGE OF WIDE FACE—AT CENTERLINE OF WIDE FACE, WHEN TWO SIZES GIVEN FOR STUDS AND JOISTS AND PLANKS; ON NARROW FACE—WIDE FACE FOR BEAMS AND STRINGERS

Flakeboard. General thickness: ¾ inch. Remarks: Most stable. No core printing. Poor edge screwholding. Heaviest panel. Exposed edge difficult to stain (but can be finished).

Lumber-core (lumber strips 1 to 4 inches wide, edge-glued together). General thickness: ¾ inch. Remarks: Easiest worked. Solid exposed edges (for stain). Stable construction. Good holding for screws into edge, for example, for installing hinges.

Hardwood

Unlike softwood, which is graded looking at a piece as a whole, hardwood is graded assuming it will be cut up to make furniture parts. Softwood is inspected after the piece has been planed smooth; hardwood is graded in the rough, and the inspector doesn't care about the defects—just the amount of clear wood between them.

The top grade is *Firsts and Seconds* (FAS). FAS is graded from the poorer side to allow good cuttings all the way through. *Select,* the next grade, is

shown are simplified; additional factors enter into grading)

LUMBER					TIMBERS				
JOISTS AND PLANKS 2" TO 4" THICK 5" AND WIDER 6' AND LONGER					APPEARANCE 2" TO 4" THICK 2" AND WIDER 6' AND LONGER	BEAMS AND STRINGERS 5" AND THICKER WIDTH MORE THAN 2" GREATER THAN THICKNESS 6' AND LONGER		POSTS AND TIMBERS 5" × 5" AND LARGER WIDTH NOT MORE THAN 2" GREATER THAN THICKNESS 6' AND LONGER	
SELECT STRUCTURAL	NO. 1	NO. 2	NO. 3	ECONOMY	APPEARANCE	SELECT STRUCTURAL	NO. 1	SELECT STRUCTURAL	NO. 1
Sound, firm, encased, and pith; tight and well-spaced	Sound, firm, encased, and pith; tight and well-spaced	Any kind, well-spaced	Any kind, well-spaced		Sound, tight, well-spaced	Sound, tight, well-spaced	Sound, tight, well-spaced	Sound, tight, well-spaced	Sound, tight, well-spaced
—	—	—	—	ALL LUMBER CHARACTERISTICS ALLOWED EXCEPT BROKEN OR SLABBY ENDS LARGE KNOTS AND KNOTHOLES, UNSOUND WOOD, HEAVY SHAKE, SPLITS, WANE OR ANY COMBINATION PERMITTED. PIECES 9' AND SHORTER MUST BE USABLE FULL LENGTH	1/2"	—	—	—	—
—	—	—	—		3/4"	—	—	—	—
1"–1 1/2"	1 1/4"–1 7/8"	1 5/8"–2 3/8"	2 1/4"–3"		1"	—	—	—	—
1 1/8"–1 7/8"	1 1/2"–2 1/4"	1 7/8"–2 7/8"	2 3/4"–3 3/4"		1 1/4"	1 1/4"–2"	1 7/8"–3"	1"	1 1/2"
1 1/2"–2 1/4"	2"–2 3/4"	2 1/2"–3 1/2"	3 1/2"–4 1/2"		1 1/2"	1 1/2"–2 1/2"	2 1/4"–3 3/4"	1 1/4"	1 7/8"
1 7/8"–2 5/8"	2 1/2"–3 1/4"	3 1/4"–4 1/4"	4 1/2"–5 1/2"		2"	1 3/4"–3"	2 1/2"–4 1/2"	1 5/8"	2 1/2"
2 1/4"–3"	3"–3 3/4"	3 3/4"–4 3/4"	5 1/2"–6 1/2"		2 1/2"	2"–3 1/4"	3"–4 3/4"	2"	3 1/8"
2 3/8"–3 1/4"	3 1/8"–4"	4 1/8"–5 1/4"	6"–7"		3"	2 1/4"–3 1/2"	3 1/4"–5"	2 3/8"	3 3/4"
					3 1/8"	2 3/8"–3 3/4"	3 1/2"–5 1/2"	2 1/2"	4"
N.A.	N.A.	N.A.	N.A.		N.A.	N.A.	N.A.	N.A.	N.A.
—	—	—	—			None permitted	None permitted	None permitted	None permitted
—	—	—	—		None permitted				
7/8"	1 1/8"	1 3/8"	1 7/8"						
1"	1 1/4"	1 1/2"	2"						
1 1/4"	1 1/2"	2"	2 1/2"						
1 1/4"	1 1/2"	2 1/2"	3"						
1 1/4"	1 1/2"	3"	3 1/2"						
1 1/4"	1 1/2"	3 1/2"	4"						
1 per 4 lin. ft.	1 per 3 lin. ft.	1 per 2 lin. ft.	1 per lin. ft.						
1 in 12	1 in 10	1 in 8	1 in 4		1 in 10	1 in 15	1 in 11	1 in 12	1 in 10
1/2 of thickness at ends; elsewhere 2' long, none through	1/2 of thickness at ends; elsewhere 2' long, none through	1/2 of thickness at ends; elsewhere 3' or longer, some through	Surface shakes permitted		Not specified	1/6 of thickness	1/6 of thickness	1/3 of thickness on one end	1/3 of thickness on one end
Length equal to width of piece	Length equal to width of piece	Length equal to 1 1/2 times width of piece	1/6 of length		Length equal to width of piece	Length equal to 1/2 of width of piece	Length equal to width of piece	Length equal to 3/4 of thickness	Length equal to width of piece
1/4 of thickness 1/4 of width up to 1/2 of length	1/4 of thickness 1/4 of width up to 1/2 of length	1/3 of thickness 1/3 of width up to 2/3 of length	1/2 of thickness 1/2 of width up to 7/8 of length		1/12 of thickness 1/12 of width 1/6 of length	1/8 of any face	1/4 of any face	1/8 of any face	1/4 of any face
1/2 of medium	1/2 of medium	Light	Medium		Very light	—	—	—	—
Not permitted	Not permitted	Not permitted in thicknesses over 2"	1/3 of cross section		Not permitted	—	—	—	—

TABLE III. Readily available APA grade-trademarked "Fir" plywood

	Grade	Use	Veneer Grade			Commonly Available Thickness
			Face	Core	Back	
APPEARANCE GRADES	A-D Interior	For painted built-ins, shelving, projects where only one side will show. Do not use where edges will be exposed or where voids in core ply under face will be objectionable.	A	D	D	¼", ⅜", ½", ¾"
	B-D Interior	Same uses as A-D Interior.	B	D	D	¾"
	A-C Exterior	For painted outdoor projects where only one side will show. Also used for indoor projects requiring a more solid plywood than A-D Interior or where edges will be veneered or finished.	A	C	C	¼", ⅜", ½", ⅝", ¾"
ENGINEERED GRADES	C-C Exterior	Unsanded plywood for roof decking, subflooring and sheathing.	C	C	C	5⁄16", ⅜", ½", ⅝", ¾"
	C-D Interior	Wall and roof sheathing, subflooring. Usually available with waterproof glue as CDX.	C	D	C	⅜", ½", ⅝", ¾"
	C-Plugged D Interior	Touch sanded. For backing wall and ceiling. Not waterproof. Not for underlayment because does not have indentation resistance. Available with waterproof glue.	Plugged-C	D	D	¼"
	Underlayment Interior	Touch sanded. Use over structural subfloor. Available with exterior glue. Provides smooth surface for resilient flooring.	Plugged-C	C&D	C	¼"
	Underlayment C-C Plugged Exterior	Touch sanded. Use over structural subfloor. Provides smooth surface for resilient flooring where severe moisture conditions may be present.	Plugged-C	C	C	¼", ⅜"

graded from the good side to allow cuttings that are good on one side. *No. 1 Common grade,* next, is graded from the poorer side and yields cuttings good on two sides, but only smaller cuttings with a lot of waste. Grades go downhill from there.

Tips on buying

• When working on a big home-improvement project where you can't estimate materials to the last foot, buy 80 to 90 percent of what you think you need. By the time you get near the end and have changed the design a few times, you'll be able to figure up exactly what additional material you need.

• Avoid economy grades of dimension lumber. If the wood is any good, it wouldn't be in that grade.

• Figure board and dimension lumber needs in standard-length pieces, rather than total number of feet. You will be surprised how planning reduces waste.

• Yards generally cut lumber without charge so you can get it into your car (if not, find another yard), but most charge to cut to dimension.

• Buy dimension lumber in as long a piece as you can handle. Long pieces tend to have less warp than short pieces—don't ask me why.

• Buy A-C EXT fir plywood in preference to A-D INT even for interior jobs. The better-quality back and core plys are worth the small extra cost, unless you are using whole plywood panels.

• For furniture making, you can generally get ¾-inch pine or birch veneer plywood at lumberyards for $12 to $15 more per panel than A/C Exterior and it can be finished without the surface preparation necessary with fir plywood.

• You have the right to expect that each piece of lumber you buy meets the standards for the grade you are being charged for.

• Need top-quality veneer plywood in less than full-panel quantities? Check local cabinet and millwork shops for job leftovers. Also a good source for small quantities of hardwood.

• If you need select-grade pine, but will cut it into small pieces, buy common lumber and cut around knots.

• While hardwood usually comes in random lengths and widths, some retailers also sell it in neatly cut pieces. Unless you can use these pieces with zero waste, you save money buying random-size pieces and paying by the board-foot—*Thomas H. Jones.*

TABLE IV. Dry softwood lumber dimensions

BOARDS				
Thickness (except Redwood)*		Width		
Nominal	Actual	Nominal	Actual	
4/4 1"	¾"	2"	1½"	
5/4 1¼"	1 5⁄32"	3"	2½"	
6/4 1½"	1 13⁄32"	4"	3½"	
7/4 1¾"	1 19⁄32"	5"	4½"	
8/4 2"	1 13⁄16"	6"	5½"	
9/4 2¼"	2 3⁄32"	7"	6½"	
10/4 2½"	2 ⅜"	8" and wider		
11/4 2¾"	2 9⁄16"	¾" off nominal		
12/4 3"	2¾"			
16/4 4"	3¾"			

*Redwood is often sold in 11⁄16" thickness rather than ¾".

DIMENSION & TIMBER	
Thickness & Width	
Nominal	Actual
2"	1½"
3"	2½"
4"	3½"
5"	4½"
6"	5½"
7"	6½"
8" and wider ¾" off nominal	

index

ABS piping, 147, 149
Acid-R grout, 48
Acorn Structures, 14, 15, 16
Adhesives
   piping, 147–149
   styrofoam, 30, 31
Air tools, 150–154
American Olean tile, 48, 93
American Society for Testing Materials, 147, 149
Anasazi Indians, 20
Antonich, George J., 13
Apple Corporation, 11
Appliance rack, 78–79
Armco Steel Co., 19
Attics
   airtight door for, 95
   condensation problems and, 50

Backyard center, 104–105
Balcomb house, 21, 22, 23
Ballal, Kris, 14
Balloon-form dome, 10–11
Barbecue counter, 104–105
Barcelo, Charles W., 13
Basements, condensation, 51
Basins, bathroom, 27–28
Bathroom built-ins, 92–93
Bathrooms, 26–28
   medicine chest, 94–95
Bathtub, 28
Bench (deck), 102–103
Berms, 122–124
Between Coat, 26
Bevco Industries, 166
Bingham, Wayne, 9
Black & Decker Mfg. Co., 154, 155, 157, 158, 163
Blowgun, 153
Boards (lumber), 172
Boise Cascade Corporation, 15
Box wrench, 164, 165, 166
Butcher-block construction, 102–103

Butler Manufacturing Company, 15
Butting, joists, 33

Cabana construction, 108
Caldera Aspen spa, 48
California Redwood Association (CRA), 101, 102
Caulking gun, 152
Chairs
   outdoor, 116–117
   weatherproof, 106–107
Chicago Pneumatic Tools Co., 154
Cleaning gun, 153
Clean 'n Strip wheel, 163
Closet, free-standing, 84–85
Closet-door pantry, 81
Cold frame, 104–105
Cold-frame hot bed, 114–115
Cole, Warren, 24–25
Compressors, 154
Computer center, 66–67
Computerized drill press, 155
Concept 2000 Inc., 19
Concrete floors, raising of, 46
Concrete waffles, 12
Condensation problems, 50–51
Congoleum Corporation, 44
Conservatory House, 16
Copper Development Association, 9
Covington Technologies, 7–8
CPVC piping, 147, 149
Crawl spaces, ventilation problems, 50–51
Crescent Tool Company, 164, 166
Crescent wrench, 164

Dalen Products, Inc., 115
Darkroom work cabinet, 86
Day, Nancy, 17
Day, Richard, 19
Deck hot-tub, 100–101
Deck bench, 102–103
Deck chair, 116–117
Deck House, 14, 16, 17
Department of Energy (U.S.), 15

Desks
   home computer center, 66–67
   rolltop-desk kit, 68–71
De Vido, Alfredo, 4
DeWalt radial-arm saw, 61
Die grinder, 150–151
Dimension lumber, 172–174
Dixie Royal Homes, 14–15, 16
Dome houses, 10–12
Door hinges, 168–171
Dow Chemical Company, 29, 30
Dowels, 130–131
Drill press, computerized, 155
Drills, 150
Drop-leaf swim deck, 119

Earth-sheltered housing, 17–19
Earth Systems, Inc., 19
Electrical cables
   garage conversion, 47
   workshop wiring, 114–146
Enercon Builders, 3
Epoxy glues, 128–129
Epsom MX-80 home computer, 66
Equality Screw Company, 158
Erekson, Allen B., 18–19
Evans Company, 164
Executive Trading Company, 154
Exxon Corporation, 136

Fairey, Philip W., 13
Fiberglass-reinforced plastic, 108–112
Fill dirt, 122–123
Fillers (wood floors), 133–134
Film-finish tests, 143
Filon Marketing Services, 108
Finishes, furniture, 141–143
Finishing, interiors, 35
Flap Wheel, 163
Floor framing, 32–34
Floors (concrete), raising of, 46
Floors (wood)
   care and refinishing of, 132–136
   squeak repairs for, 137–139

Florida Solar Energy Center, 13
Foam-core walls, 7–8
Foam dome, 11–12
Fold-up stool, 77
Footings, 46–47
Framing
    floors, 32–34
    24-inch framing, 36
    walls, 34–35
    windows, 34
Free-standing closet, 84–85
Fretz, Peter and Judy, 2
Furniture
    finishes for, 141–143
    outdoor, 116–118
    repairs for, 128–131

Garage conversion, 42–47
Garage storage units, 64–65
General Supply Corporation, 154
Genova, Inc., 147
Gold Bond Panelectric radiant heating panels, 44
Gossen Company, 126
Graham, Mark, 7
Grease gun, 152
Greenhouses, 110, 111
Grouting, 27
Guerdon Industries, 15
Gussel, Tom, 12

Halo Lighting (Div. of McGraw-Edison), 44
Hammer-chisel, 150
Hardwoods, 177–178
Hart, Harry, 3
Heath Craft Woodworks, 71
Heat Mirror insulating glazing, 14
Heflin, Neal, 127
High-tech houses, 6–13
Hinges, selection of, 168–171
Home computer center, 66–67
Home workshop, wiring for, 144–146
Honeywell Corporation, 3
Hot-tub deck, 100–101
Howard Products, 167
Hunn house, 21, 22, 23

Idaho White Pine (IWP), 174
Impac-panel houses, 8
Independence series (passive-solar houses), 14
Ingersoll-Rand Company, 154
Insulating Shade Company, 15
Insulation
    garage conversion, 47
    spa installation, 48
    super-insulated houses, 2–3
Interior finishing, 35
ITT Corporation, 13
IWP (Idaho White Pine), 174

J. C. Penny Company, 154, 157, 158
J. C. Whitney and Company, 154

Jet Engineering Company, Inc., 154
Joanna Western Mills, 78
Johnson's wax, 135
Jones, Robert, 21
Jones house, 22, 23

Kalwall Corporation, 15
Kelbaugh house, 20, 21, 22
Kenwood stereo products, 83
Kirley, Shirley and Hugh, 15
Kitchen island construction, 80
Kohler Corporation, 11, 93

Lamination, steps in, 76
Lange, Leland, 3
Lantern, patio, 117
LASL (Los Alamos Scientific Laboratory), 20–21, 22
Liftplate houses, 6
Lighting
    bathrooms, 27
    workshops, 144–145
Linton, Joseph, 9
Lo-Cal House design, 2–3
Los Alamos Scientific Laboratory (LASL), 20–21, 22
Lumber, purchasing guide, 172–178

Magazine cradle, 87
Mallary, Dwight, 26
Mallary, Susan, 26
Malmberg, Richard, 12
Manufactured Buildings Program (DOE), 15
Marvel Mystery Oil, 154
Mazria, Edward, 15
McCloskey Between Coat, 26
Medicine chest, 94–95
Middleton Place "Heartstone," 44
Milwaukee Screw-Shooter, 156–157
Minwax finishes, 135
Mobile-Modular II, 22, 23
Modular construction, 34
Modular storage units, 72–76
Moldings (wood), wall accents with, 125–127
Monkey wrench, 164
Montgomery Ward and Co., 154
Morse, Fred, 15
Mortise joints, 107
Mulvin, Bob, 8

Nailers, 152
National-Detroit Inc., 154
National Homes, 15
National orbital-pad sander, 154
Needle scaler, 151
Northeastern Lumber Manufacturers Association (NELMA), 172, 173, 174, 175
Northern Homes, 15
NuTone shower lights, 27
NuTone (Division of Scovill), 11
Nutty Company, 158

One-wall vanitory, 88–91
Outdoor furniture, 116–118
Owens Corning insulation, 48

Padding finishes, 142–143
Paint spray gun, 150
Pantry, closet-door, 81
PASCALC (Total Environmental Action), 15
Passive solar houses, 9–10, 20–23
    kit for, 14–16
Patio lantern, 117
Pearcey, Dale, 19
Pearcey, Gene, 19
PEGFIX (Princeton Energy Group), 15
Penetrating-oil finishes, 142
Pennzoil Corporation, 12
Pepper, Ken, 147, 148, 149
Perms, 51
Picnic table, 118
Phenoseal ®, 89
Pipe (plastic), solvent-welding of, 147–149
Planning, modular, 32
Planter, rustic, 113
Plastic. See Fiberglass-reinforced plastic
Plastic pipe, solvent-welding of, 147–149
Plumbing, spa installation, 48–49
Plywood, 173, 175–177
Polystyrene piping, 147
Pool dome, 112
Pool enclosure, 111
Pool-side cabana, 108
Porch addition, screened, 40–41
Poser tools, 156–158
Poston, Bruce, 7
Potting table, 104–105
Power tools
    sander/stripper, 162–163
    specialty cutter, 162–163
    wiring for, 144
Pressure washer, 153
Princeton Energy Group, 15
Privacy enclosure, 110
Propane torches, 159–161
Pueblo Indians, 20
PVC piping, 147, 149

Radial-arm saw, 61–63
Ratchet wrench, 164
Real Log Homes, 15, 16
Red Carpet Development Corporation, 13
Redwood Inspection Service (RIS), 172, 173
Reed Wallcovering, 44
Refinishing, wood floors, 132–136
Regular, Larry and Florence, 100
Repairs
    floors and stairs, 137–140
    furniture, 128–131
Retaining wall, 123–124
RIS (Redwood Inspection Service), 172, 173

Rmax Thermawall, 29–30, 31
Robinson, David, 3
Rockwell International, 154, 157
Rodac Corporation, 154
Rolltop-desk kit, 68–71
Romex cable, 145, 146
Roofs, 35–36
Rotary cutter, 163
Russell, William L., 106

Safe-T-Blow, 153
Sandblasters, 152–153
Sanders, 152, 162–163
Sander/stripper, 162–163
Sanding
    finishing, 142–143
    wood floors, 132–133
Saskatchewan Research Council, 2
Sawmill River Post & Beam, 14, 15, 16
Saws
    radial-arm saw, 61–63
    table-saw alignment, 58–60
Scafe, Dona, 18
Scafe, Gayle, 18
Scoring and snapping, styrofoam, 30
Screened porch addition, 40–41
Screwdrivers, power, 156–158
Sears Roebuck and Company, 154
Sewing center, 96–98
Shellac, 135
Shick, Wayne, 2–3
Shurcliff, William, 2, 3
Silicone caulking, 89
Silvo Hardware Corporation, 154
Simpson Timber Company, 117
Skil Tools Company, 154, 157, 158
S-K Tools, 166, 167
Sloop construction, 120–121
Smith, John, 10–11
Snap-On-Tools Company, 154
Socket wrench, 164, 165
Solar collector
    roof, 112
    wall (fiberglass-reinforced plastic), 109
Solar concentrator, 103
Solarcrete Corporation, 6–7, 8
Solar Group (Los Alamos Scientific Laboratory), 20–21, 22
Solar panels, 24–25
SolarVent, 115
Solar Woodbox house, 15
Solar Woodhouse (Sawmill River Post & Beam), 16
Soldering, 160
Solvent welding, 147–149
Southern Pine Inspection Bureau (SPIB), 173, 174
Spa construction, 48–49
Spitfire propane torch, 159
Sprayed-concrete sandwich houses, 6–7
Spray gun, paint, 150
Squeaky floors and stairs, repair of, 137–140

Staining, wood floors, 134
Stairs, squeak repair for, 140
Standard sizing, lumber, 32
Stanley door set, 84
Stanley tools, 169, 170, 171
Staplers, air tools, 152
Steel, Gerald B., 8
Stereo tower, 82–83
Stevenson Projects, 104, 120
Stool, fold-up, 77
Storage units
    appliance and wine rack, 78–79
    backyard center, 104–105
    closet-door pantry, 81
    garages, 64–65
    modular, 72–76
    tools, 54–57
Stripper/sander, 162–163
Styrofoam panels, (tongue-and-groove), 29, 30
Styrofoam TG polystyrene insulation, 30–31
Subflooring, 34–35
Sun-Tronic, 9
Super-insulated houses, 2–3
Supporting walls, removal of, 37–39
Surface finishes, 143
Sweat-soldering, 160
Swim deck, drop-leaf, 119

Tables, picnic table, 118
Table saws
    alignment of, 58–60
    wiring for, 144
Teac stereo products, 83
TEANET (Total Environmental Action), 15
Tecton Corporation, 10–11, 12
Tee, Molly, 15–16
Tennessee Valley Authority, 14
Terra Dome Corporation, 17–18
Tetrahydrofuran (THF) cement, 149
Thermal layering, 4–5
Thermatek, 12
Thermawall (Rmax), 29–30, 31
Therml Impac panels, 8
THF cement, 149
Tile, installation of, 27
Timbers, 174–175
Tire inflater, 153
Toilets, 28
Toilet tanks, condensation problems, 51
Tongue-and-groove (TG) styrofoam panels, 20, 30
Tool storage units, 54–57
Total Environmental Action, 15
Trombe wall, 22, 23
Truck-bed canopy, 111
Trusses, 35–36
Truwax, 135
Tub. See Bathtub; Hot-tub deck; Spa construction
Turner, Lloyd, 10
Tuscany Malt grout, 93
24-inch framing, 36

Vanderklaauw, Peter M., 6
Van Doren, Dave, 12
Van Doren Industries, 12
Vanitory, 88–91
Vapor barriers, 50–51
Varnish, 135, 141
Varsol, 136
Vented-skin house, 13
Ventilation
    condensation problems, 50
    stereo tower, 83
Ventilators, bathrooms, 27
von Fraunhoffer, Hermann J., 19

Waffle-Crete, 12
Wall accents, wood moldings for, 125–127
Wall framing, 34–35
Walls (supporting), removal of, 37–39
Wall-Tex, 44
Waxing, wood floors, 135–136
WCLB (West Coast Lumber Inspection Bureau), 173
Weatherproof chairs, 106–107
Welding, solvent, 147–149
West Coast Lumber Inspection Bureau (WCLB), 173
Western Wood Products Association (WWPA), 172, 173, 174, 175
Wick Building Systems, 15
Williamson house, 21, 22, 23
Wilsonart, 72, 75, 88
Window framing, 34
Windows, condensation problems, 51
Window shades, wine rack construction, 78
Wine racks, 78–79, 87
Wingaersheek Inc., 161
Wiring
    home workshop, 144–146
    stereo tower, 83
Womanized lumber, 44
Wood floors
    care and refinishing of, 132–136
    squeak repairs for, 137–139
Wood Moulding & Millwork Producers, 126, 127
Wood moldings, wall accents with, 125–127
Workbenches, 52–53
Workshop, wiring of, 144–146
Wrenches, 164–167
    air-powered, 151
WWPA (Western Wood Products Association), 172, 173, 174, 175

Xanadu house, 11–12

Yarn box, 99
Young, Gordon, 18